Iconic Figures of Modern Odisha

Iconic Figures of Modern Odisha

Editor:
Prof. Harischandra Sahoo

BLACK EAGLE BOOKS
DUBLIN, USA | BHUBANESWAR, INDIA

 BLACK EAGLE BOOKS

USA address:
7464 Wisdom Lane
Dublin, OH 43016

India address:
E/312, Trident Galaxy, Kalinga Nagar,
Bhubaneswar-751003, Odisha, India

E-mail: info@blackeaglebooks.org
Website: www.blackeaglebooks.org

First International Edition Published by
BLACK EAGLE BOOKS, 2023

ICONIC FIGURES OF MODERN ODISHA
Edited by : **Prof. Harischandra Sahoo**
41, Arnapurna Residential Complex
Shelter Chhak, Tulsipur, Cuttack - 753008
Mob.: 9438408465
E-mail : harissahoo9@gmail.com

Copyright © **Prof. Harischandra Sahoo**

All rights reserved. No part of this publication may be reproduced, stored in a retrieval system, or transmitted, in any form or by any means, electronic, mechanical, photocopying, recording or otherwise without the prior permission of the publisher.

Cover: **Sasikanta Rout**
Interior Design: Ezy's Publication

ISBN- 978-1-64560-488-4 (Paperback)
Library of Congress Control Number: 2023952341

Printed in the United States of America

Dedicated to
Droupadi Murmu
Her Excellency,
The President of India.

Editor's Note

Odisha is the land with a rich legacy. Odisha has great contribution in every field of life. In the political sphere, the freedom movement started with the Paika Rebellion (*pāika bidroha*) is a landmark. In the religious sphere, Odisha was the flourishing ground for *Buddhism, Jainism* and *Gaudia Vaishnavism* under the royal patronage of King Ashoka, King Kharavela and Prataparudra Deva respectively. Odisha has a long maritime history. Merchants of Odisha went on voyages to Bali, Java, Sumatra islands for trade and commerce. Odishi Dance is unique in the world and Sambalpuri handlooms are a favourite of most Indians. The architecture of Konark temple is a landmark. Despite all these, Odisha has been neglected and is treated as an insignificant state. Most of the people of India recognize Odisha as *Jagannāth Dhām*. But the scenario has changed now. Most of the luminaries of Odisha have contributed immensely in their own fields. Presently, most of the important posts are occupied by Odias. Smt. Draupadi Murmu is the President of India, Sri Dharmendra Pradhan, is Minister Education, Skill Development and Entrepreneurship; Dr. P.K. Mishra, holds a high post in the PMO, Shaktikanta Dash is the Governor of the Reserve Bank of India. Mrutyunjaya Mohapatra is the Director General of India Meteorological Department, Girish Murmu is the External Auditor of World Health Organisation (WHO), Prof. Kishore Basa is the Director General of ASI and Director General of National Monument Authority. Mr. Chittaranjan Tripathy is now the Director of National School of Drama. In order to carry forward the Odia identity, a humble attempt has been made to showcase some of the iconic figures of Odisha, who are reputed not only within the boundaries of the state but also across the globe; as such, they make our state glorious.

Needless to say that Odisha has a rich cultural heritage. It is time to recollect and pay our respect to the makers of Modern Odisha. On the forefront, the contributions of Utkalmani Pandit Gopabandhu Das and Utkal Gaurab Madhusudan Das come to our mind. We remember the heroic personalities like Subhas Chandra Bose. The writings of Kabi Samrat Upendra Bhanja, Adikabi Sarala Das have left indelible marks in the field of Odia literature along with the literary works of Baladev Ratha, Fakir Mohan Senapati, Gangadhar Meher, Nandakishore Bala, Radhamohan Garnaik, Mayadhar Mansingh, Sachi Routray, Kalandi Charan Panigrahi and Godabarish Mishra etc.

The contributions of Maharajas Like Krushna Chandra Gajapati Narayan Deo, Sri Rama Chandra Bhanja Deo and Purna Chandra Bhanja Deo towards the promotion of education and health services of the state are remarkable. In the field of spiritualism and literary activities, the names of Bikram Dev Burma, Basudev Sudhaladev are noteworthy.

We recollect the names of freedom fighters like Baji Rout, Saheed Laxman Naik, Birsa Munda, Chakra Bissoi, Dora Bissoi, Veera Surendra Sai, Buxi Jagabandhu Bidyadhar, Jai Rajguru, Chandan Hajuri, Chakhi Khuntia, Dharanidhar Naik and many others who sacrificed their lives for the motherland during independence movement. I salute these heros for their courage and patriotism.

In the field of freedom movement and social service, the names of Rama Devi, Sarala Devi and Malati Devi top the list. Tulasi Munda's social service and dedication for welfare and upliftment of the tribals are remarkable. Bhaktakabi Madhusudan Rao is remembered for introducing *Barnabodha* to the learners of Odia Language. Guru Raghunath Murmu is remembered for his innovative '*Olchiki*' script for the Sānthāli language. In the evenings, the *bhajans* and *cautisās* of the saint-poet Bhima Bhoi are being recited in the *Alekha Tungi* in the nook and corner of the state. Bhima's prayers to Mahima Swami for the removal of sorrows and sufferings of the entire mankind is noteworthy.

The contribution of notable figures like Surendra Nath Mohanty, Poetess Kuntala Kumari Sabat, *Pancha-Sakhas* (both traditional and modern) are worth-mentioning. The novels and short stories of Sri Bibhuti Pattnaik and Santanu Acharya, writings of Sitakanta Mohapatra, Ramakanta Ratha, Mahapatra Nilamani Sahoo and Chandra Sekhar Ratha, Srinivas Udgata and others have enriched the literary field of Odisha. In the field of music, Balakrushna Dash, Akshya Mohanty, Prafulla Kar, Pranab Pattnaik and Sunanda Patnaik come to our mind. Prasanta Nanda and Nandita Das set records in film production. In dance arena, Guru Kelucharan Mohapatra, Sanjukta Panigrahi, Kumkum Mohanty and Aruna Mohanty etc. draw our attention. The names of Raghunath Mohapatra and Sudarshan Sahoo in the field of stone-craft is worth mentioning.

In this volume, a humble attempt has been made to select some of the iconic figures of modern Odisha who have their contributed to the cultural growth of the state in different spheres like politics, science, spirituality, history, sociology, psychology, entrepreneurship, philosophy, social service, economics, sports, art and literature etc. In the category of politics, personalities like Smt. Droupadi Murmu, H.K. Mahatab, Nandini Satapathy, Janaki Ballav Patnaik, Biju Patnaik, Biswabhusan Harichandan and Naveen Patnaik have been selected and placed. In the science section, Pranakrushna Parija's biography has been placed. In the section of popular spiritual gurus, in this volume Thakur Sri Abhiram Paramhamsa and Paramhamsa Pragyanananda Giri's life and message have been incorporated. Bhikari Bala's name is cited as the *Bhajana Samrat* in the music section. Radhanath Rath and Achyuta Samanta have been recognized for their social service and philanthropic attitude. Ganeswar Mishra, Hrudananda Ray and J.N. Mohanty are veterans in the field of Philospophy and critical thinking. Radhanath Rath is a well known psychologist of our state. Baidyanath Mishra is mentioned as one of the pioneering economist. In the section on history, two important historians like M.N. Das and Jagannath Patnaik have been placed. Sreeramchandra Dash is one of the notable political scientists of our state. By publishing forty volumes of encyclopedia in Odia, Binode Kanungo has created history. In the field of language and literature we remember personalities like Gopinath Mohanty, Manoj Das, Jayanta Mohapatra, Golak Bihari Dhal, Chittaranjan Das, Kunjabihari Dash and Smt. Pratibha Ray. In the field of promotion of sports, Bhairab Mohanty is a legendary figure and the name of Dillip Tirkey comes to the forefront in Hockey. In the sand art, Sri Sudarshan Patnaik has created history. The name of Subroto Bagchi as a promising entrepreneur of the state is worth mentioning.

The personalities whom I could not takeup in this volume due to some limitations will be placed in the next volume. Since it is a valuable book especially for the younger generations, I have tried my best to see that it is free from errors. But then human errors are inevitable. I may be excused for mistakes committed, if any. My work would not have been possible without the inspiration from my friends and well-wishers like Sarat Chandra Panigrahi, Chittaranjan Misra and Chittaranjan Bhoi. They have inspired me to carry forward my mission. I am thankful to Mr. Bibhu Prasad Sahoo for typesetting and Mr. Sashikant Rout for the cover design.

I owe a lot to the esteemed contributors who have readily agreed to my proposal to contribute articles for the proposed book. All the articles are written by experts and veterans. I hope the readers will appreciate the articles. I record my sincerest thanks to my wife Bidyutprava Sahoo and my daughter Dr. Sonali Priyadarshini for their support.

I am thankful to Sri Satya Pattnaik, M/s. Black Eagle Books without whom the book could not have seen the light of the day. I welcome constructive suggestions, if any, from my readers to improve upon the book. My labour will be amply rewarded, if it gets readers approbation.

Harischandra Sahoo
Editor

CONTENT

	Subject	Author	Page
1.	**Droupadi Murmu :** Similipal Hills to Raisina Hills- The Great Leap	Preetinanda Roy	15
2.	**Harekrushna Mahatab :** The Maker of Modern Odisha	Laxmikanta Mishra	25
3.	The Saga of Charismatic Woman : **Nandini Satpathy**	Chittaranjan Bhoi	44
4.	**Janaki Ballav Pattnaik :** Politician Extra ordinary	Harekrushna Satpathy	51
5.	**Biju Pattnaik-** An Embodiment of Heroism, Patriotism & Humanism	Harihar Panda	57
6.	**Biswa Bhusan Harichandan :** A Versatile Genius	Bijayananda Singh	67
7.	The longest Reign in History : The 'Naveen' Era in Odisha	Netaji Abhinandan Soumya R. Gahir	75
8.	**Achyuta Samanta :** The Propagator of Art of Giving	Harischandra Sahoo	91
9.	Satayu Purusa : Padma Bhusan **Dr. Radhanath Rath**	Hemant kumar Parija	99
10.	**Gopinath Mohanty's** Man-Centric World View	Prafulla kumar Mohanty	109
11.	The Poetic vision of **Jayanta Mahapatra**	Durga Prasad Panda	125
12.	**Kunja Bihari Dash :** A Profile of Folk Culture and Literature of Odisha	Baishnab Charan Samal	142
13.	**Golak Bihari Dhal :** A Rare Genius	Sanatan Mallik	147
14.	**Sri Abhiram Paramahamsa :** Life and Message	Niranjan Mohanty	151
15.	**Paramahamsa Prajnananda :** Life and Message	Harischandra Sahoo	161
16.	**Pranakrushna Parija :** A veteran scientist	SibaPrasad Adhikary	171
17.	**Hrudananda Ray :** The Paradigm of Philosophising	Sarat Chandra Panigrahi	180

18. Philosopher of Excellence : **Jitendranath Mohanty**	Harischandra Sahoo	189
19. **Ganeswar Misra** : Placing Philosophy on the Logical track	Ganesh prasad Das	202
20. **Binode Kanungo** : The maker of Encyclopaedia	Pabak Kanungo	216
21. **Bhikari Bal** : Bhajan Samrat of Odisha	Sunamani Rout	225
22. **Chittaranjan Das** : Writer Extra Ordinary	Dhaneswar Sahoo	230
23. **Sreeramchandra Dash** : A Multifaceted Genius	Niranjan Barik	243
24. **Baidyanath Misra** : A Great Teacher and Institute Builder	Rabi N. Patra	258
25. **Radhanath Rath** : The Man and the Image	Udaynath Dash Sayantani Behura	270
26. **Jagannath Pattnaik** : A Nationalist Historian with a Difference	Himansu Sekhar Patnaik	285
27. **Manmath Nath Das** : A Renowned Historian	Haris Chandra Panda	304
28. **Bhairab Chandra Mohanti** : A Visionary and Dreamer of Sports	Kharavella Mohanti	316
29. Telling stories the Indian Way : The Inimitable **Manoj Das**	Chittaranjan Misra	331
30. Autobiography of **Pratibha Ray** : "*Padma Patrare Jibana*"	Basant Kumar Panda	343
31. **Harekrushna Satpathy** : Renowned Sanskrit Scholar and Academic Administrator	Arun Ranjan Mishra	355
32. **Subrato Bagchi** : "One man, one mission and a million dreams"	Disha Bhatt	360
33. Hockey Legend - **Dillip Tirkey**	Harischandra Sahoo	365
34. **Sudarshan Pattnaik** : Magical hands Capturing the beauty of sands	Kashmira Murmu	365
35. Contributor's Profile		369

Draupadi Murmu : Similipal Hills to Raisina Hills-The Great Leap

Preetinanda Roy

The arduous journey from Rairangpur to the Raisina Hills was never a walk on the bed of roses. Who could have ever imagined, even in their dreams, that a poor tribal girl, born in one of the inaccessible villages of Kusumi Block of Mayurbhanj district would ever make her way to the *Rashtrapati Bhawan* at New Delhi and become the first citizen of this great country! Neither did she nor her parents who bore this blessed child had ever thought so. None of her teachers, neighbours, the people of her district or the state where she was born had ever imagined that this sweetest flower from the wildest part of the dense forest of Similipal hills would spread her fragrance all through the world by adorning the most prestigious posting of the President of India! True it is, though the journey appears like a fairy tale. India has always given due honour and opportunity to the women leaders to showcase their potentialities. Smt. Indira Gandhi, the first woman Prime Minister, Smt. Prativa Devi Patil, first woman President or Smt. Nandini Satpathy, first woman Chief Minister are a few names who have glorified and dignified the womanhood of the country. A new chapter to this glorious tradition was added when Smt. Draupadi Murmu became the first tribal woman to become the President of India. The struggle of her life that culminated after reaching the topmost constitutional position of the greatest democratic country which is celebrating the seventy fifth glorious years of independence has added a wonderful saga carved in golden letters. The village Uparbeda in Kusumi Block of Rairangpur, Mayurbhanj became the most searched place by people from India and the world. Odisha was earlier identified as the abode of Lord Jagannath but Smt. Murmu has given a new identity to Odisha as well as to Mayurbhanj.

Smt. Draupadi Murmu was born on 20th of June 1958 to Sri Biranchi Narayan Murmu and Smt. Sinago Tudu in the consecrated village of Uparbeda of Mayurbhanj district. She had two brothers-Sri Bhagat Tudu and Sri Sarani Tudu (Tarinisen Tudu). Though her father could complete his education till class 5 and mother was illiterate, they had realised the importance of education, particularly for their daughter. Since childhood she was second to none-be it studies, sports or any other activities. This attribute of being first has always been attached to her and she became the first tribal woman President of India. She is not only the first person born in independent India to be the President but also the youngest leader to adorn that most admired position. Every Odia, every Indian is proud of this daughter of Mayurbhanj for creating such remarkable history in Indian politics. The people of Santali tribe in particular are exuberating and feeling exalted by the admirable achievement of this Santali lady.

Poverty can never create hindrance in the path of potentiality- this has been proved again and again by many great leaders, administrators, authors, artists, etc. It clearly states that the challenges of life, if used properly, can beget ultimate success. The first tribal woman President of India had a very challenging childhood amidst poverty and lack of resources. Getting a square meal a day was a dream for her on many a days. She had to walk barefoot to school which was miles away from her home. Arranging books and stationery for her primary education was too difficult a task for her. There was no electricity in her village at that time and children had to use kerosine lantern to study in the evening. But her family could not even afford kerosine for the lamp for evening studies. So she used to sleep early so that she could wake up at dawn and complete her studies. Lack of proper clothes, food or even basic needs like kerosine could not stop her from pursuing her studies. Besides studies, she used to do household chores like sweeping, polishing the walls with mud and cow dung, bringing pails of water from the distant wells, cooking and what not. The well-off students studying in higher classes in her school used to sell off their books in half price after completing a class. She used to take advantage of this opportunity and buy those books. She was enrolled in K.B.H.S. Minor school in Uparbeda village. She had to cross a brook to go to school everyday. During rainy days, the brook used to swell and the muddy road became difficult to tread. Still, she never refrained from going to school. She was the most regular student with full attendance in all the classes. She would rather reach school the earliest and sweep the classroom. She was a dedicated and sincere student in the class for which she always scored the highest marks.

There was no High school in her village or nearby villages. So, after completing her primary education at the village she expressed her desire for further education.Her father came to know about a school in the capital city Bhubaneswar where the tribal girls are provided free education and got her enrolled in Capital Girls'High School, Unit-2 , Bhubaneswar. She stayed in the hostel and completed her education from class 8th to 11ththere. Matric examination was then being conducted after 11thclass and she successfully completed matriculation with good marks. She also earned a good reputation as a sportsperson and N.C.C. cadet at her school. Thereafter she got admission in Arts in Ramadevi Women's College, Bhubaneswar. She got stipend there and continued her studies staying in the hostel. During that time, it was mandatory for the girls to wear sarees. She had only two sarees and could not buy more as she had to manage all her expenses with the stipend money. She never visited the college canteen like the other girls. She rather used the left-over rice as her snacks or breakfast in case of emergency. Being a N.C.C. cadet, she was loved and appreciated by all her classmates because of her helping nature and amicable behaviour. Most of her time was spent in the library and there also she managed by purchasing old books at half price. Such was her struggle till she successfully completed her Bachelor's Degree in 1979 from Ramadevi Women's college.

She was interested to continue higher education,

but looking at the financial constraints of her family, she decided to join as a clerk in the Department of Irrigation and Energy, Government of Odisha soon after her graduation. She worked there for four years from 1979 to 1983, got married in 1980 and blessed with motherhood during that period. Mrs. Draupadi Murmu had a love marriage. Even though Sri Shyama Charan Murmu, a bank employee, was a perfect match so far caste, occupation etc. were concerned, still it was not an easy task to make her father to accept the proposal. However, she took all the pain to make her parents realise the depth of love they had for each other after which it was materialised. It was difficult for a working woman to maintain balance between home and office. She had to quit her job in 1983 so as to take care of her son and the ailing mother-in-law. She returned to her in-law's place at Rairangpur. Shyama Charan Babu was instrumental and the main driving force behind the success of Mrs. Draupadi Murmu. He stood by her, supported every decision she took, gave her courage, shared all family responsibilities, and guided her in every step that she took in life. Destiny had in store bigger responsibilities for her and Rairangpur was waiting for her to take the first step towards that great journey of her life! During her stay in her in-law's place, she could not confine herself within the four walls and started doing social service and honorary teaching at Sri Aurobindo Integral School. This association with teaching continued till 1997. There after she contested election as Ward Member of Rairangpur N.A.C. as a candidate from the Bharatiya Janata Party (B.J.P.) and won by substantial margin. This laid the foundation stone of her greatest expedition.

Her political journey continued further when she won legislative assembly election twice in 2000 and 2004 from Rairangpur constituency. She became the State Minister for Transport and Commerce from 2000 to 2002 and the State Minister for Fisheries and Animal Husbandry from 2002 to 2004. During her tenure as the minister of state, she had obtained many accolades for her extraordinary organizational skills and leadership qualities. She was associated with the *Adivasi Morcha* of B.J.P. since 1997 and was the Vice-President of the *Adivasi Morcha*. She was given the responsibility of membership of National Working Committee and later the Presidentship of *Adivasi Morcha* of B.J.P. Among many of her remarkable achievements were the many constructive steps to increase revenue of the departments she had headed, initiatives and efforts to enlist Santali as a constitutional languages. Her political journey continued at different locations and in different capacities till 2014 when she had to accept defeat from her opponent candidate of Biju Janata Dal.

Her defeat in the assembly election turned out to be a blessing in disguise for her. In 2015 she was nominated as the ninth Governor of Jharkhand and the first woman to hold that coveted position. Even in this position, she was the first lady from a tribal community, the first lady from the State of Odisha to become the Governor of any Indian State. She completed her 5 years' tenure quite smoothly without any controversy. Keeping in mind her efficiency, honesty, sincerity, and capabilities in handling state affairs, she got an extension of a year as the Governor as well. In Indian context, it is assumed that the Governor is only a rubber stamp and does not have any opinion regarding state matters.

She has to just sign the files sent to her without any objection. Mrs. Draupadi Murmu proved it wrong by refusing to sign a bill sent to her by the Chief Minister Sri Raghubir Das. The B.J.P. led ministry at Jharkhand wanted to make amendments in the bill dealing with the sale and purchase of lands owned by the tribal to the non-tribal. The Chief Minister had discussed the matter with the supreme commands of the party at the centre to persuade the Governor to approve it without any hassle. But Smt. Murmu felt that it would be against the interest of the tribal people and refused to approve the bill. This daring refusal became the talk of the political intellectuals of the time. She proved that the Governor is not just a rubber stamp but has strong opinion, point of views and decision making capabilities for the safeguard of greater interest. During her tenure as the Governor, she had brought a lot of reforms in the education sector of the State. She herself visited approximately 300 schools, reviewed the situation, and suggested immediate action for the improvement of quality education. After holding the position of the Governor for six years and 55 days, her tenure got completed on 12th July 2021. She returned to Rairangpur and led a simple and ordinary life staying with her brother Tarinisen Tudu and her sister-in-law Sakramani Tudu.

She had to undergo a lot of struggles to get married to the man she loved. After marriage, they had an ideal and happy family life with three children. She proved to be a loving wife, a wonderful and caring mother. Though she lost a daughter when she was only 3 years old, she overcame the depression with the love ,care and support of her other 3 children. But fate had stored more devastation for her in her later life. Her elder son Laxman Murmu suddenly left all of them at the age of 25 years in 2009. His death remained a mystery till date. He came back from a feast the night before and went to sleep. The next morning he was found dead on his bed. It was neither suicide nor an accident. He was supposed to join in his new job the next day . Everything was lost. Losing a young son at the age of 25 was too difficult for a mother to accept. She was completely lost and devastated. It took around six months' time to get over this tragedy. She got involved in Prajāpitā Brahma Kumāri organization which helped her to reconcile. The ideologies of the organization changed her outlook and perception to the worldly matters. She was quitely eating vegetarian food. That was not all rather the beginning. More devastations were on their way to befall on her. In 2013, her younger son Biranchi (nick name Sipun) died of a road accident at the age of 28. He was married and the father of a son. The child also died after a few days of his father's death. But this time Mrs. Murmu was stronger and calmer. Newly adopted spirituality gave her inner strength and she had realized the real meaning of life and death. The God of death, Yamrāj did not seem satisfied with that much. He took away her brother Bharat Tudu and beloved mother in the next two months. Her life was completely shattered when she lost her dear husband Sri Shyama Charan Murmu due to a massive cardiac arrest in the year 2014. She lost her pillar of strength, the companion of all odds and evens, the assurance of her life, the solace of her paining heart, her most lovable partner . She was left with only her youngest daughter Itishree, her husband and their two children. She might not have realized at that time that her life was meant to be dedicated to the welfare of billions of people of the country.

When one reaches the topmost strand of the ladder, there is no need to climb any further. Hopefully Mrs. Murmu has arrived at that point in her political career. She was surprised to know that her name has been nominated by the B.J.P. for Presidential candidate. She was the only choicest lady for the position. Irrespective of party affiliations, she got support from people of all the states and all the parties. The entire country rejoiced with her victory. It was on 21st of July 2021 that she got elected for the highest position of the country. With her victory , she became the youngest lady and the first tribal lady to be the President of the biggest democracy of the country.

Uttering the most famous lines of Saint-poet Bhima Bhoi as the principle of her life- *Mo jibana pachhe narke padithāu, jagata uddhāra heu* (I don't care for the sufferings of my life, It's my utmost duty to help the distressed people all around), she drew attention of the entire world. 'The poor too can dream', was her statement while presenting her first deliberation as the President of India-*It doesn't matter whether you are rich or poor, dream big.*Truly, Mrs. Murmu's life is a courageous saga of inspiration and motivation preaching the truth that nothing can stop us if we have indomitable will, self-confidence, patience and dutifulness. The path is long and uncertain with many challenges but treading through that path is what is inevitable. The lines of the American poet, Robert Frost's *Stopping by the Woods on a Snowy Evening* hold absolutely good for Smt. Draupadi Murmu-

> *Woods are lovely, dark and deep*
> *But I have promises to keep,*
> *And miles to go before I sleep*
> *And miles to go before I sleep.*

It appears to be the motto of her life- a deep resolution and strong commitment to self has led her to where she is at present. She is a burning example of a phoenix who rose from its' own ashes. She is a valiant victor who could overcome all obstacles by her strong will-power, purity of heart and courage of soul. Such an inspiring lady deserves all accolades and salutes.

Harekrushna Mahatab: The maker of modern Odisha

Laxmikanta Mishra

Harekrushna Mahatab a multifaceted personality by his own making and a true representative of 20th century Odisha displayed optimism in all walks of life such as nationalist and post-independent politics, journalism, social activism, literary activity, historical reconstruction etc.his ultimate goal was to foster the progress of the Nation and successfully carve a niche for himself in the making of 'Modern Odisha' and largely in locating 'Odisha' in the political map of India and providing it an identity both in politics of nationalism and cultural hegemony of Odisha through numerous historical writings.

Born on 21 November, 1899 in a remote village Agarpara of Balasore(Bhadrak) district to Krushna Charan Das,an ordinary farmer but looking after the vast estate of his father- in-law Jagannath Mahatab who had no male heir. Originally Krushna Charan Das belonged to Asureswar village in Cuttack district but moved on to Agarpara and looked after Jagannath Mahatab's estates.

Harekrushna was in fact the adopted son of Jagannath Mahatab and thus is his surname. The 'Zamindar' family of Agarpara was said to have come from Amritsar. Although not Sikhs, they worshipped Guru Nanak. There was a 'gaddi' of Guru Nanak at Agarpara known as 'Bhaiji Bādi' which no longer exists.

During his childhood he learnt about mythological stories of the *Rāmāyan*, the *Mahābhārata* and the *Dārdhyatā Bhakti* etc. from his mother and Mahatab was deeply influenced by the idealism of Vivekananda, Ramakrishna, Mahatma Gandhi, Gopabandhu Das and Madhusudan Das. Inspired by their idealism he dedicated his life to hard work and committed himself to the service of the nation.

While pursuing his studies as a student of the second year Intermediate Science Class at Ravenshaw College, Cuttack, Mahatab came in contact with Sri Nabakrishna Choudhury, Sri Prahallad Sahu and others, who later became front-ranking leaders of freedom movement in Odisha. Mahatab and his friends thought themselves as "Free Thinkers". In their mess, Mahatab along with his friends, published "Malaya", a monthly hand written Oriya paper and "Dustbin", a weekly handwritten English paper. After passing, I.Sc. in 2nd class, he got himself admitted into B.A.Class with Sanskrit and Economics as his subjects. He was a beloved student of his teachers such as Gopal Chandra Ganguli, Baradakanta Ganguli and Artaballav Mohanty. He published a number of news items and feature articles on police atrocities at Cuttack in the "Utkal Dipika". Mahatab also became a member of "Sevā Samiti" founded by Laxminarayan Sahu and took charge of the Co-operation Department, where he learnt office management, collection of data and preparation of reports etc. which helped him a lot during his jail terms and political and official career later. On 17th May 1915, at the call of Ananta Mishra "a roving missionary" a meeting was held at Agarpara, where H.K.Mahtab evinced keen interest in the activities of the Utkal Union Conference. Thereafter he joined the "Utkal Sammillani" as a volunteer during 1918 session held at Cuttack.

It was the 'Library Movement' and its library 'Bhārati Mandir' formed around 1919-1920 by some of the students of Ravenshaw College like Mahatab, Naba Krushna Choudhury, Nityananda Kanungo, Jadumani Mangaraj and Bhagirathi Mahapatra etc. who patronised nationalism and differed radically from that of Madhusudan Das brought tremendous transformation in his life and career. Being delegated by 'Bhārati Mandir',he attended the special Session of the Congress held in 1920 at Calcutta as an observer where he had the opportunity to listen to Chittaranjan Das, Motilal Nehru, Lala Lajpat Rai, Madan Mohan Malviya and Gandhi etc. He attended the regular session of the Congress at Nagpur along with 27 other Odia delegates including Gopabandhu Das in December,1920. Mahatab was deeply influenced by Gandhian ideology and his strategy for the Non-cooperation Movement. At a time when Congress had resolved to boycott the legislature, Madhusudan Das opted to be a minister. He found himself juxtaposed and started relentlessly opposing Madhusudan. When the Utkal Pradesh Congress Committee was formed after the Chakradharpur Session of Utkal Union Conference in 1920,he became a member of the working committee. As a part of the programme of non-co-operation Mahatab boycotted the B.A. Examination in 1921.

Gandhi visited Odisha in March, 1921.Mahatab accompanied him throughout. Even whenever Gandhi visited Odisha, Mahatab remained mostly as his permanent companion. Even Gandhi derived his ideas on 'salt' from Mahatab, a fact which never received attention of the scholars at all India level. Mahatab opened a Congress office in Balasore and named it as Swarāj Mandir and co-ordinated Congress activities in Balasore first as Secretary and then as President.

During 1920-1947 this young freedom fighter nurtured the ideas of 'Nation-Making' in every sense of the term. His role in the 'Kanikā Melee' is praiseworthy.His decision of not including the 'Panchamuka region in the 'Kanikā melee' of 1922-23 and understanding with the then Superintendent of police of Balasore, although received much criticism from different quarters remained tactical and saved innocent citizens from police oppression and brought relief to them in the form of government settlement that the people were demanding.

During the Salt Satyagraha stage of Freedom Struggle, the tremendous success at 'Inchudi' was much due to him.But he was very critical of overall achievements of Civil Disobedience Movement. Mahatab admitted,

"Civil Disobedience Movement was a lesser success because, 'It was thrust upon the people'".

During 1933 to 1936,when the Congress did not have any clearcut programme and Gandhi took to Harijan uplift works, Mahatab retired to 'Gandhi Karma Mandir' at Agarpara and engaged himself in constructive activities.

After the death of Gopabandhu Das in 1928,the influence of Puri Brāhmanas in the Congress under the leadership of Nilakantha Dash had already started waning and in the Council elections of 1937,Mahatab joined hands with Nabakrushna Choudhury's group in counterposing the importance of Nilakantha Dash. Mahatab clearly emerged as a hero in the electoral politics of 1937.Soon he entered the All India Congress Working Committee, but sided with Gandhi, Nehru and others that prompted him to resign from Congress Working Committee which embarrassed Subash Bose. He played an active role in the Prajāmandal Movement (1938-1939) in Nilgiri,Balasore.

NATIONALIST DEMEANOURS AND GROWTH OF LITERARY ACTIVITY

In the aftermath of the Non-Cooperation Movement, because of his association with Kanikā Agitation and his activities in NCO,he was arrested and imprisoned in 1922 first in Cuttack Jail and then in Bhagalpur Jail.During his one year internment , he practised Yoga and read Bhagavat Gita,Bible,Tilak's Gita and some of Tagore's writings and derived much inspiration from these works.With his jail sojourn he started his literary pursuits. It was in Bhagalpur jail that he wrote the Novel *'Ajab Duniyā'* in Odia in which he depicted the psychology of jail-life. The book was seized by the British Police during search operations of the 'Swarāj Mandir' premise in Balasore in 1930.Around the same time , he also wrote a book titled *'Free Thinking'*.

After his release from prison on 16th June 1923, he went to Hazaribag jail and met Gopabandhu Das there. Immediately thereafter he returned to Balasore and on 27th June,he became the Secretary of Utkal Pradesh Congress Committee in a meeting held at Swarāj Mandir, Balasore, under the Presidency of Nilakantha

Dash. His popularity grew abound. Being a visionary, he then realised the necessity of a newspaper. Finally his dream newspaper *'The Prajātantra'* saw the light of the day on 2nd October 1923. Initially, it started as a weekly from the 'Mukura Press', Cuttack, with Bira Kishore Das as its editor to propagate the policy and constructive work of Gandhi. Simultaneously, Mahatab published an English weekly titled *'Adventure'* to focus on the exploitation of the Kanikā Rājā in particular and of the feudal lords in general.

The year 1927 witnessed two important occurences.The first was a devastating flood in Balasore which affected roughly eighty thousand people.This provided him an opportunity to understand the people and the 'Prajājatantra' got the privilege of showcasing itself through publication of different photographs highlighting the vagaries of nature and plight of the people.Gandhi's visit to Odisha and also to Balasore in 1927 provided him the opportunity of learning the deeper meaning of Gandhian Satyāgraha, Ahimsā and importance of Constructive works which he practised later. In 1928 Gopabandhu Das died ,which shocked Mahatab greatly.Around this time, he wrote *'Punyātmā Gopabandhu'*, *'Chasā Bhāi'*, *'Palasi Abasane'*.

It was during the Salt Satyāgraha phase of Civil Disobedience Movement that Mahatab created a niche for himself in the Freedom Struggle in Odisha. On 16th March, 1930, the Utkal Provincial Congress Committee met at Balasore under the presidentship of H.K. Mahatab took the decision about launching the Salt 'Satyāgraha' in Odisha. 'Inchudi' was selected as the venue for breaking the Salt Law in April, 1930. Inchudi satyāgraha turned out to be the second biggest event in Indian Freedom Struggle next to Dāndi. The fact is endorsed in the Karāchi session of Indian National Congress in 1930 presided over by Sardar Vallabhbhai Patel. Indiscriminate repression followed thereafter. The police made a search of 'Prajātantra' Press at Balasore and 'Cuttack Trading Company' and 'Sāraswata Press' of Cuttack, in connection with proscription of Mahatab's book, "*Palasi Abasane*". Coincidentally, this was the first book to be banned in Odisha on political grounds.

It was during his internment in Hazaribagh jail(later transferred to notorious Patna camp jail) that he translated Sanskrit '*Vālmiki Rāmāyana*' into Odia and wrote the Odia prose version of the '*Bhagavat Gitā*'. Mahatab also wrote a play called '*Swarāj Pathe*' which was enacted in the jail campus on a makeshift stage with blankets serving as screens and dresses and sarees borrowed from jail authorities which depicted the passage of freedom struggle.

On his return from jail in 1932 he stayed in his own village from 1933 to 1936. Along with his wife Subhadra, he undertook social works. The M. E. School in his village was raised to a High School. A dispensary was established and the entire village was converted into a khadi-clad with self-spun yarn. He converted one of his family temples into 'Vidyā Mandir' (High School) and the other into 'Karma Mandir' (Place of all the constructive works of Gandhi). Mahatab adhered to temple-entry program of Gandhi and took some untouchables into his family's Raghunāthjew temple at Agarpara and thus incurred the wrath of the neighbourhood.

He was again arrested on 9 November 1932 on charges of conspiratorial activities in connection with Civil

Disobedient Movement and was sentenced to six months' imprisonment as a 'B' class prisoner at Hazaribagh Jail. Mahatab's book, *'Dasa Barshara Odisha'* was published in early 1936 which contained details about the political scenario of Odisha from 1920 till the end of the Salt Movement in 1930-31 and the Congress activities during this period. During 1936 he involved himself in understanding issues of the peasants.

From the middle of 1938 onward, Mahatab was deeply involved in the Prajāmandal Movements in the princely states of Odisha. It was at his endeavours that Prajāmandals were formed in Nilgiri, Talcher, Nayagarh, Hindol, Palalahara, Athagarh, Tigiria, Ranpur, Bonai, Sonepur and Patna in 1938. The Nilgiri State Prajāmandal was the first to be formed in Odisha and it was the first state to start the movement on 30th June, 1938. Mahatab played a very remarkable role in the management of the movements in the states.

During the war period Mahatab was arrested and confined in the Berhampur jail as an 'A' Class Prisoner. He was released from the Berhampur Jail on 1st December 1941 and campaigned against the coalition ministry, blamed it for being bent upon helping Japan at the cost of suppressing Congress. This was followed by Mahatab's re-arrest and subsequent imprisonment for a month and a half. The individual civil disobedience, however, seemed to diffuse and lose its vitality due to the Government policy of ignoring local level activists by not arresting them but arresting only prominent leaders. However, the pace of Individual Satyāgraha slowed down by April before it was formally suspended in December, 1941.

Thereafter, he attended Committee meeting and All India Congress Committee meeting at Wardha during

13-15th Jan.1942 and at this point he thought of publishing a weekly journal called 'Rachanā' with the dominant objective of spreading Gandhian thinking and ideals.The 'Rachanā' was published as a weekly journal from 26th January 1942, when Mahatab's brain child and the mouth piece of Congress,' the *Prajātantra*' was banned. 'Rachanā' to a great extent served to fill the gap.

Mahatab attended the Congress working committee meeting on 4-6th August 1942 and on 8th August, All India Congress Committee in its historic meeting passed the 'Quit India' resolution. But, on 9th August, 1942, all the Members of the Congress Working Committee were arrested. Mahatab along with Nehru, Patel, Govinda Ballabh Pant, Pattabhi Sitarammayya, Kripalini, Asaf Ali, Dr. Prafulla Ghosh, Sayed Mohmmad, Narendra Dev etc. were put into the Ahmednagar Fort Jail. Mahatab regarded his jail-life at Ahmednagar Fort from August 1942 to April 1945 as one of the best phases of his life. During this time, Mahtab devoted himself to the learning of Sanskrit regularly for two years under the guidance of Acharya Narendra Dev. He wrote 'History of Odisha' in two volumes and a couple of novels.

In 1946 Mahatab became the Prime Minister of Odisha and took oath of office on 23rd April 1946. The Congress Ministry under him consisted of four other prominent leaders of Odisha such as Naba Krushna Choudhury, Nityananda Kanungo, Pandit Lingaraj Mishra and Radha Krishna Biswas Ray.

Mahatab's Ministry had three major achievements; (a) the Hirakud Dam Project on the river Mahanadi, (b) the creation of new Capital of Odisha in Bhubaneswar, (c) and finally the most crucial one, the merger of princely states into Odisha province.

Selection of 'Bhubaneswar'as the site of modern Capital of Odisha was the reflections of his ideas as a visionary.'Bhubaneswar' is the second planned city of Independent India. Harekrushna Mahatab, the Prime Minister decided to establish the Capital of Odisha in 'Bhubaneswar' on historical and strategic grounds.

Merger of Nilgiri state with the province of Odisha and thereby with Indian Union on November 14,1947 was the result of superb political manoeuvre. In Merger History of India, Nilgiri occupies a distinct place and Mahatab's contribution to the making of this 'beginning' earned him the distinction of being an astute and adept statesman lauded by the prominent leaders of the country.

POST-INDEPENDENT INDIA/ODISHA AND MAHATAB'S CULURAL AND LITERARY PURSUITS

In post-independence period,Mahatab dominated the politics of Odisha for over three decades until 1977 when he declared his retirement from politics.During his political career in post-independentpolitics,he remained the first and third Chief Minister (1946-50,1956-61),Governor of Bombay(02.03.1955-14.10.1956),M.P.in Lok Sabha(1952-55,1962-67),Cabinet Minister of Commerce and Industry in Nehru's Ministry(13.05.1950-26.12.1950).In political arithmetic of the state he was a great power to be reckoned with. He is considered as the father of 'Coalition Politics' in the country after the forging of first coalition in 1959.

Some of the major writings of Harekrushna Mahatab, which bear a lot of significance for constructing Ancient Past of Odisha and Contemporary history of Odisha are as follows:

Books:
1. 'History of Freedom Movement in Orissa', Vol.I-V, 1957, Cuttack.
2. 'The History of Orissa', Vol. I and II, 1959, Prajatantra Prachar Samiti, Cuttack.
3. 'Beginning of the End', 1972, Cuttack.
4. 'While Serving my Nation, (Recollections of a Congress Man)', 1986, Cuttack.
5. 'Gandhiji O' Orissa' (Odia), 1969, Cuttack.
6. 'Dasa Barasara Orissa' (Odia), 1972, Cuttack.
7. 'Sadhanara Pathe' (Odia), 1987, Cuttack.
8. 'Ārab Sāgararu Chilikā' (Odia), 1987,Cuttack.
9. 'Gāon Majlis' (Odia),   Vol. I   1977
      -do-   -do-   Vol. II   1978
      -do-   -do-   Vol.III   1980
      -do-   -do-   Vol. IV   1981
      -do-   -do-   Vol. V   1985
10. 'Gata Ardhasatābdira Orissa O' Tāra Rājnaitika Paribartana' (Odia) in Dagar (Special Issue), Aug.-Sept. 1962.)

Among his works 'the *Gāon Majlis*' is a social satire appearing regularly in his own Newspaper daily 'the *Prajātantra*', which was being published by him since 1923.Later these small pieces of writings reflecting upon contemporary social issues in the form of bazar gossips in the villages were compiled and published in five volumes. "On the spot reporting and investigative reporting is one of the main niche of *The Prajātantra*. It has therefore created a dedicated readership for decades together. Dr. Mahatab's regular columns of "*Gāon Majlis*", on the pages of the *Prajātantra*, speak volumes of his clear conscience through which he was vehemently criticising the rampant corruption and malpractices of the system. He forcefully voiced the demands and grievances of the needy and the downtrodden. At times people used to read *'The Prajātantra'* first for Dr. Mahatab's lively column *"Gāon Majlis."* It was quite scholarly and one of the compilations of this *"Gāon Majlis"* won a 'Kendriya Sahitya Academy' award for its unique contribution and the socio-political impact on the masses. The language as well as the theme and message of this column were very simple and persuasive. His style of presenting complex problems in simple and lucid language has remained inimitable sans peer.

His experience in journalism helped him in developing passion in 'History writing'. Of course history is inseparable from journalism.Today's journalism is tomorrow's history. Today has always remained the vantage point for history. During colonial times he was busy in the struggle for Odisha formation and more in Indian freedom struggle and in post-colonial period he remained pre-occupied in Odisha politics and played a major role in modernization of Odisha. Inspite of his multiple engagements, Mahatab carried forward his journalistic and literary pursuits which remained his favorite pastime activity but regular as well. "The Prajātantra, the daily newspaper, is the symbol of struggle against feudalism, orthodoxy and dogmatism. It was converted into a daily newspaper in 1930 . Although its publication was suspended in 1932 following coercive action by the British rulers at the time of said Movement, it reappeared with renewed vigour , carrying the glorious legacy of the Indian National Movement on the eve of India's historic Independence on August 8,1947 as the brain child of Utkal Keshari Dr.HarekrushnaMahtab.

He was the founding editor of the 'Eastern Times', the first weekly English Newspaper published from Odisha. The establishment of Literary Organisation named 'Prajātantra Prachār Samiti' is a land-mark not only in the personal life of H.K. Mahatab but also in the history and culture of Odisha. "Prajātantra Prachār Samiti, is a household name in every nook and corner of the state of Odisha today. This glory heritage has not been built with the Prajātantra alone. The sister publications have also contributed to enrich this tradition. They are (1)The JHANKAR, a monthly literary journal with an in built tradition upon modern mind, (2) The MEENĀ BAZAR, a children's literary monthly, liked and preserved by the young and old alike. (3) The SĀPTĀHIKI, the largest circulated Odia news weekly, (4) The PRATIVĀ, an Odia digest for the whole family and (5) The EASTERN TIMES, a premier English news weekly". The monthly Odia magazine 'Jhankār' which patronised almost all the literary figures of Odisha, did a yeomen service in creating a literary atmosphere in Odisha.

As an eminent scholar, historian and literary figure Mahatab had received a number of Degrees of Honoris Causa from different Indian Universities. He received an honorary Doctorate degree from Andhra University, an honorary D.Litt. from Utkal University and an honorary Doctorate of Law from Sagar University and the Kendriya Sahitya Academy Award. He was the founder president of the Odisha Sāhitya Academy, Sangeet Nātak Academy and Lalit Kalā Academy. The Odisha History Congress felicitated him as the "Doyen of the Oriya Historians" in 1979 as the author of 24 books and the editor of number of dailies and journals. Mahatab was a widely travelled man who has left his marks for the posterity as a freedom fighter, an administrator, a parliamentarian, a journalist, a writer, a historian, a social reformer and above all as a friend of the common people. He was a shrewd diplomat and politician. He knew well the ways to get the desired works even from rival leaders or groups. As Bidhan Chandra Ray commented "Dr. Mahatab had kept Nehru in one pocket and Patel in the other. He could know how to involve both to fight against each other by virtue of his penchant politics". In fact, the life history of Mahtab is the half-a- century history of Odisha. He died on 2nd January 1987 .This was an irreparable loss to the state and the nation. His extinguished life is a flaming torch and we have carried the memory in our heart. His was a life, lived in this world, dying a martyr's death, death which is phoenix.

He evinced interest for historical research on "History and Culture in Odisha" during the Quit India Movement, when Mahatab was imprisoned in the Ahmadnagar fort along with many national leaders including Pandit Jawaharlal Nehru and Sardar Vallabhabhai Patel. One day Nehru showed Mahatab some excerpts from Edward Thomson's book *"The Indian Beginning of Princes"* where Jagannath Temple was depicted as a "Notorious Shrine, the uncouth temple where an incomprehensible people reverenced ugliness as the personification of divine attribute and Brāhminism seems to flaunt its differences from all other religions of the modern world". Mahatab felt insulted because he failed in countering the views as he had absolutely no historical knowledge about 'Odisha'. Even he could not cite the name of a standard book on Odishan history for the views of Thomson be refuted. Before Nehru he felt ashamed and from that moment he had decided to explore the history of Odisha in order to know the ancient history of Lord Jagannath. During his imprisonment Mahtab studied the historical writings of Toynbee, Gibbon and many other historians of essence. He published the *'Odisha Itihāsa'* in 1948. The English version with the title *'History of Odisha'* was published in the year 1959. Henceforward, he dedicated his past time both in official and non-official levels for promoting historical research in Odisha. He impressed upon the contemporary scholars for locating the sources, analyse them and reconstruct the History of Odisha in a comprehensive manner.

The *'History of Odisha'* provides a comprehensive picture about the History of Odisha from ancient times up to the attainment by India of her status as a free country. He has added valuable chapters describing the condition of the country, economic, political and administrative organisation under British rule, on the basis of original documents and sources, which are utilised in their right perspective. An original contribution to history has been his account of the 'Pāik Rebellion'. Hitherto it was assumed, as was done by the late R.D. Banerjee, that it was inspired and instigated by the Marāthā population of Odisha. This assumption was not found tenable by the author on the basis of his study of original sources.

Another interesting feature of the work is that it presents the somewhat unknown history of the Bhauma Dynasty (Bhaumakāras during mid-8th century to mid-10th century A.C.E.).The period is marked the heyday of Early Medieval Odisha as is now being termed by contemporary historians.

An interesting aspect which received due attention

of Mahatab was 'Resistance of People of South Odisha from 1765 to 1803 A.D'. Resistance of the Rājā of Khalikote, Resistance Movements in the Zamindaries of Mohiri, Tarala, Jalantara, Budarshing, Surangi etc. These regions in South Odisha remained in a state of unrest and turmoil till the middle of the 19th century A.D. A proper understanding of such resistances might have provided clue about Kondh-Pāik Axis of 1817. As per his own understanding, Khallikote Resistance Movement was very costly for the English. Mahatab has discussed this considerably. The campaign of the English against the Khallikote Rājā resulted in the death of 24 English soldiers and wounding of 28 English soldiers.

Gandhiji's visit to Odisha during various periods of national movement from 1921 to 1946 has been described in greater detail in his monumental work *"Gandhiji 'O' Odisha"*. This work in a great source book for the construction of the political, economic and social history of Odisha in the pre-colonial period. This work is written completely in a different form and style. He discussed about the Gandhiji's idea on various social problems and his ideas on the constructive activities.In order to provide objective treatmentto the subject matter, Mahatab referred to the 'Young India' and 'The Harijan' and his personal correspondences.

"The Beginning of the End" (1972, Cuttack), was the work that dealt essentially with the integration of the states with Odisha. Coincidently the process of integration in India began in Odisha with the amalgamation of Nilgiri state in Balasore and ended with merger of Mayurbhanj on 1st Jan,1949 with Odisha. As per historical records, Nilgiri, formally merged with the Odisha province on 1 January 1948 although the state government had

taken over the administration of the feudatory state on November 14, 1947 following unrest and violence in this Garhjat territory.That may be the reason why Mahatab named the book as such. One of the observations of Sardar Vallabhbhai Patel has been put as the foreword of the book *"The Beginning of the End"*.

"History to the Freedom Movement in Odisha" published in five volumes between 13th August 1957 to 26th January 1959 under the General Editorship of H.K.Mahatab and written by great historians like Lingaraj Mishra, Sushil Chandra De, Prabhat Mukherjee, Sudhakar Patnaik and Ghanashyam Das is a *magnum opus* and is still considered as the storehouse of information.In due course these volumes turned out to be primary source material without which no research on any aspect of freedom struggle is inconceivable.

HarekrushnaMahatab wrote his autobiography in two volumes entitled as *'Sādhanāra Pathe'*, (Published in 1987, Cuttack), and *'Arab Sāgararu Chilikā'* (Published in 1987, Cuttack) covering the entire period of his life from 1899 to 1977 A.D., were two valuable documents which were utilised by the historians not only for the construction of Modern Odishan History but also Contemporary history of post-colonial period. Both the books are highly valuable for writing Social History of Odisha. In the first chapter of the book entitled *'Sādhanara Pathe,'* he discussed about the utility of history by stating, *"The past provides us necessary guidance for carving out our path for the future."*

He patronised historical research both at individual and institutional level.He extended the state patronage for organisation of Associations of History such as Indian History Congress and Odisha History Congress. The 12th session of the Indian History Congress along with a special session of Indian Historical Record Commission was held at Ravenshaw College, Cuttack from 25th to 28th December 1949. Then Mahatab was the Chief Minister of Odisha. Eminent historians like R.C. Majumdar, K.K.Dutta, R.P. Tripathy, D.C. Sircar, Bisweswar Prasad, A.S. Altekar participated in both the meetings. Here Nilakantha Das gave the theory of Jain origin of Sri Jagannath which drew the attention of the scholars, which was refuted by Mahatab who mooted theory of Buddhist origin of Sri Jagannath.

It was under his patronage that Odisha History Congress came in to existence in 1969. He attended almost all the sessions of the Congress beginning with the second session held at G. M. College, Sambalpur in 1970 till 1983 which was held at Baripada. He attended the Bhubaneswar session of Odisha History Congress, 1979 held at B.J.B. College. Among others Dr. Radhanath Rath, Dr. Herman Kulke were present. At the age of 83, Mahatab attended the Baripada Session of Odisha History Congress in 1982. There he presented a well-prepared speech which dealt with certain important aspects of historiography like dangers of tinctorial research and serious misgivings of the NCERT in its direction for text book preparation and teaching of history.

The contribution of Mahatab to Odishan Culture, Literature, Historiography and Jounalism is immense and immeasurable particularly in view of his multifaceted personality and multifarious academic activities and public service. Proper analysis of his works would lead us to conclude that he initiated new ideological orientations to historical research. He believed that Journalism and History are inseparable from each other. Although he was sharing his opinion with Arnold J. Toynbee's fatalistic theory of 'Challenge and Response' as regards the origin, growth and decline of civilization but his approach was more like R.G. Collingwood. The position claimed by D.D. Kosambi in Indian Historiography may be ascribed to Harekrushna Mahatab as far as Odishan Historiography is concerned. His scholarly acumen would continue to shed lusture in historical knowledge construction for centuries together.

REFERENCES
1. Mahatab,H.K., "Sādhanāra Pathe", (Odia),Cuttack, 1972, p.314
2. Soma Chand, "Hare Krushna Mahatab and Freedom Struggle (1920-47)", 1997, Calcutta, p.XIII.
3. Soma Chand, "Hare Krushna Mahatab and Freedom Struggle (1920-47)", 1997, Calcutta,p.XIII.
4. Ibid. p.XIV.
5. M.N. Das and C.P.Nanda, "Builders of Modem India: Hare Krushna Mahatab", 2001, Publication.
6. Division, GOI, New Delhi, pp.18-19.
7. Ibid. pp. 29-31.
8. Desa Kathā, 6 March, 1930 (Odia Newspaper).
9. G.C. Mohanty, 'Swādhina Pathe Sangrāmi', Bhubaneswar,1988, p-4.
10. Soma Chand, Hare Krushna Mahatab And Freedom Struggle 1930-1947, Calcutta, 1997, p-XII.
11. S.C. De, Diary of Political Events in Orissa, Bhubaneswar, 1964, p.42.
12. http://www.theprajatantra.org/about-us.html
13. http://www.theprajatantra.org/about-us.html
14. The Samābesha (Odia), 334th issue, 1987, p. 173.
15. H.K.Mahatab, Odishā Itihās, Cuttack,1948, P.2.
16. 'The Ganjam District Manual', pp. 99-101.

The Saga of a Charismatic Woman: Nandini Satapathy

Chittaranjan Bhoi

A true successor of a literary stalwart, Nandini Satapathy alias 'Kuni' was born to a well-to-do Odia family of Pithapur village of Cuttack district. The gifted child, Nandini was born to Padma Bhusan Kalandi Charan Panigrahi and Ratnamani Devi on the 9th June 1931. Nandini's childhood was action-packed. She was brought up in a family that was considered as the temple of learning. Under the tender love and care of Kalandi and uncle, Bhagabati, she grew up as a model. Nandini was influenced more by Bhagabati Charan Panigrahi who was a left-wing thinker, a Marxist idealist and a revolutionary. She was simple but exquisite. As has been rightly said, "Great mind germinates in great environment", the upbringing of Nandini was in a disciplined environment that helped her to move on and on. She was given ample freedom and liberty to take life as she wished. She was free from male supremacy. Indeed, the father, the mother, the uncle and all other members of the family trusted her very much. All of them ignited her spirit and inspired her to take up the cudgels of life.

From the very childhood she was conscious of self-respect which she inherited from her father. At the age of five, when she was studying in a school in Mayurbhanj district, she was forced to chant the morning prayer which she did not like. The prayer reads :
*This is my Bhanja soil, this is the king
I shall worship him life after life.*

This distasteful prayer wounded her sentiment and she felt like losing her self-esteem which consequently forced her to quit the school. The congenital transmission of quality from Kalandi to Nandini is quite evident. The father Kalandi who was resisting and sentimental was also conscious of his self-esteem. This conciousness has been found from the lines :
*We are born in human race but have no respect and dignity,
Our daughters are everyone's sister-in-laws and we are scoundrels.*

The aforesaid lines signify that both the father and the daughter were conscious of their self-esteem. Like father, like daugher.

The stream of consciousness and creativity were flowing interminably in Nandini's family and she, from the childhood was drowned into the sweeping sway of the influence of the family members.

Like "Morning shows the day", Nandini's patriotic feelings oozed out in her adolescence. At the age of eight, she came out alone to see and hear Subash Chandra Bose speak at Municipality Ground, Cuttack. Many such instances were there where Nandini was found joining the rallies and meetings of the freedom fighters.

Nandini's inclination towards literature and politics are due to the influence of her family members. She obtained her Master of Arts (MA) degree in Odia Literature from Ravenshaw College, Cuttack in 1951. She emerged as a student leader dropping out Union Jack, National Flag of Britisher at Ravenshaw campus.

. Nandini loved people and was loved by them. Her love for people and her promise to give justice to the destitute millions made her a politician. Nandini held important political positions such as Union Minister of India and Chief Minister of Odisha.

The voice of the poor echoed in Nandini's heart which probably insisted her to join public service through politics. Indeed, she began her formal political journey in 1960 and appointed as Odisha Pradesh Mahila Congress President by the then President of Odisha Pradesh Congress Committee (OPCC), Biju Patnaik and then after she has not seen back. In 1962, Nandini became a Member of Parliament (MP, Rahya Sabha) from Odisha. Her flamboyance and systematic presentation of issues in parliament drew the attention of Jawaharlal Nehru, the then Prime Minister and other parliamentarians. Nandini became a popular leader during Indira Gandhi's tenure as Prime Minister. Her maturity and ripeness in politics made her the President of Odisha Pradesh Congress Committee (OPCC) in 1966. She further became the Union Minister of State in Prime Minister Indira Gandhi's Government in 1968. Nandini was elected for the second time (MP, Rajya Sabha) from Odisha with a portfolio of Union Minister attached to Prime Minister's Office (PMO) during Indira Government. In 1972 Nandini was elected as MLA from Cuttack assembly seat in a by-election defeating Biren Mitra and then became the Chief Minister of Odisha. From 1972-74 and 1974-76, Nandini became two times Chief Minister and only women Chief Minister of Odisha.

During her tenure as Chief Minister she undertook

many developmental works. Odisha Land reform act is one of the significant initiatives of Mrs. Satapathy. She took steps to provide patches of land to the landless Odias. She also introduced rehabilitation scheme to help the distressed who lost their kith and kin. Bringing 'Anti-dowry' act was a remarkable step of Nandini establishment in Odisha. Her empathy for the subaltern and homeless poor is evident when she provided houses to them through *Indirā Ābas Yojanā*.

Alongwith her successful political career, Nandini could accelerate her literary acumen to a substantial height. The busy political schedule could not dissociate Nandini from literature. She was not only a poet and story-teller but also a flourishing translator. Her literary contributions such as *Ketoti Kathā* and *Sapta Darshi* (Collection of short stories) *Uttar Purusha* (Collection of poems)and translations such as *Gandhi Kathāmruta* of Krishna Kripalini, *Selected Stories* of Mahaswata Devi, *Lazzā (novel)* of Taslima Nasreen, *Revenue Tiket* of Amrita Pritam earned her great reputation as a literary figure. Most of her stories depict the plights and predicaments of the impoverished people of the society. She was maligned by some of her contemporaries for translating *Lazzā*, the book which was banned in Bangladesh. But she did not care for it.

The translated stories such as- *Jagannath Car festival, Sishu, Churi, Kabi patni, Arjun, Gandha, Choli ke Pichea, Bhata, Jalachatra, Bishma nk Pipasha, Urbashi & Jani, Janmadina, Sanja o Sakal ra Maa, Sindhubala, Bhiti, Bhārat Barsha, Sunyastān Purankar, Jannavi Maa, Bannya, Nishant Mājhi ra Bhutan Jātrā* got readers approbation.

Nandini was not detached from family-life despite her eventful career in politics and creative writing. She married her Ravenshaw College friend, Debendra Satapathy of Dhalpur, Dhenkanal. Sri Satapathy was elected two time's Member of Parliament (MP) from Dhenkanal Lok Sabha constituency, Odisha. Her conjugal life was decisive. Her male counterpart was of same wave length. The understanding between them was excellent.

She had two sons, Nachiketa and Tathagata. Nachiketa was working in a Multinational Company at New Delhi. Tathagata Satpathy, the elder son of Nandini is the Editor of a leading Newspaper, 'The Dharitri' and 'Odisha Post', one time MLA from Dhenkanal and four times Member of Parliament (MP) from Dhenkanal Lok Sabha Constituency of Odisha. He is also a flamboyant speaker.

The recipient of many coveted awards, Nandini bagged Kendra Sahitya Akademi Award for Translation, Odisha Sahitya Akademi Award, Sāhitya Bhārati Award, Prajātantra Sanmān and many more.

Nandini was jailed for her involvement in freedom movement. She was an ardent follower of Marxist ideology. She confronted many challenges and trounced all those boldly. Nandini was daring and honest. She was not at all compromising.

Nandini passed through a critical phase of life when she barely needed a job. She cracked Public Service Commission but rejected by the panel because she had many police cases. Naba Krushna Choudhury, the then Chief Minister of Odisha assured her a job but could not guarantee it for the same reason. Though the rejections disappointed her for quite some time yet, became a blessing in disguise. Her search for job ended and quest for better future began with those rejections.

The boldness of Nandini is no secret. Her encounter with the Naxalites in Odisha was horrific. Her perception about the radical leftist ideology was different from the others.

She ventured to engage them for a talk and thus, could able to negotiate many of their issues. She assured to provide them their fundamental needs and eventually fulfilled all those and could restore peace. This daring act made Nandini stand apart from her contemporary politicians.

Nandini was a devotee of Shreema (The Mother). She influenced Indira Gandhi to follow her spiritual outfit. Of course she was maligned by her contemporaries for being driven by her impulse and conscience without caring for what people think. She was straightforward and truthful. Under no circumstance, she compromised with her resolution. A case in point, Nandini voted for Indira Gandhi against Morarji Desai going against Biju Patnaik's will.

During her term as Chief Minister, Nandini used to travel extensively to different regions of the Odisha to strengthen her connect with the people. Once she became emotionally drowned on her visit to Kalahandi and Koraput during famine. She literally cried for the famished in front of her lieutenants. This shows her compassion for the distressed.

Many of her contemporaries conspired against Nandini to oust her from the position as Chief Minister and became successful. But the exuberance and indomitable willpower of the great leady made her invincible. However, the following lines of Radhamohan Gadnaik have a great semblance of the life history of Nandini.

I will follow the untrodden path, I will
You may reprimand me as much as you can
I will explore
What on earth is unexplored
Accept all praise and insult bowing down,
Confront all impediments spreading the chest.
Time will come and that day
You will offer me the reward.

However Nandini is a national property. The great Odia breathed her last on 4th August 2006, leaving behind the footprints on the sands of time. Odisha lost a great public leader, a literary stalwart, a woman with humane heart. But she will be ever remembered for her invaluable contribution in politics and literature. She will remain alive in the memory lane of all Odias for her courage, kindness, empathy, boldness and dogged determination. Let us pay tribute to the legendary daughter of the soil, Nandini Satapathy.

REFERENCES

1- *"Matira Nandini"* by Sri Ashis Ranjan Mahapatra, the biography of Nandini Satapathy, 1999

2-Krishna Kripalini's book *"Gāndhi Kathāmṛuta"* translated by Nandini Satapathy into Odia Language.

Janaki Ballav Patnaik: A Politician Extraordinary

Harekrishna Satapathy

Age long traditions believe that Lord Rama, while on exile for fourteen years wandering forests after forests came to this place and installed a "Shiva Linga" on the bank of river Mandākini (Malāguni in common parlance) which is being worshipped today as "Rāmanidhi Deva" in a temple from time immemorial. Other ancient traces of Lord Rama's arrival to this area of present Khordha district are also available on the top of the adjoining hills and rivers that enhance the scenic beauty of this place that is named after Lord Rama and hence called "Rameswar". Shri Janaki Ballav Patnaik (Hereafter JB) (1927-2015) was born here in the village of Rameswara, to his father Gokulananda Patnaik and mother Rambha Dei. Gokulananda Patnaik, an eminent poet and writer of the first half of the 20th century and the then Head pundit of the village U.P. School. After his marriage, he got extremely worried because he did not have any issue for a long time. As per the dictates of his inner voice, he started to worship Rāmanidhi Deva and he was blessed with a baby (son) and as per his promise, he named the new born baby "Janaki

Ballava", a synonym of Lord Rama. He had further promised to write a *"Mahākāvya"* in the praise of Lord Rama. And he fulfilled his second promise by writing a *"Mahākāvya"* entitled *"Jānaki Ballabh Vilāsa"* after the birth of Janaki Ballabh to offer his humble salutations at the lotus feet of Bhagavan Rama. At present, *"Jānaki Ballabh Vilāsa"* is a popular literary creation in the contemporary history of Odia literature.

Morning shows the day. Janaki Ballabh started showing the signs of divinity in each activities from the very childhood. His father admitted him in village primary school, where he himself was under the direct supervision of his father, as a result he excelled in the class like a rising sun. He was selected for scholarship examination from Khordha district and stood first in the entire district. In 1938, he was enrolled in Rameswar M.E. School and subsequently in 1940 in Khordha High School under the stewardship of eminent educationist and creative writer, Sri Baikunthanath Patnaik as the Head Master. Apart from academics, the Head-Master was taking steps for the allround development of the students. Once, when JB was asked regarding his aim in life, he expressed to become an 'editor of news paper'. The school atmosphere was congenial for JB to manifest his inner talents. His first poetry "Ashoka" was published in school magazine *"Avakāsh"*. The tender mind of JB expressed his love for motherland. He was writing articles on contemporary issues. Mahatma Gandhi, Jawaharlal Nehru and Spiritualism of Swami Vivekananda, Madhusudan Das and Gopabandhu were his ideals.

JB completed I.A. and B.A. (Hons.) from Ravenshaw College and went to Benaras Hindu University, Varanasi for doing M.A. in Political Science. But his ambition was to become a *"Desh Bhakta"* (true patriot) although he has secured 1st postion in his subjects. But his interest was to know the history, culture and literature of his country.

Soon after his M.A. he came back to Cuttack and joined *'The Prajātantra Organization'* and became the editor of "The Eastern Times" and the 'Prajātantra'. He came in contact with Dr. Harekrishna Mahatab, a great leader and historian of his time and then started the journey in developing his literary activities. He became the first editor of Odia Magazine *"Pourusha"*. It was a golden opportunity for JB to showcase his editorial efficiency, academic excellence and he became very popular in and outside Odisha and established a base to build career both in politics and literature.

JB became a candidate for Loksabha Election in 1971 and got elected to the Parliament from historic millenium city, Cuttack. His main purpose was to ensure the allround development of his home state, Odisha. JB quotes Kavibar Radhanath Ray who describes Odisha to be a petal in the lotus of India.

"Bhārata Pankaja dalamida
Utkala mandalmiti viditam yat"

This means India is a Lotus and Utkal or Odisha is known to be an integral part of the country. JB drew the attention of Govt. of India for the allround development of the state. His debating skill was unique in the Parliament for which he was praised. JB's remarkable speech drew the attention of the then Prime Minister, Indira Gandhi and other Central Ministers and in course of time he could become an unparallel leader of National Congress Party. He was inducted as Deputy Minister in Indira's Council of Ministers (1973). He was elevated to the Minister of State in 1975 with important portfolio like "Defence". The INS Chilka, Missile Training Centre at Gopalpur (Ganjam), Naval Armament Depot in Koraput, Jakhapura-Bansapani Railway Track are some of the significant contributions of JB to Odisha. For his efforts in 1978, he was made the President of Odisha Pradesh Congress Committee assigned to lead the party in Odisha. During that period, he is known as the "*Chā ṇakya of Odisha*". He led the party and party got unprecedented majority. In 1980, JB was again elected from Cuttack Loksabha Constituency. He joined as Cabinet Minister in Indira Gandhi's Cabinet and was given the portfolio of Cabinet Minister for Tourism and Civil Aviation, who gave vibrant direction to his ministry. JB was also given the responsibility to lead Pradesh Congress Party to fight Assembly election in May 1980. As per the direction of the Party High Command, he came to Odisha and became Chief Minister on 10th June 1980. Replacing Smt. Nandini Satpathy. JB continued as Chief Minister for a full term of five years. Needless to mention that JB had to handle various issues of dissidents with patience, courage and conviction to maintain stability and he was considered to be a pathfinder till his third term from 1995 to 1999. Odisha witnessed stability and unprecedented growth in Health, Education, Industry, surface transport, Animal Husbandries.

During the tenure of JB, Tourism Industry got boosting. For the first time in the country, hotels of Odisha were declared to be industry and entrepreneurs were encouraged and tourists were attracted to Odisha. The establishment of Chandaka Elephant Sanctuary near Bhubaneswar became first elephant sanctuary in the country. Bhitarkanika was declared ot be marine park or marine sanctuary. Puri,

Konark and Bhubaneswar were connected as a *Golden Triangle* and attracted a number of tourist to Odisha. In the capital, JB had undertaken many steps for public welfare. Development of Chandaka Mancheswar Industrial Estate, setting up of Indira Gandhi park, construction of Kalinga Stadium, establishment of state's first planetorium (in the name of Samanta Chandra Sekhar), establishment of N.K. Chaudhury Centre for development studies, Kalinga Studio (one and only one film making institute), XIMB (now a university), National Institute of Physics were established and Bhubaneswar emerged as a capital with vigour. Similarly in Cuttack (the old Capital of Odisha), a huge ring road was made to check the flood. A new Bidānāsikatak was created to provide residential facilities for aspirants to reside in historic millenium city. His contribution in Agricultural sector is commendable; agriculture was given the status of industry; irrigation facilities increased 33%. with canals and lift irrigation increased subsequently.

IPICOL was established to encourage Industry Sector and APICOL was created to promote agriculture sector of state. Along with industrial revolution, JB gave due attention to the promotion of Odia language and literature and encouraged to Sanskrit study and research through establishment of a Sanskrit University in Puri. JB brought name and fame to state of Odisha during 1980-90 and another five years from 1995-2000.

JB travelled a number of foreign countries not only as Chief Minister, but also as a newsperson with a research attitude to unearth the traces of Indian culture and tradition in those countries and to find the best policies and practice to be emulated for the development of his own state and many foreign investors were attracted to Odisha. The most important dimension of JB's personality was his creativity for which he has been immortalized. He is known as a poet, author, translator and overall a "Sāraswat Sādhak". As a poet, he has composed "Sindhu Upatyakā" in Odia and "Vāni" from "Nilakandareswaram (Sankrit), *Swapna O Samkalpa, Rāmāyaṇa, Mahābhārata, Srimad Bhāgvat* and *Gautam Buddha*. He has translated three Satakam (*Sringara Satakam*) composed by Bhatruhari. He edited "Gokulānanda Granthāvali', an anthology of the writing of his father and translation of Bankim Chandra Granthāvali from Bengali to Odia.

Because of JB's literary creation he received Sahitya Academy Award and other prestigious awards. He was conferred with D.Litt Degree (Prajñā Vācaspati) *Honoris causa* by two reputed institutes like Shri Jagannath Sanskrit University, Puri, and National Sanskrit University, Tirupati. JB also served as Governor of Assam from 2009 to 2014 and was adjudged as most popular Governor.

JB was an embodiment of peace, patience, an epitome of Indian value and culture. He had command over languages like Odia, Sanskrit, English, Hindi and Bengali. He loved the philosophy of plain living and high thinking from Gandhi, courage and conviction from Swami Vivekananda, Statesmanship from Nehru. He had good relations with personalities like Pranab Mukherjee and P. V. Narasingha Rao. JB will be remembered as "*Rājarshi*" (A seer like leader) in the field of politics, social services, domestic behaviour and above all a personality determined for the allround development of the state of Odisha.

Biju Patnaik - An embodiment of heroism, patriotism and humanism

Harihar Panda

Biju Patnaik, a very popular name on the lips of every Odia, is regarded as one of the makers of modern Odisha. His sad demise on 17 April 1997 created a great vacuum in the political scenario of Odisha. A multifaceted personality, Biju Patnaik left an indelible imprint not only in the heart of Odia multitude but also of India and abroad. Regarded as the 'Tall Man' and admired as an epitome of courage and bravery he galvanized the political platform of pre-independent and post-independent India. As a man of high ambition, he created history, changed history and also shaped history. As a lover of Odias his body, mind and soul were dedicated for the upliftment of the people of this land – a practice which he maintained till his last breath.

Childhood days

Biju Patnaik, the living legend, was born on 5th March, 1916 at Tulasipur in Cuttack as a worthy son of Laxminarayan Patnaik and Ashalata Devi. Biju had two brothers – the elder one, Sraddhananda, better known as George Patnaik, a notable Dentist and Jayananda alias

Siju Babu who met premature death, Biju's only sister Mukti Devi and an M.A. during that period. Biju's rudimentary schooling started in Mission Primary School, Mission School (present Christ Collegiate School) and the prestigious Ravenshaw Collegiate School. In 1932 he passed Matriculation with First Division. In 1930, when he was a school boy, he jumped into the flooded river to rescue the umbrella of Gopabandhu Das who hugged him and blessed him to be a greatman in future. In 1931 an aeroplane landed at Kaliaboda, Cuttack and being curious, Biju went to touch the plane and was lathicharged by Hergreaves and blood tickled out of his head. From that day, Biju resolved to be a pilot.[1]

At College

After qualifying an entrance examination in Patna in 1932, Biju was admitted into Ravenshaw College and read I.Sc.. Accompanied by his friends – Amar De and Bhramarbar Sahu, Biju went to Peshwar by bi-cycle and returned back. His adventurous journey has been reflected in *Bulanisa*.[2] Besides his daring journey to Peshawar Biju had exhibited an uncommon skill of a sports man and earned the majestic title of "Ravenshaw Blue".[3] Leaving B.Sc. from Ravenshaw Biju entered into Aeronautical Engineering College in 1934 and took aeronautical training for three years in Aeronautical Training Institute of Indian and Delhi Flying Club and became a Cargo Pilot. He married Gyan Devi, the grand daughter of Radhashyama Singh of Rawalpindi on 6.12.1939.

Kalinga Airlines, Dacota Plane and adventures

Biju started Kalinga Airlines and after independence in 1949 it was given a licence for operating a purely freighter service on the Calcutta-Agartala route. His Kalinga Airlines Dakotas were very famous during that time what he had brought from Panagarh Surplus Depot as a Government Pilot. During the Quit India Movement Biju secretly performed works like airlifting of revolutionary pamphlets, posters and leaflets in support of Netaji's INA, airlifting of leaders like Jay Prakash Narayan, Ram Manohar Lohia, Achut Patwardhan, Aruna Asaf Ali and others stealthily to a clandestine spot and he was caught by the British Police and imprisoned and released from jail in 1945. During the World War II when Russia was surrounded by the Nazi brigades, Biju as a Pilot of Royal Air Force supplied weapons to Russian soldiers. During 1947-48 Indo-Pak war he was able to land Indian trops at Srinagar airstrip and rescued many Kashmir Pandits including Ramanand Sagar, the famous T.V. serial maker of *Rāmāyana*. His help to Nepal's insurgents against Rana's regime was remarkable. With matchless brvavery Biju rescued the life of Sukarno, Hatta, Siahriar and others bringing them from Jakarta to Delhi and was conferred the title of '*Bhumiputra*' in Indonesia in 1950.

Entry into Politics and career as a Politician

With the conclusion of the World War II, Biju was released from the jail in 1945. In the election to second pre-independent Assembly held in 1946, Biju was elected as an MLA from Orissa Sadar seat. With the establishment of Orissa Textile Mill and Kalinga Refrigerator began his career as an industrialist. In the election of 1952 Biju was elected to Assembly from Jagannath Prasad constituency. Since 1952, the politics of Odisha was a synonym of politics of instability.[4] In the 1957 election Biju was elected from Sorada and Dr.H.K.Mahatab formed the Ministry with the backing of other parties but the stability was questionable on the grounds of brittle ethics that went behind it.[5] Biju played a vital role to patch up the antagonism between Mahatab and R.N.Singh Deo. In 1961, Biju became the President or the Pradesh Congress Committee after defeating Banamali Patnaik which sealed the fate of Mahatab's coalition regime.[6] During the devastating floods of 1961 and 1962, Biju played a vital role by airdropping of tons of cooked food like puri, paratha, boiled potato, flattened rice and jaggery, candles, match boxes, salt, etc. and won the hearts of the downtrodden.

Biju as Chief Minister

After a short spell of President's rule in Odisha, the mid-term election was held in June 1961 and Biju Patnaik came with a scripting success grappling 82 seats out of 140 in Odisha Vidhan Sabha and became the Chief Minister. The Congress orgnisation got a juvenile touch under the magic leadership of Biju. He was instrumental in making monumental achievements like the establishment of Paradeep Port, Express Highway, Industrial Development Corporation, Ferrochrome Plant of Jajpur road, Regional Engineering College of Rourkela, Sainik School at Bhubaneswar, Mig Factory at Sunabeda, Balimela Dam, Thermal Power Plant of Talcher, Charbatia Airbase, CRP Centre, Orissa Flying Club, Engineering College of Burla, Medical College of Berhampur, Regional College of Education, Orissa University of Agriculture and Technology, Tikarapada Multi-Purpose Dam, hundreds of educational institutions for boys and girls etc. During this period the role of Biju Patnaik and his

Kalinga Airlines rendered habitual service for the nation in the Sino-Indian War of 1962. In 1963 Kamraj Plan was executed and Biju resigned from post of Chief Minister. Morarji Desai, the ex-Prime Minister of Indian had written in the autobiography that Biju Patnaik was instrumental for this plan but it came in the name of Kamraj.[8]

The fury of 1964, CBI Report and Biju's debacle

In 1964 a students' strike originated from Cuttack and spread all over Odisha as a conflagration which put the last nail on the coffin of Biren Mitra's Ministry. By the advice of H.K.Mahatab, the students gave derogatory slogans against Biju-Biren-Nilamani. Biju tried his level best to appease the students but he failed stupendously. Biju's house was ransacked by the police. To add to his plight, a memorandum of Shri R.N.Singh Deo, the leader of opposition of Odisha Legislative Assembly and 62 others submitted to the President against the corruption of Biju, Biren and others was seriously taken by G.L.Nanda, the Home Minister. After CBI's report Lal Bahadur Shastri formed a sub-committee of Union Cabinet to persue the report and submit the decision. At this juncture Biju and other Congress leaders of Eastern India met at Ranchi in November 1964 and condemned the steps taken by Nanda. Of course, the committee had taken some unjudicious attitude[9] for which Biju had to resign from the Chairman of the State Planning Board. In 1965 Indo-Pak war due to Biju's initiation the attack of Seventh Fleet on India was sagaciously avoided.[10] Odisha's political condition from 1961-1966 had reached the nadir point of degeneration with frequent change of Chief Ministers like Biju Patnaik, Biren Mitra and Sadasiv

Tripathy which destabilized the "political stability" of Odisha.[11] Biju's fate was doomed in 1967 election when a school teacher Chakradhar Satpathy who defeated Biju at Patkura who only got 16,690 votes and lost hope for his comeback in future.

The Khanna Commission and Elections from 1971 to 1990

In 1967 election when Biju could not be allowed to contest for Rajya Sabha, he formed Utkal Congress with his friends and criticized the step-motherly attitude of the Central Government for Odisha.[12] After the formation of the non-Congress ministry in 1967, Justice Khanna, the then Judge of the Delhi High Court came to enquire about the corruption levelled against Biju Patnaik and other Congress Chief Ministers and Deputy Chief Ministers of Odisha who had abused power. After examining all the allegations against Biju Patnaik concerning the sale of Kalinga Iron Works, purchase of Tabular process from Kalinga Tubes, Daya Bridge contract, reduction of premium of land leased to OTM, Choudwar and appointment of Sundergarh Public Prosecutor, the Khanna Commission exonerated Biju Babu. In 1971 election Biju's Utkal Congress was rejected by the people of Odisha. However, in 1971 by-election Biju Patnaik won from Rajnagar due to his help to the public during the devastating cyclone of 1971. He was arrested during 1975 emergency who was booked under MISA and RAW and sent to jail but his spirit was never broken which he regained after his victory in 1977 and became the Minister of Steel and Mines of India and was instrumental in setting the plant of NALCO in Angul. During that period under his initiation, the Aluminium Factory at Damanjodi, Koraput and the Second Steel Plant at Paradeep were initiated. With the debacle of Janata Party in the Centre, Kendrapara Parliamentary Constituency proved to be his political bastion in the elections of 1979, 1980, 1984 and 1985. He resigned from Lok Sabha seat in 1985 and remained as Leader of Opposition in Odisha Assembly from 1985 to 1990. When heinous scandalous deals were flashed against J.B.Patnaik, the then Chief Minister of Odisha on the pages of *Illustrated Weekly*, forgetting the bitter enmity with him, Biju gave a statement to the news-reporters that they should not poke their nose in the private life of the politicians. However in 1989 Lok Sabha election Biju's Padayātrā led Lok Dal to bang 18 seats out of 21 although he did not contest. In 1990 Biju's Lok Dal banged 123 seats out of 147 of the Odisha Legislative Assembly[13] and Biju became the Chief Minister after a gap of twenty seven years.

Biju's second term as Chief Minister

During his second term as the Chief Minister, although his dream for the second steel plant at Jakhapura near Daitari was shattered on the rock of frustration due to the withdrawal of Swaraj Paul from the project, but his spirit and reformative zeal did not diminish. Talking on women empowerment, he said, "Do you waste yourselves away into the 21st century? Make the 21st century a standard bearer for your strength of mind to meet all kinds of challenges, specially the challenges of your own society ... Where ever you may light a lamp as I have lighted here and remove the darkness from the society where you live. If you have done this, you have done a great service to yourself, to the society and to the nation".[14] He issued instruction that if a government servant receives dowry, he should be put under suspension and after inquiry will be dismissed from service[15] During this period he undertook several welfare measures for people like 'Kalinga Kutir Yojanā', 'Wage hike for labourers', 'anti-corruption drive', 'beating of corrupt officials', 'dealing with Naxalites', 'castration of rapists' etc. He also faced several upheavels like strike of Secretariat employees, liquor tragedy of Cuttack (1992) which took away 300 lives and so on.

The last journey

On 29.03.1997, Biju Babu was hospitalized at Ram Manohar Lohia Hospital, New Delhi for the treatment of aggravated Bronchial Asthma. He was shifted to Escort Hospital on 30.03.1997. On 17.04.1997, on the day of *Sudashā Brata,* the tall man crumbled and left the world for good. Entire Odisha became dumb. On the next day his mortal body was brought to Bhubaneswar in a defence aircraft.[15] His wife Gyan Patnaik, sons Prem Patnaik and Nabin Patnaik and daughter Gita Mehta were present. After last *Darshan* at Nabin Nivas, he was cremated at Swargadwār at Puri. More than five lakhs of people were present there. Odisha Government announced seven days mourning for their departed leader. Many eminent personalities of India assembled at Puri to bid farewell to their leader once for all. They were the then Prime Minister A.B.Vajpeyee, Chandrasekhar, L.K. Advani, Devi Lal, Madhu Dandavate, Pramod Mahajan, M.G. Ramachandran, N.T. Rama Rao and many others including all the great leaders of Odisha.[16]

The cremation ground was echoed with the slogans like *"Biju Babu Amar Rahe"*, *"Kalinga Samrat Amar Rahe"* etc.

Biju Patnaik was a leader par excellence. His attitude was to play with fire. His service and sacrifice, trails and tribulations, dare and dash to wipe out the tears of motherland, his mission and message for a resurgent India are all exemplary to make him a firebrand nationalist. By dint of his entrepreneurial ability he could be an avowed industrialist and dreamt to industrialize Odisha. A champion of women empowerment he brought laws for their protection and to punish the persons harassing women in any manner. The humanistic touch, he projected during his life cannot be erased by the ironical smile of the time. It is better to conclude with Soumya Ranjan Patnaik who paid tribute to Biju Patnaik in these words:[17]

His chief contribution belongs to the world of spirit where an Odia boy born seven decades after him felt proud that he belonged to the same race as Biju Patnaik. No other Odia has even bridged such a generation gap and no one will in foreseeable future".

REFERENCES

1. "Dāmbhika O' Duhsahasikatara Pratika Biju Patnaik' in *Parjyabekshyaka* (Odia), Bhubaneswar, dt.6.3.1990.
2. *Samaya*, Bhubaneswar, dt.27.4.1997.
3. "Kridābit Biju O' Kridā Puraskar", *Dharitri*, Bhubaneswar dt.5.3.2005.
4. S.Nanda, *Coalition Politics in Orissa*, New Delhi, 1997, pp.33-36.
5. D.Patnaik, *'Role of Congress Ministry in Orissa 1950-64'*, Unpublished thesis submitted to Utkal University, p.38.

6. N.Routray, *Smruti Anubhuti* (Odia), Cuttack, 1986, p.47.
7. A.K.Lenka, 'Biju Patnaik : A Profile of a Leader and Administrator (1947-1963)', unpublished thesis, Utkal University, 2007, pp.39-40.
8. G.Patnaik, "*Biju Tānka Pari Pilā Dinu*" (Odia), *Ananya*, p.8.
9. S.Ghosh, *Orissa in Turmoil*, Bhubaneswar, 1991, p.140.
10. P.Mohanty, "*Kie Ehi Biju Patnaik*" (Odia), *Adyapi*, Paradeep, 1987, p.18.
11. Tiwari, *State Politics in India : A Study of Orissa (1961-1971)*, New Delhi, 1994, p.85.
12. For details see, J.K.Mishra, 'Government and Public in Orissa', a thesis submitted to Sambalpur University, p.57.
13. *Sun Times*, 2.3.1990.
14. Biju Patnaik's address at the Conference at Delhi on 14.9.1992, *Orissa Review*, October Issue, 1992, p.4.
15. J.Mangaraj, "Janatā Nuhen Jana Samudra" (Odia), *Sun Times*, 18.4.1997.
16. J.Mishra & B.S.Mishra, *Kalinga Keshari* (Odia), Cuttack, 1999, p.32.
17. *Sun Times*, 18.4.1997, p.4.

Biswa Bhusan Harichandan: A Versatile Genius

Bijayananda Singh

Biswabhusan Harichandan is an illustrious son of the worthy father Parsuram Harichandan, who had wide acclamation in the state as a dramatist, a literary figure and a freedom fighter having political affinity and was the first Vice-Chairman of Zilla Parishad of undivided Puri district. On 3rd August' 1934, Biswabhusan Harichandan was born in village Godijhar of Banpur belonging to the district of Khordha, a centre of revolution against the British Raj. Since the childhood, he was distinguished from others as a brilliant student with uncommon qualities. In course of time, the young mind was nurtured and nourished with honours subject in economics in S.C.S College, Puri, the religious citadel of Odisha. After graduation he decided not to go for P.G. in economics and switched over to do graduation in law at Madhusudan Law College, Cuttack.

Biswabhusan's versatile genius and towering personality made him an eminent advocate in High Court and renowned political leader in politics simultaneously. Hard work, dedication, strong determination and punctuality placed him in extraordinary position in public domain. The spirited Biswabhusan joined Jayaprakashji's "Sampurna Krānti Movement" and fought against the throttling of democracy by the then Prime Minister Smt. Indira Gandhi which resulted in his imprisonment during the time of Emergency, for months together. As reformation was the dream of Biswabhusan, he could not abstain from revolting against any sorts of social injustice. In the capacity of Chairman of High Court Bar Association Action Committee, he led the Lawyer's agitation in Odisha against the supersession of judges in Supreme Court in 1974 and aroused public opinion against the dictatorial regime of Smt. Indira Gandhi, the then Prime Minister.

Being a politician, he had incessantly tried to perform the best for the betterment of people irrespective of party politics. The voters' regards, respect, affection and great expectation from his politics, elected him to the Legislative Assembly of Odisha for five times viz. 1977, 1990, 1996, 2000 and 2004. People's love was reflected, when Biswabhusan won the 2000 Assembly election in the state capital Bhubaneswar by a margin of 95000 votes against his nearest rival in breaking all the previous records in Odisha.

Biswabhusan has always been in high estimation in the Government. Whenever he is elected to State Legislative Assembly, his personality has become the centre of attraction. While in government, he was offered the dignitary portfolios of Cabinet Minister in the years, 1977, 1990, 2000 and 2004 and continued as such till 2009. As cabinet minister his important portfolios were Revenue, Law, Rural Development, Industries, Food and Civil Supplies, Labour and Employment, Housing, Cultural Affairs, Fisheries and Animal Resources Development Departments. He had laid the foundation of BJP in Odisha and became the founder President of the party in 1980 by Shri Atal Bihari Vajpayee, the national president and then elected as the state President of BJP consecutively for three more terms till 1988. He was also elected as the leader of the BJP legislature Party in state Assembly for 13 years i.e. from 1996 to 2009. All the people of Odisha agog over the pivotal role being played by Biswa Bhusan with all efficiency and prominence in the Government and remained in the public's gaze. He is an epitome and icon in politics for fighting the people's cause, for which he is highly admired and respected by the people, administration and politicians, irrespective of their party affiliation.

Power, in itself is neutral. In Biswa Bhusan's hand it became a blessing. Power is condemned by non-politicians but this power, in hands of Biswa Bhusan needs to be realised with sense of all respect so that he has cleaned of all the ugly instincts that biding within them. Biswa Bhusan knows himself, understands his own being, understands the meaning of life. Therefore, he has no inferiority complex at all, like all other politicians. He is so full, so contented, and so utterly blissful; there is no reason for him to feel any ambition to have power over others.

No politician is remembered after power is over unless the politician has the affinity with the culture and literature. Biswa Bhusan babu has not spent all his time in politics, rather he has created his own time for literature. As a columnist he has wide name and fame in writing articles on contemporary political issues, historical, social and cultural matters which have been published in all leading newspapers of Odisha and some leading English weeklies published in Delhi. Biswa

Bhusan babu who has taken bold step with all justifications and concrete evidence that there was no war like Kalinga war, that ever fought in 261 BC. That war was rather fabricated by some historians with beautiful literary descriptions that a river of blood was created.

His tributes to the world of encyclopaedia are innumerable but we can quote some of them out of many. They are *Mahā Sangrāmara Mahānāyak*, a drama on Buxi Jagabandhu, the Supreme Commander of Pāika Revolution of 1817, six one act plays,like *Rānā Pratāp, Shesha Jhalak, Mahārāni Padmin of Mewar, Astha Sikhā on Tapang Dalabeherā's heroic war and sacrifice, Mānasi* (social) and *Abhisapta Karna* (mythological) *Swachha Sāsanara Gahanakathā*, an anthology of twenty six short stories and 'Ye *Mātira Dāka*', a compilation of some of his selected published articles, *Sangrām Sarināhin*, his autobiography, which has focussed on his struggles for the common and down-trodden people of the society in political, administrative, social, cultural and other fields during his long public career of more than half a centrury.

Politicians are sort of different people but so far as Biswa Bhusan babu is concerned, he is a politician in true sense of the term. He, with all rationality and the mind set of sacrifice to humanity is something divine, what is most appropriate in case of Biswa Bhusan Harichandan. In deep observation, to his political career, one will come upon religiousness in his political life but not religious. His cosmopolitan outlook has made him unique and transparent in muddy water of politics.

During his tenure as a Cabinet Minister in 1977, the essential commodities, which were scarce during emergency, were not only freely made available but were available at economic price and the price-line was steadily maintained. His stringent actions against the black marketers and hoarders made him very popular in Odisha.

As Revenue Minister, he laid emphasis on computerization of land records, simplification and codification of revenue laws for convenience of administration and took bold steps for restoration of Adivasi land which are illegally and fraudulently transferred by amending Regulation 2 of 1956 and making it more stringent. He reorganized the revenue administration by making it more pro-people. He stood as the saviour of Tribal people.

As Industry Minister, he took initiative in introducing single window system and got the Industry facilitation Act passed. The much sought for R.R. Policy of the State which brought a revolutionary change in the field of rehabilitation and re-settlement of the displaced persons was the brain-child of Sri Harichandan who in his capacity as the Chairman of the Cabinet Sub-Committee gave it final shape which was then the best R.R. Policy of the country.

During his tenure as a Minister of Culture Affairs, he made some significant contributions. It was the usual practice that the Minister of Culture remains in charge of the Dept. of Culture as Ex-officio President of Odisha Sahitya Academy. But Sri Harichandan changed the tradition and amended the rule; divided the Sahitya Academy into three Academies such as Sahitya Academy, Sangeet Natak Academy and Lalitkala Academy, by placing eminent senior persons like writers, artists and persons excelled in their field to be appointed as President of such Academy. It is a new approach in which scholars, eminent personalities in their field are encouraged to become the President of the Academy.

Due to his stiff opposition, the State was saved from selling away all the surplus government land for repayment of Government's loans for which the State Cabinet had already taken a decision while he was absent from the head quarter. He expressed his strong reservation on it stating that such transfer was not only illegal, but also unethical. He said that state is the owner of the land and not the government which has limited powers like Trustees. He vehemently opposed the sale of all the surplus govt. lands and was able to get the decision changed. Another cabinet meeting was convened at his insistence and the decision was annulled.

As a patriot, he took keen interest in giving stress on the historic war for freedom by the people of Odisha known as "Pāika Bidroha 1817" under the leadership of Buxi Jagabandhu, which continued for long 8 years till 1825. Biswa Bhusan Babu wrote articles on this Paika Bidroha in leading news papers, magazines and encouraged the historians to write on the same highlighting the heroic acts of Pāika Bidroha. In 1978 when along with all other portfolios, cultural affairs department was with him, he planned to celebrate the martial tradition of Odisha, specially highlighting the glorious Pāika Revolution. He involved all the political parties in this Martial Tradition Celebration where more than one hundred Pāika Ākhadā Groups had joined and sword fencing and other competitions were held for 3 days in parade ground of Bhubaneswar. The mammoth procession of Pāikas and the horse riding pāikas from Barunei hill, the centre of revolution to the parade ground in the state capital holding their traditional weapons swords and shields with their war cries was not only attractive was very sensational. People in both sides of this 25 km. long road were shouting slogans and encouraging them. For 3 days sword fencing and other competitions of the Pāikas were exhibited in parade ground and in Soochanā Bhavan. The historians and research scholars read and discussed about their articles on the martial tradition and history of Odisha. The political stalwarts like Dr. Harekrushna Mahatab, Biju Pattnaik, Dr. Radhanath Rath, and Rabi Ray were encouraging Biswabhusan Babu for this great celebration. There were two big public meetings in the parade ground one on the inaugural day of the celebration and another on the closing day where all these leaders and Chief Minister Nilamani Routray and President of the celebration Biswa Bhusan Babu addressed the mammoth gathering with their thunders applause.

This sort of celebration were organised under his leadership from time to time where politicians of different parties, historians and Central Ministers were participating. The entire aim of Biswa Bhusan babu was for enkindling the spirit of patriotism amongst the people who would come forward to serve the people of the motherland. Pāika Revolution got National recognition as a freedom movement by the Hon'ble Prime Minister Shri Narendra Modi in 2017 and budgetary provision was made for the bicentenary celebration of it and to build a memorial at Barunei hill, the centre of the revolution. The bicentenary celebration of Pāika Bidroha was held in Delhi and in other places of the country with all pomp and ceremony.

Biswa Bhusan became the Governor of Andhra Pradesh from 2019 to 2023. In Andhra Pradesh he was loved by one and all. He was called as *"Peoples' Governor"* very close to the hearts of people of Andhra Pradesh. At present, he is the Governor of Chhattisgarh with effect from February-2023. He takes interest in the public welfare and safeguards Indian Culture and tradition.

Biswa Bhusan babu is a powerful orator and in most of his inspiring speeches, he tries to sensitise the people to serve the nation. He is the son of the soil of Odisha but every bit of his action is dedicated for the cause of people of the state and the Nation. He is really a legend, a true patriot, a milestone of the progress and prosperity of the motherland. His service to the nation for more than five decades in every field will be remembered for all time to come. The footprints that he leaves in sands of time will certainly be followed by the people of coming generation.

The Longest Reign in History: The 'Naveen' Era in Odisha Politics

Netajee Abhinandan | Soumya Ranjan Gahir

Twenty-three years and counting. Five consecutive terms and twenty-three years. The record set by Naveen Patnaik is nearly impossible to break. He is not only the longest-serving Chief Minister of Odisha but also one of the longest-serving Chief Ministers of any Indian state, holding the post for over two decades, and only the third Indian Chief Minister after Pawan Chamling and Jyoti Basu to win five consecutive terms as Chief Minister. He has not faced a single electoral defeat since entering the political arena in 1997 after the demise of his father, Biju Patnaik. The consistent, continuous and steadfast support of the people of Odisha over more than two decades has made Naveen Patnaik the tallest-ever leader in the political history of the state, even shadowing the glorious achievements of his father, legendary Biju Patnaik. Someone who had no relation with politics-direct or indirect-turning master of the art and craft of politics in 20 years is an amazing story in itself.

The people who have known Naveen in his pre-political life could observe a sharp change in his lifestyle and people-to-people approach. Being a grounded person with an acute sense of social justice, he was eager to learn the ropes of Odisha politics. He took a humane approach by intermingling with people and taking an interest in their lives. Further, he gave up wearing tees and trousers, started wearing white kurta-pyjama with Kolhapuri chappals, and started giving speeches in Odia, however short it may have been at the start. These small changes imbibed by Naveen enabled him to achieve what he could for Odisha in 25 years of his political journey.

Naveen Patnaik's Legacy: Fulfilling Father's Dream for Odisha

With a vision to build a modern, empowered, and progressive new Odisha, Naveen Patnaik has launched numerous welfare programs over the years and ensured that all the development benefits were passed on to the people at the grassroots level. Naveen has rendered committed service to the state's population and created a people-oriented governance model. He has adopted a unique charter of 5T as the guiding principles of his government; these are-Team Work, Technology, Transparency, Transformation, and Timeliness.

During Naveen Patnaik's five-term tenure in Odisha, the state has made rapid strides in development and has become a role model in many fields, some of which are:

Women Empowerment

Women's empowerment is very close to the Chief Minister's heart. His women empowerment model focuses on providing women equal rights and opportunities to empower them and live with dignity in society. Naveen has reserved 50 percent of seats for women in gram panchayats and urban local bodies to ensure holistic empowerment. In the recently concluded local body elections, more than 55 percent of women have got elected. Notably, India stands behind 140 countries in its low representation of women in Parliament. However, Biju Janta Dal reserved one-third of the seats for women in the 2019 Lok Sabha elections, which showed their commitment to gender equality.

Women's Transformation through Mission Shakti

The *'Mission Shakti'* program was adopted in 2001 as a critical women empowerment strategy and was initiated as a women's self-help group initiative. Mission Shakti aims to empower women through gainful activities by providing credit and market linkage. Nearly 70 lakh women have been organised into 6 lakh groups in all blocks and urban local bodies of the state so far. To further the SHG movement in the state and consolidate and deepen the efforts around the SHG movement, a separate Department of Mission Shakti came into existence on 1st June 2021.

Self-Help Groups

The Odisha Government provides interest-free loans of upto 5 lakhs for these SHGs. This has helped scale up finance for women-run businesses. After empowering 70 lakh women through Self-Help Groups (SHGs), the Odisha government announced transforming the SHGs into Small and Medium-Sized Enterprises (SMEs) and turning them into vibrant financial hubs. The Chief Minister said, *"I truly believe that no household, society, or state and no country has ever moved forward without empowering its women."*

Sports

With the vision of 'investment in sports is an investment in youth', the government prioritised the development of sports infrastructure in the state. With the declining popularity of hockey, a sport in which India has won eight gold medals, Naveen Patnaik took a historic step to support and sponsor the national men's and women's hockey teams for five years, and the result was for all to see at the Tokyo Olympics. After four decades, the Indian men's team brought home a medal, and what is perhaps more significant is that Mr. Patnaik announced sponsoring Indian hockey for ten more years. Moreover, this partnership was not restricted to hockey alone but gradually extended to Rugby, Swimming, and Football. The Odisha government's efforts were recognised and awarded Best State for the promotion of Sports awards in 2023.

Furthermore, Odisha is acknowledged as *'The Sports Capital of India* for successfully organising the Asian Athletics Championship in 2017, two consecutive Hockey Men's World Cups in 2018 and 2023, and other major national and international sports events. Odisha is investing significantly in developing an inclusive and all-accessible sports ecosystem. Kalinga Sports Complex, located in the heart of Bhubaneswar, is known as one of the best sports hubs in India for its world-class infrastructures and facilities for Hockey, Athletics, Football, Sport Climbing, Weightlifting, Swimming, Sport Science, etc. In Rourkela, the Birsa Munda Hockey Stadium was recently inducted into the Guinness Book of world records as the largest fully-seated hockey stadium in the world, with a seating capacity for over 20,000 spectators.

Tourism

Odisha, often referred to as *'India's best-kept secret,'* has tremendous potential in the tourism sector because of its golden history, strategic geographical location, diverse demography, and profound bounties of nature. Odisha is known for its scenic beauty, exquisite temples, extraordinary monuments, exquisite craftsmanship, wildlife sanctuaries, natural landscape, and pristine beaches worldwide. The Odisha government is making concerted efforts to develop Odisha as a global hotspot for tourists, provide livelihoods and employment opportunities, and make the state attractive to investors. Over the past decades, tourism has continuously expanded and diversified to become the fastest-growing economic sector. Tourism is now one of the main contributors to the economy of Odisha, accounting for 13% of its GDP.

To promote sustainable and responsible tourism to create employment opportunities and bring socio-economic benefits to the stakeholder community Naveen Patnaik has invested his spare time and resources into promoting Odisha tourism. He has taken a particular interest in his fifth term in preserving and promoting heritage towns like Puri and ancient temples like Jagannath temple, Konark temple, and Lingaraj temple of Bhubaneswar. The government has breathed new life into tourism by redeveloping pilgrimage centres, beaches, and other tourist attractions, propelling Odisha as one of the most travelled places in the country.

In the last six to seven years, tourist arrival to the state has increased. However, the COVID-19 pandemic and subsequent travel restrictions have affected the tourism sector the worst, not only in the state and country but across the globe. Therefore, to re-emphasis tourism sector aftermath of the pandemic Odisha government has launched Tourism Policy 2022, which envisages an aggressive, dynamic, and long-term approach to achieve the growth potential in tourism by initiating identified policy measures, framing the required statutory framework, ensuring large-scale investment support through professional management and private participation. It has implemented the award-winning Single Window System (Go SWIFT) that facilitates the appraisal of investment proposals without any physical interface.

Furthermore, Naveen Patnaik hosted a roundtable discussion in Kyoto focusing on opportunities for collaboration between Japan and Odisha in Tourism and Sports. During the discussion, the Chief Minister highlighted the immense potential of Odisha as a tourist destination, with a particular emphasis on leveraging Odisha's rich Buddhist tradition, especially the heritage sites in *Dhauli, Lalitgiri, Ratnagiri,* and *Udayagiri.* He urged stakeholders in the sports and tourism sector to explore opportunities for collaboration between Japan and Odisha.

Secularism

Naveen Patnaik has proved his secular credentials by breaking BJD's ties with the Bharatiya Janata Party ahead of the 2009 general elections after the Kandhamal riots 2008. He made the famous declaration that every drop of his blood remained secular.

When the Union government declined to renew the FCRA registration, Naveen Patnaik stood by Missionaries of Charity (MoC) and reaffirmed his secular outlook. Patnaik appeared as a Robinhood to Missionaries of

Charity by allocating 79 lacs from the Chief Minister's Relief Fund. He understood the gravity of social service and the role of Missionaries of Charity in tribal areas of Odisha, hence extending humanitarian and monetary services. Patnaik's decision on the MoC affirms his commitment to religious pluralism and secularism and his vision to build a secular society.

Naveen Model of Governance: Welfare of One and All

When Naveen Patnaik took over as Chief Minister in 2000, the state suffered a severe crisis after the 1999 *Super Cyclone*. The state's finances were in a mess, and all developmental activities had ceased. Poverty and hunger all over the state made its condition worse. Nevertheless, soon after assuming the chief minister's office, he moved into action mode by chalking out strategies and rolling out a series of welfare measures for all categories of people and all-around development work. Decades ago, the state was in the public spotlight because of poverty and hunger. However, it has become one of the largest food producers in the country and a leader in poverty reduction. The poverty rate has dropped from 63% to 29%. During the next five years, the state expects poverty to drop drastically to just 10%. 1 rupee per kilogram of rice to the poor has been a game-changer in this direction.

Madhu Bābu Pension Yojanā

The Madhu Bābu Pension Yojanā (MBPY) is a pension scheme introduced to provide financial assistance to destitute, elderly, and disabled individuals in the state. It was initiated under the Department of Social Security and Empowerment of Persons with Disabilities for the disabled and old age persons in Odisha by the Chief Minister of Odisha in 2008. Under this scheme, beneficiaries will be provided a monthly pension of up to Rs. 700.

Mamatā Scheme

To alleviate the issue of maternal and infant undernutrition, the Government of Odisha, under the Department of Women and Child Development, launched a scheme initiated for pregnant women and lactating mothers called MAMATĀ in 2011. It is a conditional cash transfer maternity benefit scheme where Rs 5000 is transferred to the bank account of mothers. This scheme provides monetary support to pregnant and lactating women to enable them to seek improved nutrition and promote health-seeking behaviour. Pregnant and lactating women of the 19 & above age group can avail of the benefits under this scheme for the first two live births.

Biju YuvaSashaktikaran Yojanā

Launched in 2013, "Biju Yuva Sashaktikaran Yojanā" is a scheme by the Department of Higher Education, Govt. of Odisha. In this scheme, Rs. 30,000 per student is transferred directly to the bank accounts of 15,000 meritorious +2 students through Direct Benefit Transfer (DBT) to purchase a laptop.

Odisha Food Security Scheme (SFSS)

In reaction to the 2013 Food Security Act not covering certain groups in Odisha, Naveen Patnaik's government is revising. The Food Security Scheme launched under the National Food Security Act, 2013 would cover 25 lakh people in the first phase who were leftout under the National Food Security Act (NFSA)-2013. Beneficiaries under the State Food Security Scheme (SFSC) would receive 5 kg of rice at Re 1 per kg. The Odisha SFSC will spend Rs 442 crore per year.

Biju Sishu Surakshya Yojanā

The Odisha Government launched the Biju Sishu Surakshyā Yojanā, a scheme to facilitate the care and protection of orphan and HIV-infected children residing in different childcare institutions and orphanages. It was launched under the Women and Child Development Department in the Government of Odisha in 2016.

KĀLIA Yojanā

To develop agriculture and improve the conditions of landless farmers and sharecroppers, a direct benefit scheme named KĀLIA (Krushak Assistance for Livelihood and Income Augmentation) was launched in 2018. With this scheme, the state Government aims to lend farmers an all-inclusive and flexible support system, ensuring accelerated agricultural prosperity. The scheme envisages financial assistance of Rs.25,000 per farming family over five seasons to small and marginal farmers so that farmers can purchase inputs like seeds, fertilisers, and pesticides and use assistance towards labour and other investments. It will provide crop loans upto Rs.50,000 at 0% interest for the vulnerable landless labourers, sharecroppers, cultivators, and agricultural families identified by Gram Panchayats. Proposed by the Government of Odisha, the KĀLIA scheme brings 92% of state cultivators and almost all needy landless cultivators, significantly boosting the state's agricultural sector.

SAFAL Scheme

Farming is Odisha's most prominent occupation and its mainstay. A comprehensive agriculture strategy and government actions have prioritised the farming sector's growth. The Chief Minister of Odisha opened the SAFAL Common Credit Portal on 26th October 2022. Safal stands for Simplified Application for Agricultural Loans. The launch of Safal was done to improve the lives of farmers. Through the common credit portal, the farmers and *agri-preneurs* can access 500+ loan products offered by 40+ banks. They can apply for the loan online, track the submitted loan application and receive regular notifications on their application process.

Biju Swāsthya Kalyān Yojanā (BSKY)

'Every life is precious,' with this guiding principle, Naveen Patnaik launched the Biju Swāsthya Kalyān Yojanā (BSKY) smart card scheme on 15th August 2018, which promises cashless healthcare coverage of upto Rs.5 lakh per family and an additional 5 lakh for women members of the family. Smartcard holders can get cashless health coverage in more than 200 empanelled hospitals in the state. The state government will bear the cost for over 96.5 lakh economically vulnerable families. Around 45 lakhs of instances are recorded each month where the beneficiaries have availed free health care treatment under Biju Swāsthya Kalyān Yojanā.

Khushi Scheme

Khushi scheme of Odisha launched on 26th February 2018, aims to provide good menstrual hygiene care to women of the state. The initiative aims to promote health and hygiene among school-going adolescent girls leading to higher retention and greater women empowerment. Under the scheme, the government will provide free sanitary napkins to 17 lakh girls studying in Classes 6 to 12 in government and government-aided schools. The scheme is being implemented by state's Health and Family Welfare Department at a cost of Rs 70 crore per year. It was launched in 2018.

Jāgā Mission

The state has been taking drastic measures to make all the urban centres slum-free through the Jāgā Mission, which launched on 8th August 2018. The state passed the Odisha Land Rights for urban poor and Homeless Act to recognise slum dwellers' contribution to the cities' economy. This landmark piece of legislation, which aims to benefit every landless person who lives in a slum in municipalities and notifies area councils, is the first of its kind in the country. The Jāgā Mission is being implemented in all the 2,938 slums in 114 urban local bodies. 1.75 lakh families were given land rights under the scheme, and 585 slums were converted into model colonies.

Basudhā Scheme

Naveen Patnaik gave the Green Signal to the Drinking Water Project in 2018. He laid out the foundation stone of the Buxi Jagabandhu, assuring drinking water to all habitation'. Basudhā Odisha Drinking Water Project is one of the much-awaited projects of the state. After the completion of the project, the state government will provide clean drinking water to 147 districts in Puri and Ganjam villages.

Sumangal Scheme

The Odisha government has launched the scheme to encourage people to marry in inter-caste. Under this scheme, the inter-caste couple would receive a financial incentive of 2.5 lakhs. The Chief Minister also said those inter-caste marriages are the backbone of bringing social harmony to society. One of the main objectives of this scheme is to provide social integration and remove untouchability.

Mukhyamantri Karma Tatpara Abhiyān Yojanā

Odisha government has developed a new scheme called *Mukhyamantri Karma Tatpara Abhiyān Yojanā* to decrease the unemployment rate in Odisha state. On 1st February 2021, the Chief Minister launched the wage scheme, which creates an opportunity for poor urban people and migrant labours. This *Abhiyān* would engage the labouers in occupations like construction of stormwater drainage, rainwater harvesting, green cover, increased sanitation, creation of community centres, etc., for the poor urban locals, who will help them earn their livelihood.

ĀSHIRBĀD Scheme

The Department of Women and Child Development of the Government of Odisha, on 20th June 2021, launched the ĀSHIRBĀD scheme for specially cared children who are facing difficulties due to the death of both parents or the death of a primary bread earner in the family due to this COVID-19 Pandemic. Āshirbād aims for in-situ rehabilitation and continuation of their life in a similar family-based, non-institutional socio-cultural environment, where ever feasible and in the best interest of the child, and to ensure that caregivers and other kith and kin are encouraged to provide the best of care to these children. Under this scheme, up to Rs.2.500/- per month will be provided to the beneficiaries till the child attains 18 years of age or till adoption, whatever is earlier.

Gangādhar Meher Sikhyā Manakbrudhi Yojanā

The Odisha government has launched Gangādhar Meher Sikhyā Manakbrudhi Yojanā 2023 for the students. In this GMSMY Scheme, the state government will provide students with school uniforms, shoes, bags, free bicycles, and books. CM Naveen Patnaik, who led the state government, has allocated a sum of Rs. 430 crores for Gangādhar Meher Sikhyā Manakbrudhi Yojanā in Odisha Budget 2023.

Nirmān Shramik Puccā Ghar Yojanā

To provide the pucca house to the building and construction workers, the state government has started Nirmān Shramik Puccā Ghar Yojanā (NSPGY) in 2023. Under this scheme, the state government will subsidise the puccā house built by the beneficiary. To avail of the benefits of this scheme, it is mandatory to register under the Odisha Building and other construction workers' welfare boards. The unit cost under this scheme for the new house construction is Rs 120000 for the non-IAP district and Rs 130000 for the IAP district. Beneficiaries will also get a wage share under MGNREGA for 90-person days in non-IAP and 95-person days in IAP districts.

Harischandra Sahāyatā Yojanā

The Government of Odisha initiated *Harischandra*

Sahāyatā Yojanā in August 2013 to provide financial assistance to the poor and destitute to conduct the last rites of their family members and for the cremation of unclaimed dead bodies. Through this scheme, financial assistance of Rs 2000 is provided in rural areas, and Rs.3000 is provided in urban areas to the poor for conducting the cremation of the diseased.

Conclusion

Naveen Patnaik assumed office as Chief Minister at a time when coastal Odisha was in a shambles in the aftermath of the 1999 super cyclone. Millions of people were in need of relief and rehabilitation. The State's economy was also in a precarious condition. The situation has undergone a sea change since then. The state that was earlier known for its backwardness has been rated by international monitoring agencies as one of the advanced States in fighting natural disasters.Learning from its experience of handling frequent cyclones, floods and droughts, the government started adopting a zero-casualty approach in the event of natural disasters. Evacuating lakhs of people from coastal areas and providing them safe shelter ahead of cyclones has helped prevent loss of human lives in as many as seven cyclones since the super cyclone. Naveen, who started his political journey after the death of his father, Biju Patnaik, in 1997, has been working silently to script the success story for Odisha. His first stint as Chief Minister was marked by proactive and detailed planning, which resolutely underscored the government's intention to establish a positive, welfare model of governance. Following this planning stage in the first two years (2000-2002), the government moved to a proactive action mode that covered almost all realms of life. Naveen Patnaik has stuck to this proactive mode through five consecutive terms as Chief Minister. He worked steadily and steadfastly to realise his dream of a new Odisha that would meet the aspirations of its people by transforming the State in various spheres, be it the welfare of vulnerable sections of society or promotion of sports.Odisha is one of the fastest growing States in the country at present, boasting a growth rate much higher than the country's GDP growth rate of 8.8 percent. Its per capita income grew by 16.8 percent in 2020-21. The average growth of per capita income over the last 10 years has been 10.3 percent, against the national average of 9.15 percent.

Naveen Patnaik is undoubtedly the most popular leader in Odisha today. His popularity soars over all his colleagues and opponents. Though he began his political journey as an outsider, Naveen's sharp political acumen and deft political management have ensured the decimation of all his opponents, both within and outside the party. It is his charisma and emotional connect with Odias that have driven Biju Janata Dal's success in last five state elections, than anything else. Despite being a small talker and not very vocal, Naveen holds such sway over the people that he has never faced anti-incumbency and has trounced his opponents by a significant margin to stay in power for around two and half decades. While the entire country was gripped by pro-Modi wave during 2014 and 2019 general elections, Naveen managed to hold his ground and win absolute majority for his party to form government. What has endeared him to the masses is his successful implementation of pro-people policies and welfare schemes for all sections of society, especially the downtrodden and the women.

Naveen Patnaik has scripted a wonderful transformation of Odisha making it the most progressive and empowered State by delegating power to the grassroots and making governance transparent. The transformation is visible in all corners—be it community health centres, schools or the major religious centres that attract a large number of pilgrims and tourists.The only thing that has remained constant in the two and half decades of his political career is that he has remained uninfluenced by such lavish praise and preferred to let his work speak for his commitment and zeal for the betterment of Odisha and its people.

REFERENCES
1. Barik, S. (2022, December 3). Odisha transforming women SHGs into SMEs. *The Hindu.*
2. Datta, R. (2022, June 6). *The Quiet Performer: Recounting Naveen Patnaik's 25 years in public life.* India Today.
3. *Odisha bags "Best State for Promotion of Sports" award.* (2023, February 27). ANI News.
4. *Odisha promotes itself as the sports capital of India with huge investments | More sports News—Times of India.* (2022, October 5).
5. *Odisha: The Sports Capital of India—Hindustan Times.* (2023, December 2).
6. *Odisha Tourism Policy, 2022.*(2022). The Odisha Gazette.
7. Ramakrishnan, P. D. (2022, May 6). *Naveen Odisha: State witnesses transformation under CM Naveen Patnaik.*
8. Senapati, A. (2023, January 21). Govt. making efforts to develop Odisha as global hotspot of tourists: CM Naveen Patnaik. *The Times of India.*

Achyuta Samanta: The Propagator of the Art of Giving

Harischandra Sahoo

Born on 20th January 1964, in a remote village of Kalarabanka, twenty kilometers east to Cuttack city, Dr. Achyuta Samanta, the legendary figure grew up in abject poverty. Just when he had started knowing about the world around him, he lost his father (Anadai Samanta) at the tender age of four. His mother and seven siblings passed through financial hardship, the death of the father was a bolt from the blue. But his mother, Nilimarani was bold and courageous enough to face the situation. Though he was a child, about to go to the school, he came forward to help his mother and was determined to face the challenges of life. It is often said that "Behind the success of every man, there is a woman", to name a few - the mother of Lal Bahadur Shastri, Rani Laxmi Bai or Chhatrapati Sivaji. All the mothers were guiding spirits who used to nurture them to stand bold to face the difficult situations of life.

Early life through turbulent waters

Dr. Achyuta Samanta was committed to helping his mother, often he calls her (Nilamarani) as his *'hero'*. She shaped his life and acted as *'a friend, philosopher and guide'*. She acted as a beacon at the time when he was at cross-roads, facing difficult situations. When Achyuta was loitering, the school master looked at him, he saw a simple, innocent child having craze to learn and came to school, that's when the school master decided to lend a helping hand. It is only because of the village school master's good impression on him Achyuta started going to school and rest of the time was engaged in helping his mother in household chores. It was a difficult and trying time for the entire family to manage their livelihood. As time rolled on, Achyuta completed his schooling in the village school, pursued higher education and finally completed his Masters in Science from Utkal University in Chemistry with much financial hardship. But like Lalbahadur Shastri he never expressed his financial problems to anyone. At a tender age, he was a great support system especially during his sister's marriage and brother's job. The financial situation of the family improved, and he had a sigh of relief after getting the job of a lecturer in Chemistry in a local college in Bhubaneswar.

Dr. Achyuta Samanta always speaks of his ideal mother who was brave and courageous enough to face the hard-core realities of life. His father's words, "To serve the mankind" remained imprinted in his mind. He was determined to serve the society, to help the distressed for which he decided to remain a bachelor to serve the mankind.

The professional career began as a lecturer in Chemistry but there was a dire need for technical education in Bhubaneswar. He opened an ITI with a handful of students in a tin-roofed house. While managing the ITI, he saw the children of the workers and labourers of the vicinity moving here and there, being deprived of getting an opportunity of pursuing formal education. He then planned to open a school for them. This is how, the idea for expanding the horizon of education germinated in his mind, especially for the poor tribal children of the inaccessible forest areas of Odisha. These children are not only neglected due to the lack of education but also deprived of the basic facilities of life. Dr. Samanta believes that *"education is the third eye of a child"*. Thus, his determination and dreams were translated into reality by opening two educational institutions. Now his dream projects - KIIT and KISS have turned out to be the biggest institutions of the state as well as the country. Dr. Samanta is the founder of these institutions. KISS is the only residential institution of the world where 30,000 poor tribal students are pursuing education starting from kindergarten to Ph.D. and 20,000 alumni have been registered so far. It is a milestone in world history. Because of Samanta's hard labour and vision for expansion of education among the deprived tribal children, they could see the light of the day. There are many satellite campuses of KISS in different districts of the state. The tribal children (especially girls) are trained how to earn while they learn in order to become self-reliant in life. World leaders, nation heads, and dignitaries while visiting KISS express their bewilderment for the commendable leadership of Dr. Samanta during their visit. Recently, KISS has been awarded with International Green Gown – 2023 award. KIIT is one of the reputed educational institutions and recently celebrated Silver Jubilee of it's glorious existence with the tagline – *'From Soil to Silver'*. KIIT has occupied

13th Position in All India Ranking as well. He is also associated with KIMS as mark of immense contribution in health care.

Respect for Mother and Motherland

Dr. Samanta emphasizes on the views that *"Charity begins at home"*. His mother was a hero and icon for him. At the age of 89 years when she left for heavenly abode on 2nd Aug 2016, Dr. Samanta was deeply saddened owing to the demise of his beloved mother. She was like a strong wall behind him. While paying tribute to the great soul, he expressed with spontaneity that she shaped his life and it was because of her, he could afford to become a man. He furthermore suggested that one should not forget one's mother and the motherland i.e. the village where one is born. He has converted his village Kalarabanka into a smart village, and a model village with facilities like hospital, roads, post-office, bank, English medium school along with all ultramodern facilities like electricity and water supply. He humbly reminds us of our duties for the upliftment of the village that has worked as a spring board to jump high. The changing life-style has taken away the concept of simple living. Man has become self-centered. The joint family is replaced by unitary lifestyle. Samanta reminds us regarding Gandhiji's dream of going back to village and to try to uplift the standard of living of the villagers.

The Propagator of Art of Giving

We all know about 'Art of Living' advocated by Sri Sri Ravishankar, the spiritual Guru of India. But here we come across a new concept of "Art of Giving" by Dr. Samanta. He advocates and propagates "Art of Giving".

Every year "International Day of Art of Giving" is celebrated on 17th May with the slogan *"Live to Give, Give to Live"*. The "Art of Giving" aims at inculcating a hope for the needy, promoting *Happiness* and *Harmony* among all. Human life is the most valuable on the earth. Looking at the sub-human conditions of the people of India, Swami Vivekananda once said that God has given man, a head to think, a heart to feel and hands to work for the downtrodden, the illiterate and the destitute. God is not in the temple, Mosque and Gurudwārā. Every human being is a temple of living God. Dr. Samata reminds us of our rich cultural heritage where charity (*Dāna*) is considered to be one of the noble virtues. We have heard of rishi "Dadhichi" who sacrificed his life for the survival of the *devas*. King Shibi was ready to donate his own flesh. Karna was a great giver; even King Harischandra sacrificed his wife Sabya and only son Rohita as a token of *Dāna*.

Now the question is, to whom are we going to donate or give? Answer is very simple – we should donate to the poor, the needy, the deprived, the helpless, the destitute and distressed people. By serving them, donating something as per one's capacity, one does a great job. Dr. Samanta throughout his lifetime comes forward to help others. A simple example can be taken into account. In the recent train tragedy (at Bahanaga Rly. Station) many people lost their lives. Many children lost their parents. Immediately Dr. Samanta announced that he was ready to give free education and take the responsibility of the children and give employment to them who have lost their earning members of their family as per their qualifications. One can't simply believe unless one sees how thoughtfully he was feeding the stray dogs and animals during Covit-19 pandemic period. He is a man of action, a man of simple living and high thinking.

Political Career

Dr. Samanta marked his way to politics in the year 2019. His political journey began as a Member of Parliament from Kandhamal constituency. Dr. Samanta took many a steps for improving the socio-economic condition of the people of his constituency. He invited the Managing Director of MDH Group of Companies to Kandhamal to set up an industry to create employment. As a Member of Parliament he has participated in debates and given proposals for all-round development of the state. As a free-thinker, he regularly writes columns and articles in the newspapers to express his views and sensitise people. He is the founder of *'Kādambini'*, a magazine dedicated for the cause of women empowerment and *Kuni Kathā*, a magazine for the small children. He is founder of *Kalinga TV* and *Kalinga News Channel*.

Love for Sports

Dr. Samanta is a lover of sports. He has dreamt of making both the institutes KIIT and KISS as the hub of sports. World's first runner, Dutee Chand is the product of KIIT who always expresses her indebtedness to Dr. Samanta. At present Dr. Samanta is the President of Volleyball Federation of India. He is the President of Odisha Volleyball Association and the Chief Patron of All India Chess Federation. He is also one among the Board of Administrative Members of Central Asia Volleyball Association (CAVA). All these positions show his love and commitment for sports. He has created world class sports infrastructure like ultramodern stadium and sports complex provided for games like Rugby, Football, Archery and other games and sports in KIIT and KISS Campus. The aim is to promote spirit of sports among the tribal students to set records at national and international level.

Honours, Prizes, Awards and Accolades

Dr. Samanta has won a lot of national and international awards and honours for his social work and philanthropic attitude. He always emphasizes to be a good human being and not to be ungrateful in life. He always suggests to dream big and translate dreams into reality. He has received 50 International Awards, 55 Honorary Ph.D.s and more that 200 state and national awards besides the civilian award from Royal Kingdom of Baharain and Mangolia. He is the first Odia to be the Member of UGC and AICTE. Many eminent Nobel Laureates have acknowledged the activities of Prof. Samanta and their testimonials are a stellar example of the significant achievements of this towering personality.

Prof. Richard R Ernst, Nobel Laureate in Chemistry, (1991) writes, *"Dr. Samanta is a Life Model for me"*. Prof. Ferid Murad, Nobel Laureate in Physiology of Medicine (1998) remarks: *"What is Education? Education is very precious. What Dr. Samanta has done is more than Couple of pounds of Gold"*. Sir Richard John Roberts Nobel prize winner in Physiology of Medicine (1993) states *"I am overwhelmed with admiration to witness what Prof. Achyuta Samanta has created through his vision, dedication and passion"*. Prof. Hiroshi Amano, Nobel Laureate in Physics, (2014) states: *"Your (Dr. Samnata's) achievements is just incredible and extremely difficult to emulate for generations to come"*

A personality worth emulating

Dr. Samanta is a simple man wearing Jean Pant, white shirt, chappals and taking vegetarian meal. But he is very meticulous and systematic in his work. It is hard to believe that physically a short statured man like Dr. Samanta could do multiple social activities and carry so many things in his mind. His commitment for the promotion and development of the standard of living of the indigenous people by providing education is praiseworthy and eye-opener for others.

REFERENCES :
1. Achyuta Samanta, *My Mother My Hero*, Rupa New Delhi (2021)
2. *Art of Giving*, World Leadership Academy (2022)

Satāyu Purusa Padmabhusan Dr. Radhanath Rath
(1896 – 1998)

Hemant Kumar Parija

Born and brought up in poverty Dr. Radhanath Ratha was destined to play an important role in Odia print media for about eighty years. He had the good fortune of receiving the paternal guidance of Pandit Gopabandhu Dash, who founded the 'Samaj' on 4th Oct. 1919 to serve the poor Odias who lived in abject poverty in inaccessible villages. Prominent nationalist leaders like Pandit Nilakantha Dash, Pandit Godavarish Mishra, Acharya Harihara Dash, Pandit Lingaraj Mishra and others served as editors of the Samaj at different times. Radhanath Rath left the Government service at Chainbasa and came to Satyabadi at the invitation of Pandit Gopabandhu Dash in 1919 and got himself involved with the publication of the Samaj. Once he joined the press he never thought of leaving it till his death in 1998. He served as Manager, working editor and Editor of the Samaj and made it so popular that it became a synonym for news paper. However, he served under the guidance of Pandit

Gopabandhu for only nine years as the latter died in 1928. But this short association with Gopabandhu had so much influence on him that he remained a loyal follower of his master throughout his life.

Radhanath was the eldest son of Jagannath Rath and Kamala Devi, who originally belonged to a brahmin village named Biraharekrushnapur near Puri, which was considered a place of culture and religious activities. In those days the brahmins enjoyed a prominent place in the society and were noted for learning. Rājā Biswanath Devavarma, the ruler of the tributoary state of Athagarh, decided to invite some learned brahmins form villages around Puri. On his invitation five learned brāhmin families of village Biraharekrushnapur and nearby villages left their village and moved to Athagarh. The Rājā give them land and established a village near his royal palace and named it Radhanathpur Sāsan. Radhanath's father Jagannath who was one among those learned brāhmins, who moved to Athagarh with his families. At that time his wife Kamala Devi was pregnant. Soon after reaching Athagarh Kamala Devi gave birth to her first child Radhanath. Pandit Jagannath Rath was blessed with five sons and two daughters. With meager income it was very difficult on the part of Jagannath to manage a large family and to take care of the education of his children.

Radhanath had his early education at the Mohanty '*Chāhāli*' at Athagarh. An intelligent boy, Radhanath always stood first in the class but to appease an influential person of the area, his son was made first and Radhanath was degraded to the second position. Radhanath felt insulted and humiliated and decided never to go to the '*Chāhāli*" any more. One day he left his home and fled away towards the forest. His worried parents searched him in and around the area and finally traced him sleeping under a tree in the jungle. His father now sent him to Balasore for further study, where a close relative Pandit Lokanath Mahapatra was working as a teacher at the Zilla School. After passing the 7th class, Radhanath joined Cuttack Collegiate School for higher studies. Since his father was financially very weak and was not in a position to finance Radhanath, the later had to depend for help from prominent persons of the time like Janakinath Bose (father of Subhash Chandra Bose), Gopala Chandra Praharaj, Pandit Akuli Misra and Utkal Gaurav Madhusudan Das. In 1916, he passed the high school examination in first class but the financial condition of his family compelled him to discontinue his studies and to search for a job. As per the custom of the time he had to marry before appearing the High School Examination. At that time he was only 16 years old and Savitri Devi, the bride, only 11 years.

In search of job, Radhanath first went to Sambalpur and joined a private press as a worker. Later on he got a job in the Police Department due to his proficiency in English language and typing skill. There he drew the attention of the English police officer for his honesty, sincerity and proficiency in English. Before leaving Sambalpur to join the army, the English officer Mr. Butter Field recommended his name to his friend. Mr. C.F.K. Maccins, who was working as an officer in the Forest Department at Chainbasa, now in Jharkhand. Radhanath joined there as a clerk with a salary of Rs. 75/- per month. It was here that he met Pandit Gopabandhu Das for the first time on 6th Sept 1919. This meeting proved to be a turning point in the life of Radhananth. Gopabandhu was charmed by the behavior and integrity of Radhanath, who in turn was greatly influenced by the magnetic personality of Gopabandhu. Gopabandhu wanted to take Radhanath to Satyabadi in Puri district where he had a press and was planning to start a newspaper. He needed the help of Radhanath. Radhanath decided to leave the job at Chainbasa and to join the new assignment at Satyabadi. Pandit Gopabandhu writes in his diary dated 6th Sept 1919 – *"Radhanath is a nice young man, active, honest, energetic, straitforward and patriotic. He is now a clerk in the Forest Department, but has decided to come to Satyabadi."* Within few days, Radhanath left Chainbasa and reached Satyabadi on the Kumāra Purnimā day in 1919. After a brief stint as a teacher at the Satyabadi School, he joined the Satyabadi press when Gopabandhu started the weekly Samaj on 4th Oct. 1919. A new phase began in the life of Radhanath and was never separated from the Samaj till his death in 1998.

Radhanath served under the paternal care and guidance of Pandit Gopabandhu only for nine years (1919 to 1928) as he died on 17th June' 1928. But his association with Gopabandhu for nine years moulded his personality and established him as a man of integrity and honesty. In June, 1927 the Samaj and the Satyabadi Press were shifted to Cuttack. The then Manager of the press Satyabadi Tripathy could not come to Cuttack due to personal difficulties. Radhanath had to serve both the press and the Samaj as Manager. Gopabndhu in the last will handed over both the Samaj and the Satyabadi Press to the "Servant of the people Society" for the smooth functioning of the Samaj. After the death of Gopabandhu many eminent personalities like Pandit Nilakantha Dash, Pandit Godavarish Misra, Acharya Harihara Dash,

Gopabandhu Choudhury and Pandit Lingaraj Misra took over the charge of the Samaj as Eidtior for sometime and left the institution. But it is Radhanath who continued to serve the Samaj in different capacities and made the paper popular. In 1930, the weekly Samaj was converted into a daily newspaper to serve the people better. But during the freedom movement the publication of the Samaj was stopped on several occasions and Radhanath had to mortgage his wife's ornaments to pay salary to the employees.

Radhanath got himself so much involved in the management of the Samaj that he got little time to be involved in other activities yet he contested elections, become a minister, took part in prajāmandal movement and involved in literary pursuits.

In the pre-independent period there were 26 Garjāt estates which were ruled by Rajas and Maharajas. They were autocrats, people had no freedom or rights and were subject to a lot of illegal taxes. In some states people organized themselves under the banner of "Prajāmandal Samities" and revolted against their autocratic rulers. The people of Athagarh formed a Prajāmandal Samiti under the Presidentship of Radhanath Rath. In 1938 they organized a very big meeting at Khuntuni and raised their voice against the Raja. Radhanath babu encouraged them to revolt against the autocratic Raja. Hearing this the Raja became furious and sent his police to arrest him from his Athagarh residence. Radhanath babu could know the secret plan of the Raja and before the arrival of the police, he escaped to Cuttack in a bicycle. His family members, too ecaped to Cuttack the same night. From that day he organized the movement from his Cuttack residence and the office of the Samaj became the centre of the activites of the Prajāmandal movement. During this period he had to collect information about the Prajāmandal movements and publish in the Samaj. In the mean time, a state peoples standing committee was formed with members selected from the Garjat States. Radhanath babu was selected from Athagarh and he took up the responsibility of organizing the movements. He met the political agent of the Government in 1938 and apprised him of the torture of the people at the hands of the Rajas. Unable to withstand the inhuman behavior and torture of the Raja's servants, many people form Athagarh had left their homes and taken shelter at Cuttack and Banki. His discussion with the Political Agent proved successful. A meeting was organized at the Athagarh palace where the Raja (Radhanath), President of the Athagarh Prajāmandal Radhanath Rath and the political Agent Mr. E.C. N. Ciffin were present. It was decided to grant some concessions like holding meetings, reading newspaprers and granting ownership over land were given to the people. As a result the Prajāmandal movement gradually calmed down. The kingdom of Athagarh was finally merged with Odisha on 1st Jan. 1948.

In spite of his deep involvement in the Management of the Samaj, Radhanath also took interest in politics. He was elected to the Odisha Legislative Assembly thrice in 1946, 1952 and 1957 and served as minister of Finance, Education, Agriculture, Animal Husbandry, Forest and Health at different times from 1952 to 1961. In 1946, Pandit Lingaraj Mishra, the then Editor of the Samaj, became a minister in the cabinet of Dr. H.K. Mahatab and served upto 1952. During this period Radhanath served as the Editor of Samaj. In 1961 the ministry of

Dr. Mahatab collapsed and the Assembly was dissolved. Radhanath was disgusted with the nasty politics and took retirement from politics. He once again took over the charge of the Samaj as its editor and worked for the cause of the common people.

As a minister, Radhanath also took up some important steps for the benefit of Odisha. There was a proposal to establish a steel plant at Rourkela in collaboration with the government of Germany. While the proposal was in discussion stage many provinces like Madhya Pradesh opposed the proposal and demanded to shift the place from Rourkela to some other place in Madhya Pradesh. The Chief Minister of Odisha Sri Nabakrushna Choudhury deputed Radhanath to place the case of Odisha before the Cabinet Sub-Committee presided over by Pandit Jawaharlal Nehru. Choudhury was confident that Radhanath would place the cause of Odisha better than anybody else. Radhanath so forcefully argued that the Cabinet Sub-Committee ultimately accepted his views and the Rourkela Steel Plant was established later on.

When Radhanath was the Minister of Forest, he took steps for the establishment of a Zoo near Bhubaneswar. A suitable place near Baranga was selected and the zoo come into existence. Chief Minister Mahatab inaugurated it in 1959 and named it *"Nandan Kānan"*. Today it has earned national fame and people from all over India visit this place regularly.

The economy of Odisha was primarily an agricultural economy, where 80% of the population depended on agriculture. 65% of our state's income came from agriculture. The Government of Odisha felt the need of an agricultural university in Odisha, where our agricultural scientists and technologists would be trained in modern mechanized agriculture. That was the time when India's first Agricultural University had been established at Tarai in U.P. in collaboration with USA. It was named Govinda Ballav Panth Agricultural University. The then Agriculture and Development Minster Radhanath Rath visited the newly built University in U.P.; discussed with the American and Indian experts and came back with the impression that a poor agricultural state like Odisha needs such a university. On the basis of his report the Govt. of Odisha decided to establish a similar university in Odisha. It started negotiations with the Govt. of USA as well as with the Govt of India and finally decided to establish such a university near the Chilika lake in collaboration with the Missouri University of USA. Unfortunately while the project was being worked out, Chief Minister Nabakrushna Choudhury resigned and the project was put in cold storage. Later on, when Biju Patnaik became Chief Minister and Pabitra Mohan Pradhan became the Agriculture Minister, the Project was revived. But the original plan of establishing the university near the Chilika Lake was changed and the Orissa University of Agriculture and Technology (OUAT) was established at Bhubaneswar in 1962. Later on Radahanath Rath became the Pro-Chancellor of this University.

Soon after independence, the existence of 565 native states created threats for the future of India. Negotiations continued with the native states for their merger with India. Out of 26 native states which existed within the geographical boundary of Odisha 25 signed the document of merger with the independent dominion of India and came under the control of Odisha on 1st Jan. 1948. Mayurbhanj however, signed the document of merger with Odisha on 1st Jan. 1949. But before the merger of Mayurbhanj, the two states of Saraikela and Kharasuan were handed over to Bihar by the arbitration of the states ministry on 18th May 1948. This became the bone of contention between the two governments of Bihar and Odisha

The Govt. of India appointed a States Reorganisation Committee (SRC) in 1954 under the chairmanship of Sayeed Fazl Ali, the then Governor of Odisha, to bring about a solution to the boundary disputes among different states. Chief Minister Nabakrushna Choudhury assigned the responsibility on Radhanath Rath to prepare a memorandum and to put forth our case before the SRC for the merger of the two disputed native states with Odisha. In the memorandum it was argued that the two native states of Saraikela and Kharsuan were merged with Bihar in May 1948 as Mayubhanj had not been merged with Odisha by then and which as a buffter state separated Odisha from the two states. Moreover, the two native states were situated within the Singhbhoom district, where the population of the Odias was more than the Hindi and the Bengali speaking people. The Adivasis of Odisha had strong social cultural and matrimonial relation with the Adivasi of Singhboom. Therefore, the memorandum demanded the merger of he whole district of Singhboom with Odisha. But unfortunately our genuine demands could not influence the SRC members. The Biharis created trouble in the two states. The Adivasis became violent, attacked our leaders. Our case was lost before the powerful lobby of Bihar. The two purely Odiya native states were merged with Bihar as per the SRC report. Odisha lost the two native states for ever.

When Radhanath babu was put in jail for two years at Berhampur duing the 1942 Quit India Movement, he got time to devote himlf to litearay pursuit. He translated the *Mahābhārat* of Vyasadeva and the *Das Capital* of Karl Marx into Odia. His *"Bandira Marmavāni"* is written in memory of the mentor. He wrote about his jail life and named it *"Mo jail smrutilipi,* which he published in the Ravivār Samāj serially. He introduced a new feature in the daily Samaj and named it *"Jhitipiti Kahe"* on January 7, 1962. Here he criticized sarcastically the social evils as well as corruptions in the Govt. It became popular and the common people who read believed the contests to be true.

Radhanath Babu is a household name in Odisha. Twice he was offered the Chief Minister post – once in 1965 and second in 1971. But on both the occasions he politely declined and himself suggested the names of Sadasiv Tripathy and Biswanath Dash. It is said that once he was offered the post of Governor of Assam by Lal Bhadur Sastri, but again he politely declined. Like his mentor, Pandit Gopabandhu Das, he joined the Servants of the People's Society as a member but later on rose to the position of its Vice-President and President in 1981. As a journalist, legislator and minister, Radhanath Babu led a simple and honest life. Corruption never touched him. In recognition to his services, the Govt. of India honored him with *"Padma Bhusan"*.

REFERENCES :
1. *Utkal Ratna : Radhanath* (Ed.) Ananda Pani and Arun Kumar Panda, Gopabandhu Sahitya Mandira, Cuttack (2002).
2. *Radhanath Rath : Gopabandhu Aitihara Bāhaka*, Ananda Pani and Arun Kumar Panda, Gopabandhu Sahitya Mandira, Cuttack (1996).

Gopinath Mohanty's Man-Centric World View
(1914 – 1991)

Prafulla Kumar Mohanty

Gopinath Mohanty is, in my view, one of the all time greats in the world of literature. By confining his greatness within the limits of Indian Literature, we do injustice to his seminal contributions. He created a language-simple, poetic yet mysterious. He created a world of man, palpable yet spiritually mystical. In his works he has resorted to man his sense of *Being*.

Gopinath Mohanty's primary focus is on man and how best he can make the world his home. It is a Dostoyevaskian paradigm. Dostoyevasky in *Brothers Karamazov* has given us a true picture of man's search for home in the universe. Man is not confined to a family – joint or neuclear. Man's world does not end with a *forty foot* or *five hundred foot wall*. There is a larger world beyond his family. Gopinath makes his men and women move in a cultural unity inherited and practised over centruries.

The human condition imposes on man three

constraints – hunger, sickness and war. Man has to fight the predatory animals, fight for his hunger and also for his survival. For this, man lives in groups for he cannot survive alone. The group develops a culture where his fight continues. His quest for food continues and his fight for physical survival continues. His inner conflicts and internecine wars continue. Gopinath Mohanty was the most conscientious person of his time in Odia literature. As such, he analyses the available cultures, languages, food habits according to the situational dynamics in different geographical conditions of men.

To study Gopinath Mohanty as a writer with socio-cultural and civilizational awareness, we must notice the progression in his novels. Gopinath Mohanty belongs to a serious phase of psychic transformation of the Odia, however, I may quickly add that he is an Odia and also a universal man. Gopinath knew that the old cultural patterrns were gradually being transformed into new forms of *Psycho-social reality*.

The rural culture, the tribal culture were gradually being changed because of the impact of modernity, – colonial and post-independence. In 1936, the Odia had his own geographical territory, his map of identity for the first time after about 200 years, even before that Odia never had any assured survival. Poverty and clusters of culture kept him non-communicative and also fearful. After 1936, althouth identity came, the Odia never had access to good or standard education. Health care avenues and opportunities of economic self-sustenance were not available. After 1947, the national freedom gave the Odia some national pride but there was no immediate change in his inherited culture. Civilization dawned on Odisha like a blazing sun slowly piercing the cloud cover of ignorance. Gopinath definitely went through the slow and painful changes that came to his Odisha.

Gopinath Mohanty can be studied under three contexts of culture and civilization, namely, Tribal, Urban and Existential. In the tribal context, I will place three novels namely *Dādi Buddhā, Parajā* and *Amrutara Saṇtān*. In the urban context, I will discuss only two novels i.e. *Danāpāni and Māti Matāla*. In the existential context, I will discuss *Laya Bilaya*, which I consider to be a true masterpiece. Gopinath served in Koraput district as an administrative officer. The creative writer, Gopinath however, moved around the beautiful mountain valleys, rivers and dark forests trying to understand the meaning of tribal life.

In *Dādi Buddhā*, we have a God-like Ancestor who defines life, culture and ways of the relationship between man, nature and God. Dādi Buddhā himself was considered to be diety. But between Dādi Buddhā and Sarubu Saonta, we have Sukṛu Jāni in *Parajā* who differs from both the deities like an awakening soul. Sukṛu Jāni inherits a culuture that is optimistic in nature. He believes that this world, this langer, danger, tanger, mountains, forests and streams and valleys are meant for man's enjoyment. *Darmu* above, *Dartani* below – the Sky and the Earth are the original parents of man. They bless us to live with freedom and enjoy life.

The word 'Parajā' is derived from '*Prajā*' (means the ruled) But there is also a class of tribals known as 'Parajā'. They have numerous festivals. Sukṛu had his own family – two sons (Tikrā and Māndiā) and two daughters (Jhilli and Billy). He drinks and dances in all festivities, but the land under his possession was inadequate to meet the growing mouths in his family. He thinks, he can cut the trees and prepare farm land as it is a divine gift for man. His sons also grow ambitious. They cook illicit liquor and sell in the village fair. And from here begins Sukṛu Jāni's problems.

Sukṛu Jāni is caught by the forest guard, an agent of late colonial civilization, as he violates the new regulations. He is shocked. His shock intensifies when his sons also are arrested by the police for making illicit liquor. He descends to the depths of ignominy to bribe the new agents of civilization. The money-lender, the *sāhukār* is also another agent of the rudimentary modernity that dawns on Sukṛu Jāni's innocent cultural belief systems. His *Darmu* and *Dirtani* do not come for his rescue. He is involved in a law-suit and for that also, he had to go borrowing to pay the lawyer, another new agent of modernity in his innocent territory. There too, he is cheated, loses the suit and suffers what follows.

The *sāhukār*, the builders paving new roads absorbs his family. He serves as a labourer. His children too serve the new masters as bond slaves. Slowly but surely Sukṛu Jāni loses his faith, looses his reality and inherited belief-system. But a new awareness comes to him. He realizes that he has his own life, he has a sense of justice and he can play God in his own arena of life. When his daughters are also taken away by the *sāhukār*, and the new system, the awareness in him prompts him to act. He kills the *sāhukār* and surrenders at the police station.

Gopinath Mohanty takes off where Fakir Mohan left. Fakir Mohan in 'Chhamān Āthaguntha' has given us a world-picture where the moral energy of the universe controls human destiny. Man choicelessly surrenders. *Chhamān Āthaguntha* is a story of victims. The only good human being in the novel, namely Mangarāj's saintly wife also is victimized by her own goodness, by her own belief in the laws of God. All the other characters including Champā, Govinda, Bhagiā, Sāriā and Mangarāj himself fall victim to the universal moral energy. Man is unable to rise up with any awareness of his rights and sense of justice. The temple and its modern substitute 'Law Court' cheat him. A cheated man 'Bhagiā' victimised by his own simplicity, could have killed Mangarāj, if he had an awareness of his rightful position in the world. But, he merely bites Mangarāj in a demented state.

Gopinath in *Parajā* had shown the rise of Odia pride. The new Odia in Sukṛu Jāni kills although he knows that by killing the sāhukār, he cannot transcend the new law, the new civilizational dynamics, but the Odia pride stands out as Sukṛu Jāni becomes an agent of justice himself. In the history of Odia novel, *'Parajā'* is a new landmark.

Gopinath's reputation as a great novelist mostly rests on *'Amrutara Santāna'*. Here too, an outsider, enters (Pegoti) a beautiful fair skinned woman, artful, beautiful and ambitious. She was a small time actress but was quite attractive in the territory of the novel. Diyudu and Puyu, Sukṛu Jāni's son and daughter-in-law never had an amicable conjugal life. But they continued in Kondh Society despite their unspoken conflicts. But then Diyudu comes in contact with Pegoti. He transgresses the charm of Sarubu Saonta's moral kingdom. Sarubu Saonta in the lineage of *Dādi Buddhā* was smart, the original ancestor of a divine deity but was a patriarch who upheld the values of Kondh society and culture. This culture, however does not sustain the value of family, Puyu is neglected. We see, nuclear family breaking down. If Kalandi Panigrahi has shown in *Mātira Manisha* the crack of the joint family, Gopinath has shown the falling apart of the nuclear family, but Puyu is shown as a woman with a strong will power. She was not ambitious like her husband but she had determination not to drift apart from her culture. Gopinath has shown that man is of immortal energy. Man is the child of immortality. Whatever comes, he faces, failures or success, without loosing the identity of human being.

In this context, I am tempted to recall a tea-table conversation I had long years ago at Delhi. I had delivered the key-note address at a Sahitya Academy National Seminar at Delhi. The great scholar and critic, the late Namwar Singh casually asked me what 'I thought about Gopinath Mohanty's *Amrutara Santāna*? I said, the first chapter of *Amrutara Santān* tells everything. It's a long chapter describing the end of '*Chaiti Parab*' (Spring Festival) and death of Sarubu Saonta. With the end of the spring festival, Sarubu Saonta's spring of a benign human culture also ends. Prof. Namwar Singh smiled and said, "Yes! That's it". Why I remember this as a personal tea-table conversation with the great professor, I am still convinced that the whole of *Amrutara Santān* is encapsulated in the 1st chapter as in Hardian Novels, the new winds of change blow apart a great cultural pride practised by men and women. "Things fall apart."

As the family cracks, the great cultural pride is crushed by the new, however rudimentary, values of civilization. In the tribal context, Gopinath has shown that the inner resistance because of cultural pride to the imposed values ultimately makes the individuals more aware of his reality. Change is not accepted but brings about a change in perceptions of man's position in the new order.

II

In the urban context, we will consider two novels of Gopinath Mohanty; *Dānāpāni* and *Māti Matāl*. Bali Dutta in *Dānāpāni* is an improved version of Ramachandra Mangaraj. Ramachandra Mangaraj was an 'outsider' who enters the chaotic society with his native ambitions of 'manipulate and succeed', not by following the morals and related regulations of the natural order but by assuming the obtaining reality as chaotic and manipulable. Bali Dutta is an half-educated man; has a family, i.e. a beautiful wife and tons of material ambitions. He is an ordinary employee but desires to reach the top by methods which one may say were immoral. He uses his wife Sarojini as a pawn on the chess board of his ambitions. He tries to please his boss and thereby to have material gains. His name indicates that he sacrifices the given values of life. But it so happens that he achieves his ambitions of material prosperity and the accompanying muscle power. But his wife moves away from him. He is left alone, high and dry. Sarojini becomes a queen bee and Bali Dutta is left with nothing that ultimately comforts the human soul. In another sense, Bali Dutta sacrifices his soul to get a pompous material self. His wife turns into almost courtesan moving from lakh to lakh and sitting over every one's head. Technically the novel has an *Hour-Glass – pattern* where the protagonists Bali Dutta and his wife are transposed as in hour-glass.

Gopinath understands what modern civilization brings to man. Individualism unsavoury ambition ultimately diffuse the society. The family is wreaked, the soul of the individuals turn into *nothingness* and human being loses his ultimate *essence*. This novel almost criticizes the future of the new civilization.

In the tribal context, Gopinath has shown how man turns into a victim when a new civilization with its own inbuilt culture impacts the obtaining culture of an old settlement of people. The victim either turns a victimizer or runs away to find out his own destiny in another place or just surrenders to his/ her fate. Gopinath being a man of global understanding of the political and economic currents of the world, tries to construct a new idea of economic and political value-structure. During the period of his youth and his growing intellectual contacts with different wings of new ideas he had definitely formed a construct of a man in his own. Odisha particularly in his favourite Cuttack – Jagatsinghpur area where he had spent his childhood. In the 40's, of the 20th century there are two major idea constructs emanating from two great minds. One was the father of the nation, Mohandas Karamchand Gandhi and the other was Karl Marx, who gave a new way of looking at human economy, especially in a war –torn world. After independence, maxism however did not have any impact on India's newly form democratic structure. But Nehru was somewhat left leaning and some of the Marxian ideas were incorporated into the economic system of India – five year plans, mixed economy etc. At the sametime, one of the most loyal followers of M.K. Gandhi, Binoba Bhave started his 'Bhudān Movement'. The left wing idea of co-operative farming was gaining ground. The *Zamidāri* system was on its ways out. Gopinath wanted to have an experiment with all these current ideas in his Gyanapitha Award Winning Novel '*Māti Matāla*'. Odisha was always a poor state, flood-cyclone prone and illiteracy coupled with poverty of body and mind. Gopinath in his *Māti Matāla* wishes to change the structure of the society, culture and economy within the frame-work of the traditional value-structure of Odisha as well as the new bureaucracy of the new independent government. He had shown that an Odia graduate, a rare specimen in a contemporary term – with a mind of his own cannot contribute anything towards the formation of the new order. Ravi, the hero of the novel *Māti Matāla* gets a government job that to the job of an Administrative Officer after clearing the administrative service examination. But he decides not to join. He had seen how the farm lands are divided and subdivided by the inheritors of a joint family and becomes smaller and smaller. Money for investment in farming normally came from the money-lender who was always a non-Odia, in other words – an outsider like the '*sāhukār*' in *Parajā*. People did not have any real education particularly, the women, never had any scope because of parental restrictions. In fact, women were not free even to express opinions. There were followers of Gandhism and Marxism in different pockets of Odisha and also in his own district. There is a tacit reference to 'Gopabandhu Choudhury', a Gandhian, an honest and upright man. But his decree did not run as a new administrator. However, the short staffed and inefficient adminstrative officers, if not corrupt attracted the attention of the poor villagers. The police administration was poor. The police behaved like the new masters. Schools were practically non-existent and those which were running were unattractive and inefficiently managed. Ravi thought if he could unite the people and induce them towards the new idea of co-operative farming, the yield would be better and people will have a sense of comradery and mutual friendship. Many people of the area, particularly Mr. Choudhury appreciated the youngman, but no one came forward to help him. But by great efforts he created a viable atmosphere conducive to cooperative farming and it began in earnest. But the human being is always possessive. He is not prepared to give up what he inherits from his forefathers. He never wanted to donate any land. Moreover, man is not that creature who lives only on two simple meals a day. Each human being has the ambition to create a personal world which was not possible in this system.

The idea of Bhudān Movement and cooperative farming which had started in Andhra Pradesh was captured by the communists and Gopinath's fictional area too. It did not grow firm roots. Floods, losses of life in the obtaining conditions of physical infracture almost broke the backbone of the new movement. Ravi and Chhabi worked together and delayed their marriage only for public service, but to no avail. Of course finally, they married but Gopinath's focus was not on love, married life or single individual's rise in the society. He wanted man to grow in prosperity and dignity by collective effort. Several factors including intellectual apathy, social apathy and administrative indifference could not lead the human society to grow up together as a whole. The individual grows. The individuals' personal ambitions becomes fruitful. Mankind cannot sustain itself holding each other's hand. Each human mind is different and that is to be respected. However, sacrifice alone cannot alleviate mankind as a whole. Gopinath's character also fails in his pursuit of truth. *Ahimsa* and love of mankind can never become a single unit.

Each human being wants to make his world his own. Like Walt Whitman, each man thinks, "I am vast, I contain multitude". But no man says the multitude is one and i.e. man. The earth is our home; No, the earth is mine and mine alone. And such attitudinal clashes cannot make the '*Loamy Earth*' a field of diamond.

Gopinath's narrative has an epical sweep in *Māti Matāla*, words made into sounds and sounds into rhythms and ultimately, we get the poetry of life. The descriptions of landscapes, the development of his characters, the eye for details, in short, common words carve out the architecture of life which is seldom found in world literature. The detailed description of floods, suffering of people, the description of boats and their movements not only capture the reality but become reality itself. The human sympathy what Gopinath shows is incomparable. The way he analyses the minds of his characters are inimitable. Gopinath treats the human beings as divine agents. Even the course, ill behaved, rash individuals are not condemned. Gopinath loves human beings and always thinks of raising man to a higher level of *being*.

In the urban phase – man fails as both as an individual and as a group. Bali Dutta by following wild methods to become powerful loses his family, love and even self-respect. In *Māti Matāla*, the individual alone rises to leave his stamp behind but ironically what he perceives is that goodmen who follow truth and honest values, suffer, if not physically at least mentally. The world perhaps is not yet prepared to accept human goodness as the new divinity. The authorial dream does not succeed but how wonderful is that dream !

III

The existential context is used here without any reference to existentialism as a philosophy which was quite popular in the west, particularly in Europe during Gopinath's middle age. Existentialism refers here to pure and simple existential issues of human beings. This is true of all phases of the novelist's growth. In the tribal context, man was totally immersed in the faith but due to existential pressures, he comes out of his innocence in a state of awareness of reality. In the urban phase, there was no middle class. In *Māti Matāla*, we have the beginning of the middle class, which however was sporadic. In *Laya Bilaya*, which I consider to be one of the greatest works of Gopinath, we see, the middle class. Tarun Roy was a clerk in north-east of Calcutta. As a new member of middle class (lower), he was not fully settled in his mind. Like all human beings, he wanted to use his power and authority which he found in his boss. Like all human beings, he wanted to live a very happy family life with wife and lovely children. But his low salary coupled with authoritarian behavior of his boss in the hierarchical system of bureaucracy, he felt small and inadequate. His boss never liked him, colleagues did not respect him and he too was restless, sitting in a clerck's chamber. To add to his external, societal problems of his maladjustment at his place of work, he does not like his wife gathering fat. His daughter's education and future life constantly bothered him. He was a malcontent. He was almost growing cynical. He lost all his desire to live in coordination with his immediate society. He was growing violent, irritable and at times wild. In this state of mind, he comes with his family i.e. wife and daughter to Puri. The train stops at the outer signal from where he tries to see the contours of Jagannāth temple but fails. He goes to the city, takes a room in a small hotel. Next morning, he watches the sunrise at Puri beach and somehow gets fascinated. Gopinath's description of the beach, the tourists taking sea-bath and the rising Sun radiating an exhorting joy are unique in Odia Literature. He sits there for some time, sees the fishermen packing their baskets, the sun rises up and up. The shades changed. The colour of sunlight changed. The sand dunes rise and fall like ant hills. All these disturb him joyfully for sometime, but he is not reconciled yet.

He goes to see the Jagannāth temple for which he came all the way from Calcutta. He sees Jagannāth, the large dark eyes penetrates his heart. But he is not fully satisfied. He observes the evening sky on the beach, goes to temple again, suddenly in the presence of the wooden icons, he has something akin to epiphany. His inner-darkness, cynicism and negative feelings seem to be disappearing for a while. He goes to the roof of the top floor of the hotel and looks at the temple again. Also looks at the sky, the sea and evening scene. He feels a change and when his wife comes to room, she appears to be a new woman, her fat, her own disgruntling loneliness all appear to be pleasing. He accepts her as his mate, thinking that whatever she is, she is – his wife, his woman. He has sex with her on the roof and embraces his wife as his world. Some positive news, he receives about his daughter's marriage and he raises his hand to Lord Jagannāth. His being is no more cynically non-participating in the affairs of life, he accepts life, he accepts his reality, everything of the world appears to be pleasing and inspiring. He does not think of his boss as a tyrant. He is now determined to work hard, behave amicably with his friends and neighbors and live as a true human being. He looks back from the train while returning to Calcutta at the receding contours of the temple, of the sea- beach and looks forward to meeting life with reinvented vitality.

In this novel Gopinath convincingly suggests that man, nature and spirituality are a whole-sum being. Life needs a touch of the beautiful and the divine without which life is not livable. Tarun Roy is transformed from a cynical being into a man in society accepting all existential conditions. He would beat all challenges of life meaningfully with nature in his heart and spirituality in his psyche.

In the tribal phase, man looses spirituality and also nature. Sukṛu Jāni loses his faith but does not find an acceptable alternative in new order. He tries to pray God. In the urban phase, the societal environment has changed. The uncoming civilization is beginning to have its effects on man. Bali Dutta tries to manipulate the society, thereby losing his own worthy-possession. He does not accept his own reality. He wants to manipulate reality and the result is a psychic fall of having everything, but enjoying nothing. In *Mati Matāla* a few saintly –men educated in modern values try to find an alternative to the new civilization. They succeed to a great extent but finally succumb to the new values as this soil is not amenable to the experiments which Ravi made to make life more pleasant and better than what it could have been in its own process. Man does not fail but success does not crown him. The ideas remain but the implementation does not find its goal. In *Laya Bilaya*, Gopinath has shown that man and nature without spirituality can not function and move towards any tangible life form. Tarun Roy is in a metropolis in Calcutta where the large human order and the fragmented isolationist power groups are beyond the beauty and grace of nature. There is no God and the Calcutta sea-beach is not for sun – watching or wave –surfing. It is full of ships and boats, trades that are legitimate and illegitimate. In this atmosphere one has to accept his allotted field of life and work to the best of his ability surrendering his baser self to God.

Gopinath is a visionary poet. He envisions life in different contexts and shows that unless man keeps on changing his attitudes and adjusts with the unfolding reality, he cannot survive in the world with any trace of happiness. Moreover, happiness is indefinable. Man has to create his own happiness which carved only by accepting reality as the grace of God. All his works are experiments with life. His *Ākāsh Sundari* however, is an experiment with the stream of consciousness technique which was practised by people like James Joyce. Gopinath makes a beautiful experiment with the technique and suceeds. But *Ākāsh Sundari* does not belong to the carve of Gopinath as a novelist of visionary artistry. Gopinath was writing to raise human beings to higher levels, to bring nature and spirituality to human beings and to alleviate man to a higher level of consciousness. His sensuous apprehension of reality is unique. No other Odia story teller / narrations of life can be compared with him. He stands apart like the brightest star in lonely splendour.

REFERENCES:
1. Gopinath Mohanty, *Māti Matāla*, Vidyapuri, Cuttack, 2015.
2. ——, *Parajā*, Vidyapuri, Cuttack, 2012.
3. ——, *Amrutara Santāna*, Vidyapuri, Cuttack, 2021.
4. ——, *Laya Bilaya*,
5. ——, *Dādi Buddhā*,
6. Fakir Mohan Senapati, *Chhamān Āthaguntha*, Friends Publishers, Cuttack, 2011.

The Poetic Vision of Jayanta Mahapatra
(1928 - 2023)

Durga Prasad Panda

In the crowded Tinikonia Bagicha area of Cuttack city away from the Literary heat and dust of the metropolis, poet Jayanta Mahapatra (hereafter 'Jayanta')—has found -a place for himself, somewhat secluded and cornered in a 'metaphoric sort of way'. Celebrated and feted throughout the world, he could easily slip into the role of the local eminence grise of English letters. But when asked by an interviewer if there were words of wisdom- he would like to pass on to younger poets, Jayanta quipped. "Am I any different from them? l still receive rejection slips from prestigious journals abroad". The first thing that strikes one about Jayanta is his hallmark humility and a persona which is intensely human.

Born in 1928, Jayanta himself admits having had a traumatic childhood. His mother, a strict disciplinarian, imposed a strict regimen of chores and duties on a young Jayanta, the eldest in a family of two, leaving him utterly lonely and helpless. Educated locally and at Science College, Patna, he went on to become a teacher of Physics who taught in different colleges of Odisha till his retirement in 1986. A popular teacher and a highly respected academician, he is very fondly remembered by his students. Although it may sound strange, but Jayanta started writing late in life. After many rejections, his first poem 'Girl by the window' was accepted for publication in *The Illustrated Weekly of India* in the year 1969 when he was already 41. In his words *"at a time when most other poets would have produced more or less their best work"*. For someone like him with a difficult childhood, he found solace in the arms of his father who from his touring school inspector job spent time with him occasionally. As if to make up for this late start he went on in quick succession to produce a substantial body of outstanding poetry. For him poetry was destined to be "an anchor to his perception; for a life time". The poet himself admits candidly, *"the very act of writing poetry is a liberating experience and fulfils a certain inner need which takes the poet past himself and the mundane necessities of life; I believe, poetry still stretches the non-existent membrane of the mind"*.

Reviewing Jayanta's "A Rain of Rites" in the famous American Journal, *The Hudson Review* the eminent critic Vernon Young wrote:

"The manner of his apprehension in wonderful, sensate poems inevitably brings to the tongue the word 'sophistication'; evident in every cadence is the long over-ripening of a sardonic wisdom. Few contemporary poems in our world impress me more than these".

Ironically, Jayanta insists on being called an Odia poet who incidentally writes in English. His poems, he says, "are just attempts to hold a handful of earth to my face and let it speak for me, so the poems reveal who I am". To him "the very act of writing a poem is like being caught up in the net of time" and the poem itself becomes "a precise moment of truth, a creation that remains true to the human conscience".

Somewhat ridiculed initially as a 'physics poet', international recognition arrived when his poems started appearing in the pages of much coveted literary journals such as Critical Quarterly, The Hudson Review; The Kenyon Review, The Sewanee Review, Queens Quarterly, Poetry (Chicago) and the The Times Literary Supplement.

Jayanta's poetry is deeply rooted in his own soil and infused with a built-in sense irony. For instance, in a poem 'The Lost Children of America' with the 'hippi' culture of the early 70's as a theme, the reader feels as though he is the one wandering around the narrow, filthy streets of Cuttack city in Odisha:

Here
in the dusty malarial lanes
of Cuttack where years have slowly lost their secrets
they wander
in these lanes nicked by intrigue and rain
along river banks splattered with excreta and dung
in the crowded market square among rotting tomatoes
fish-scales and the moist warm odour of bananas and
piss
passing by the big-breasted, hard-eyed young whores
who frequent the empty silent space behind the local
cinema
by the Town Hall where corrupt politicians still
go on delivering their pre-election speeches
like -the unreal stirrings
of incense smoke in a darkened shrine
like the languid movements of mangled lepers

> *around a temple of the goddess Chandi at dawn*
> *like a wounded whale drifting away*
> *sadly in unknown seas*
> *like the dark winds of Asia*
> *which murmur joylessly in slums but do not answer*
> *they wander, these lost children -of America,*
> *flaunting their long unkempt hair and their bare feet;*
> ("The Lost Children of America")

Cuttack, the city Jayanta is passionately in love -with, the temple city of Bhubaneswar and the religious town of Puri appear as oft-repeated landscapes in his poetry. He writes:

> *At Puri the crows.*
> *The one wide street*
> *lolls out like a giant tongue.*
> *Five faceless lepers move aside*
> *as a priest passes by.* ("Taste for Tomorrow")

As one traverses through the large body of Jayanta's poetry, it is easy for the discernable reader to enter into his mental landscape; one that is invaded by a horde of anxieties and uncertainties, tormenting memories and pangs of his growing up. The everyday concerns of poverty; hunger and death, give his poems a distinctive, ruminating tone:

> Cliches still;
> the filarial water, amoebic dysentery
> bodies ribbed and packed with hunger
> It has always been like that
> The hard sky stares everywhere like a God.
>
> ("Orissa Landscapes")

Though some critics have this tendency to see Jayanta's poems as over sentimentalized kitsch, one tends to see them as an attempt to negotiate and mediate through a maze of conflicts, contradictions and confusions; both within and without; learning on some complex symbols and images. It is pretty difficult to pin his work down to any specific literary theory. His poems thwart any attempt at thematic straight-jacketing and bulldoze any stylistic stratification. Very much rooted, Jayanta maintains that it is one's immediate experience which gives the much needed "flesh to one's skeleton of imagination". Thus, his poetry is a prolonged process of coming to terms with the reality around himself. His somber voice is an outcome of a critical and complex 'Filtering through' of his experience which relentlessly oscillates between the abstract and concrete:

"All the poetry there is
appear to rise out of ashes
for there is nothing like the ashes
to remind as how little there is to say".

("All the poetry there is")

His use of sharp -metaphors, juxtaposed with very personal and unusual symbols creates a tension around the poems where the reader is left alone, more often than not flabbergasted, to draw suggestions or inferences for himself. Maybe this whole exercise makes the poem somewhat obscure, but then this succinct style of his creativity sets him apart from other Indian English poets. Sometimes, his poems read like an explosion of sharp edged questions flung at none but himself:

"Why does one room invariably
lead into other rooms?" ("The Moon Moments")

And yet again:
"*where is the good reason
that says a moral can't be sold?*"
("Tonight I hear the water flowing")

In Relationship, the long poem which got Jayanta the Sahitya Akademi Award, for the first time in the category of Indian English Poetry, he embarked upon an inward journey where he identifies his subconscious self with a tradition to which he belongs, but not comfortably; a past which he inherits, but not wholeheartedly and tries to establish a rapport in between:

"*It is my own life
that has cornered me beneath the stones
of this temple in ruins, in a blaze of sun.*"
("Relationship")

Thus, his engagement with an uncomfortable past, his exploration of the complex relationship between tradition and modernity, manifest in many of his poems. Jayanta's tormented self, crushed between a past he could not extricate himself from and an overbearing weight of the present ultimately finds recourse in his signature tone of ambivalence and obscurity, ensuing thus a ceaseless process of synchronization. His critical and unconventional response to 'time' and 'space', his deft negotiation between myth, tradition and modernity, finally decides the coarse texture of his poetry. In this context, Jayanta has this to say:

"*Often the human mind can take wild, awesome leaps into the unconscious, and come out with metaphors of dizzying dimensions. Here is the dram mind's unbelievable ability to create its own, beings*".

Traversing thus, through the wilderness of Jayanta's words and images, it is not unusual for the reader to bump sporadically into the shadows of both mystic and mythic elements that dwell all too often across his literary landscape.

"on the trunk of an old banyan
A mutilating knife celebrates
The agenda of love,
Elsewhere, a two thousand years old edict
Of peace stares, heavy with useless remorse."
(Violence)

As the reader moves through the sweeping body of his poetry writing over half-a-century, he finds himself confronted with a summation of events and turmoils that very much characterize Jayanta's weid and grim private world. An absurd poetic landscape dotted with recurring and powerfully creative images of shadow, darkness, door, bone, rain, light, death, Gods stones:

"Beneath the bloodied walls of history
Nothing can happen more dreadful
Then stones turned to gods
Through prayers."
(The Stones)

It would not be wrong to say that in a number of ways, Jayanta seems very much like his own poems – meditative, morose and always anxious of dark possibilities. Through his poems he holds up to us a somewhat bleak world. His poetic vision hinges on the topography of pain and pathos so much so that it virtually mocks the much touted beauty of the inherent both within and without. Except for the occasional 'glee' in the eyes of his poems, one hardly comes across a poem of Jayanta where he seems to have been carried way by the happiness and pleasure. This celebration of pain in his poems doesn't necessarily mean that 'pleasure' did not exist in his life at all. Rather, in the rugged terrain of his imagination it always exists 'elsewhere' somewhere beyond his poetic realm; may be in the act of 'writing' itself.

Jayanta is not much of a 'rebel' in his poems though there are streaks of 'anger' in this words. Feeble voices of defiance and dissent apart and overtones of protest notwithstanding; he is never 'loud' in his protests, rather somewhat 'subdued' in his tone but unsparing in his critique.

The poet's land, Odisha, finds a powerful presence in most of his poems, for him, Odisha is not just a 'place', but a 'state of mind, a dream space' his muse prefers to inhabit amidst all the meaninglessness and the chaos. Reading his poem one gets the feel of the place where the smell of paddy ripe for harvest mingles easily with the reek of starvation-deaths:

"*The rice has lost its wings.*
It doesn't tremble in the wind
as I feel my way
along the defeating distances of hunger."   ("Rice")

And in another poem he writes very evocatively about the pilgrimage town of Puri:

"*Hr Puri, the crows.*
The one wide street
loll: out like a giant tongue." (Taste of Tomorrow)

Ironically, Jayanta loves to be called an 'Odia' poet who incidentally happens to be writing in English. This speaks volumes about the 'rootedness' of his poetry to the soil on which he has firmly planted his feet. The strength of his voice lies in his ability to be 'universal' without losing its ideological moorings and thematic grip on the 'local'.

About his Odia poems, one could easily say that they are more like branches stretching divergently from the same tree—independent in their own search for a separate sky yet inextricably linked to the solid trunk. When Jayanta started writing in Odia, a few murmurs of dissent were heard, eyebrows were raised, and some snide remarks made by the Odia language -puritans; who found fault with his knowledge of Odia syntax, grammar an diction; but over the years, with half a dozen collections of Odia poems and soon after the publication of a brutally honest and beautifully written autobiography, he has proved his mettle as a bilingual poet who could mould both the languages with equal ease to suit his own private needs. Jayanta himself says that "his 'Odia' poems could not have written in English as there are certain things which one could say only in one's mother tongue." His involvement with both languages has only enriched the total poetic effect on his Odia poems as well, consequently *"imparting an altogether different taste, gloss and shine to modern Odia poetry"*.

Having gone through the poetry of Jayanta Mahapatra written over five decades one tends to ask; "has Jayanta's voice changed over all these years of writing?" The answer is both an emphatic 'yes' and a resounding 'no'. His richly textured voice still broods meditatively over centuries of decay and sufferings, an acute sense of loss, haunting memories that refuse to go, a sense of disillusionment, grim realities of hunger and starvation, and suppression of women.

For sometime it may appear that nothing at all has changed and yet the change has been phenomenal! Towards the later phase of his poetic journey -the reader comes across yet another voice of Jayanta which has moved away from his earlier, somewhat esoteric-surrealistic – suggestive mode of writing to flat, lucid statements of poetry; from being the poster boy (boy?) of abstractions and modernist incomprehensibility to a concrete poetic speech and one who has abandoned the acutely inward tone of his poetry for an all new transparent voice. Be it 'abstract' or 'concrete' Jayanta's world remains all the same; complex relationships, defeated dreams, painful memories, mingle together to create a typical Indian 'stoic' self who accepts things mutely in a fatalist sorts of way:

"This is a man who talks of pain
as though it belonged to him alone.
May be he had invented it himself
and made at virtue of it."

("Of A Questionable Conviction")

In his anthology, 'Twelve Modern Indian Poets', Arvind Krishna Mehrotra, the celebrated Indian English poet has rightly remarked about Jayanta- *"There are no poets he seems to be touched by and there is none he is likely to influence"*; thus indicating the free-standing universe of his poems. In his inimitable style another celebrated poet and critic of our times, K. Satchidanandan aptly makes this observation about Jayanta's poetry:

"He is committed without being dogmatic, sensitive without being sentimental, native without being insular, indignant Without being cynical and beautiful without being decorative. He knows that poetry, like Picasso said of painting, is not meant to adorn the drawing rooms but a means to express the sad truth of its times. His concern for the dispossessed rustic that is tare among the urbanized Indian poets writing in English marks him out as a tragic rebel."

How true is the above statement! While most Odia poets dabbled in ancient myths, celestial love, mysticism and churned out reams of 'escape' poetry using heavily' personalized and obscured symbols maintaining all along a safe distance from grim, socio-political realities, trying to sound 'politically correct' in their voice; this man chose to write poems about life on the margins, oppression of women. displacement of tribals, starvation deaths, prostitutes, violence and the low "life around -himself with a rich and intense local flavour." Subtleties of vision, deft handling. of language, a built-in sense of irony, evocative images, contemplative and meditative voice make Jayanta's poems what good poetry ought to be; -thus setting new benchmarks of quality poetry at a global level. A very seasoned poet like him knows only too well how to deliver, not just in style but in substance too.

Jayanta is a meticulous keeper of records relating to his long literary innings. By the time I had embarked upon this grand job of editing this volume, he had already donated thousands of his books, magazines and other documents of significance amassed over half a century to a college library where he taught in his early teaching years. Thus, I narrowly missed a veritable treasure trove of literary materials. Of course there were some treasures still remained with him, as waiting for me for this volume to happen.

To say that Jayanta Mahapatra is the foremost Indian English poet today would not just be a cliche but a 'literary sacrilege' of sorts; a huge understatement in terms of how actually our words convey. However, this comprehensive volume on Jayanta's writing is supposed to be a richly deserving tribute to his creative genius, as well as a celebration of his poetry, critical essays, conversations, correspondences, critical appreciations of his works spread across nearly half a century of his creative journey.

The section 'Close Encounters' includes among others a fond and detail reminiscences by the novelist Amit Choudhuri about an unexpected visit to Jayanta's Cuttack home. Long back, Jayanta had apparently published four of Choudhuri's poems in his prestigious *'Chandrābhāga'* when the novelist was just 18.

Jayanta is not an easy poet to be understood. His poems are not meant for easy consumption that don't yield to any straightforward meaning where the baffled reader is left to himself to draw some suggestion and references that give him a 'feel' of the poem. No doubt excessive dependence on 'symbol' makes his poems disturbingly surrealistic and obscure, but that is how his poems are — complex in a beautiful sort of way. What then make Jayanta's poetry difficult and different, but beautifully mysterious? This question has been dealt with by several acclaimed critics in the section 'Through critical lenses'. A rather longish article published in *Contemporary Literary Criterion* Vol.33" (1985) by the Gale Research Company (Detroit, Michigan, USA) includes astute observations by many distinguished poets who focus on the intricacies of Jayanta's early poems. This comprehensive essay brings together important reviews of his poems that appered in various prestigious journals around the world. For this section Prof. John Oliver Perry sets the tone by harping upon the chronic and somewhat shaky existence of Indian English poetry which took a turn around for good with Jayanta receiving the Central Sahitya Akademi Award for the first time in such a category in 1985. In the volatility of a mixed culture will live in, in India, Perry tries to understand the specificities and intricacies of Indian English poetry writing, placing Jayanta's poetry in its "broad world context."

While Dr. R.P. Raveendran, scholar and critic, scrutinizes Jayanta's poem looking for steaks of the decolonization process; the late critic Dr. Krishna Rayan noticed a dramatic shift in Jayanta's poems over the years from *'suggestions'* to *'statements'* affirming that his voice has moved from 'abstract' to somewhat 'concrete', from. incomprehensible esoteric to a mundane plain. This essay had to be culled down from one of his long essays for reasons of 'space and context.'

I have a strong fascination for Jayanta's work of prose for the simple reason that they are often to be the logical extension of his poetic vision and thought. His prose, too, is "for its mature and lyrical beauty" much the same way as his poems. They also serve as 'doors' to enter into his imaginative realm. These deeply contemplative, ruminative and reflective essays also reveal the scholarly side "his persona and also give a significant insight into his complex poetic craft, his passionate love for his roots and the milieu that surrounds him. Richly lyrical, these essays included here form an invaluable addition to the contemporary poetic discourse. Skewed a little in favour of his prose work, some of his finest writing which 'ranges from travelogue, literary criticism, memoirs and reminiscences, encounters and astute observations of a deeply-lived life. It would be no less a revelation for many to know that Jayanta started his literary journey (I hate the word 'career') short stories, but getting them published turned out to be an uphill task. His bumpy ride on the crest of his stories included outright rejection as well as 'cold' acceptance.

He then switched over to 'poetry'. His stories started getting published in well known magazines only after he made a name for Indian English poetry. In his large creative output, his stories could be seen more like a welcome, and 'delicately done aberrations'.

Though widely travelled across the world, unlike others, ironically, Jayanta seems least interested in the lure and gloss of New York City for instance; or of Manhattan and the likes, when he visited USA. Instead he gets drawn into the remote and the silence of Americas wilderness. The readers will find a typical Jayanta revealing in, "extraordinary quite radiance and piercing silence", where even his careful, light footfalls appeared to defile the pristine purity of the forests. 'America's magical showpieces lie inside the country's womb; they leave no signs in the accessible city landscape. The doors are there for anyone who chooses to open them", says Jayanta ruefully. Both the pieces included in the travelogue section testify to this.

I have included as many as six interviews; and as they reveal for Jayanta, 'poetry was not, just a spontaneous overflow of powerful feelings, rather appear carefully structured act of painstaking labour." He also took it upon himself that it was his moral duty to explain the intricacies and complex thought process that went into the making of his poetry. One significant feature of these talks is that the poet seems humble enough to admit his ignorance whenever he felt he wasn't sure about his specific answer. One could see him taking shelter behind words like 'may be', 'I don't in-row', 'perhaps'; taking every care not to impose his thoughts on the reader.

Jayanta is not much of a talker - he is reticent, concise and to the point with his words. But once the dialogue is initiated and achieves a desired level of seriousness, he doesn't hesitate to pour his heart out.

From the most recent conversation with him by Dr. Sukrita Paul Kumar to the very first ones, spanning almost forty years, these conversations throw rare insights into Jayanta's craft, vision and his take on life and letters. The 'Reader' also includes an interview done by Prof. Satchidanand Mohanty, one which is an exhaustive version containing elaborate talk and anxieties that dominate his muse.

Jayanta used to reply to almost, every letter (and he still does) he receives from his readers, scholars, critics and friends across the World; responding to their quarries and other simple things — both artistically written in long hand and typed. These letters brimming with the language of love, concern and tenderness- have an 'epistolary' value -as well as a soothing effect on the part of the 'reader. In one of the many letters he had written to me he had reflected and lamented about the hassles of bringing out his brain child, the prestigious journal *Chandrābhāga*' single handedly against all odds. His long correspondence with Prof. Norman Simms and other critics reveal a lot about his craft, style and how he concerns and engages himself vis-a-vis his poetry writing. "These letters are precious because they had to be virtually excavated from the old, dusty cartons lying for years in his attic. They provide a rare glimpse into a gentle and innocent personality.

Now something about Jayanta, the editor. I found him to be the toughest editor so far as editing a literary journal is concerned. Once, in a letter to me, he had somewhat jokingly described himself as the 'harshest editor' alive in India. *'Chandrabhāgā'* the prestigious literary magazine, finely brought out by him had a two-series run: the first from 1979-1985 (14 issues) and then from 2000-2007 (15 issues). Before that, in the early 70s he also edited a journal called 'Gray Book' for sometime. I have seen his passion in bringing out *'Chandrabhāgā'* even as the magazine was taking a toll on his health. In her frail heath, his wife Jyotsna was also assisting him in sorting things out, helped by the poet Rabi Swain. Funds were low; costs were mounting, advertisements were very few, subscribers were dwindling. Bringing out a serious magazine of poetry was ever so difficult for Jayanta. Once Jayanta had confided to me how one subscriber cancelled his subscription when poems he had sent were rejected by him. Let me take this chance to say that, after rejecting dozens of my poems, when he finally accepted two of my poems. The minor changes he made to them were acceptable to me! I couldn't sleep that night in some excitement. Jayanta was so passionately involved in *'Chandrabhāgā'* that once he went as far as Kolkata searching for a certain quality of 'paper' for *'Chandrabhāgā'*. Finally, in 2007 (issue 15), *'Chandrabhāgā'* (2nd series) ceased publication.

It would be worthwhile to note that Jayanta has written some significant poems on his fellow poets (some essays too!). 'When I consulted him about including some of them in the 'Reader', he was reluctant on the plea that he was unsure about their 'quality'. For me, however, it was reason enough that a well-known contemporary poet, blow-struck by the death of one of his fellow poets, would come out with a moving poem, giving a creative vent to his grief. Despite Jayanta's reservations about these poems, I felt they had to be there in this 'Reader' for posterity and for their contemporariness, if not entirely for their poetic quality as Jayanta believes.

On the other hand complementing this matter, are a number of poets and critics who have also written-" poems dedicated to Jayanta. Yet no "Reader" could claim to be definitive and be expected to include everything memorable that the poet" has churned out in his lifetime. 'Besides, the choice is pretty difficult especially when the 'body of work is quite vast and diverse. The choice of material to be included in the 'Reader' from such a vast writing-bound *"life is bound to be somewhat subjective and erratic too. One lives forever with the regret of many notable omissions due to unexplainable reasons much against. one's own wish,"* resisting one temptation or another. Perhaps I will carry a feeling of incompleteness of Jayanta's work within me all my life.

* Courtesy : *Jayanta Mahapatra : A Reader*, Ed. – D.P. Panda, Sahitya Academi, New Delhi (2018)

Lokaratna Kunja Bihari Dash : A Profile on Folk Culture & Literature of Odisha (1914-1995)

Baishnab Charan Samal

Lokaratna Dr. Kunjabihari Dash was a man of integrity. He was a sympathetic humanist. From his very childhood he was loving his own village and people of the countryside irrespective of caste and creed, rich and poor and was attracted towards the natural beauty during his youth. He was born in the year 1914 in the village Inchudi Shasan of Puri district in a traditional brāhmin family. His father was Chintamani Dash and mother was Taramani. He had also one younger brother Udayanath to whom he loved much and by his help and inspiration, Udaya became a famous doctor, remained in America, But divine brotherly affection between them continued till their last. By the help of his younger brother Kunjabihari, establised Chintamani Vidyapitha and a charitable hospital in his village. This proves his love and philanthropic mentality towards his village and rural mass.

Kunjabihari was a genius. He got his primary education in his village. During his youth he felt the heat of independence struggle of India led by Mahatma Gandhi with the sharp weapon of Truth and Nonviolence. Also he had seen two divine angels, one was Kulabruddha Madhusudan Das and the other one was Utkalmani Gopabandhu Das. These two dedicated personalities impressed him immensely. He foresee the establishment of Naba Utkal i.e. Odisha Pradesh in 1st April 1936 and that thrilled him deeply. He also came in contact with revolutionary poet and novelist Kuntala Kumari Sabat and afterwards compiled her granthābali and published in two parts and wrote a meticulous preface regarding the life history of Kuntala Kumari and her literary talent. His intellectual acumen is still now the inspiration to the readers, researchers and the critics.

Kunjabihari was very much studious and labourious. He had also deep sensibility in search of truth, history and culture due to his intimate inspiration and introspection. He went to Calcutta for higher studies. Inspite of intense financial difficulties he was determined to fulfil his aim. He became a teacher in the Night School established by Utkalmani Gopabandhu Das for Oriya labourers staying at Calcutta and continued his studies. He passed M.A. in Sanskrit honourably and also passed M.A. in Oriya under Calcutta University.

His service career started as an inspector of Sanskrit in the education department in Orissa (1946). Then he joined as a lecturer in Oriya in Fakirmohan College, Balasore in 1947. He was very popular there. By his sincere effort in the memory of Fakirmohan Senapati 'Fakirmohan Smruti Sansad' had been established in the year 1950 and that literary Institution is now a glorious institution in Odisha. In 1950, he went to Visva

Bharati on deputation and joined there as the Head of the Oriya department. Due to his effort and personality, he became very popular among the learned professors of various faculties and students. The then Upāchārya became his friend. He opened the B.A (Hons) and M.A. in Odia there. He started his Ph.D. work at Visva Bharati on Odia folk literature and got Ph.D degree in 1954. He was the first Ph.D holder in Odia language and literature. He also founded there 'Odia Sahitya Samaj' and published a research oriented book '*Adhunika Oriya Sahitya: Bhumi O Bhumikā*'. His thesis '*Oriya Loka Geeta O Kahani*' was published in 1958 and still is an outstanding work on Odia folk culture and literature. While he was at Visva Bharati, he read various books on folk-studies of Rabindranatha Tagore and also came in close contact with Prof. Tusarkanti Ghose and others. There he came in contact with Annada Sankara Roy, the Odia poet of Sabuja Juga, afterwards became an outstanding novelist in Bengali language. Meeting with Annada Sankar time and time again Kunjabihari wrote one valuable book on Annada Sankara.

During that time he travelled throughout Odisha and the detached areas like Sadeikala, Kharasuan, Dhal Bhumi, Manbhumi, Tikra, Nuagada, Manjusha and met various old men and women from whom he collected folk tales, poems, proverbs, legends and folk dramas. Prior to him one Kāyast lady had collected some folk songs and the eminent writer and scholar Gopal Chandra Praharaj had collected a number of folk-tales. *Utkal Kāhāni* is his valuable collection. Then Chakradhara Mahapatra collected many folk-songs and published them as '*Utkal Gāunli Geeta*'. But Dr. Kunja Bihari Dash surpassed all for his vast collections. His excellent collections are *Palli Geeti Sanchayan* (vol 1,2,3) *Lokabāni* (vol 1,2,3) *Loka Galpa Sanchayan, Dhaga Dhamāli, Prabachan* etc. He also participated in various National and International seminars on Folk Culture and Literature. For his noble contribution in this field of folk literature the 'Akademi of Folklore, Calcutta', bestowed upon him the honour 'Loka-Ratna' in 1978.

Lokaratna Kunjabihari Dash was not confined only in folk studies but he had shown his talent and excellency in writing poetry, travelogues, short-stories, novels, criticisms, essay and Ramyarachanā, children literature. He was a poet at first and continued writing poetry till his last- *Pāsāna Charane Rakta, Bagra, Birashree, Naba Māllika, Se Eka Lomasha Nila Hata, Mati O Lāthi* etc are his poetry collections. His poetry collections are published in three volumes. As he was lover of human society and people, his poetry contains natural beauty, sympathy for poor and the distressed people, the cultivators, labourers and animals. He had also written prose, poems and ballads. Musicality is the essence of his poetry. He had written various short stories and one collection has been published 'Hasha Kānda Gapa' (the stories of smile and cry). He has contributed four novels, such as 'Rāmāyan', 'Ki kathā Kalikata', 'Manimā Sunimā heu', 'Mashāni Tulasi'. All his novels and stories are imprint of Odia society, culture and everywhere one finds the tears and struggles of the people. He is famous for his travelogues. *Lankā Jātrā, Mo Swapnara Kāshmir, America Europe Africa. Diga Digantara Kāhāni, America Punascha.* He had written criticism also. *Odia Loka Geeta O Kāhāni, Samālochanā, Sāhityika, Sāhitya O Samālochanā* etc are his criticisms. In his criticisms one observes his originality and insight. His Ramyarachanā are *Srimanta. Jibanayan, Jibana 0 Jibani* are his prominent books written on the lives and contributions of different eminent persons of Odisha. .

The Autobiography of Dr. Dash is *'Mo Kāhāni'* which has been awarded by the Kendriya Sahitya Akademi. As he was very philanthropic, humanistic, sympathetic and affectionate, he inspired some his friends to write autobiographies. Among them the notable personalities are Prof. Krushna Chandra Panigrahi and Faturananda who confessed the same in their autobiographies. He also adorned the Presidentship of Utkal Sahitya Samaj, the oldest Odia literary Institution, He was the Founder President of 'Sāralā Sansad' which was founded by the philanthropic and lover of Odia literature Late Ila Panda and Bansidhara Panda by their sincere participation along with Dr. Kunjabihari Dash and Dr. Nityananda Satpathy.

Prof. Dr. Kunjabihari Dash was really a man of high morality and worshipper of aesthetics. He had respect for values, culture and common people. His has deep sense of emotion. But he has never been swept away by emotion. Very often his inner being is attracted towards the reality. So he is a romantic realist. His love for soil and people, village and the working people was immense. His social consciousness and sense of humanity, especially his love for folk - culture, and literature, folk–language and their struggling life are very deep and dense. He took heavenly abode in 1995 but he is still alive among the people and will reamin alive in future too. In fact he is the profile of folk-culture, literature and people of Odisha.

Golak Bihari Dhal : A Rare Genious

Sanatan Mallik

Prof. Golak Bihari Dhal is a rare genius in the field of comparative linguistics. As a phonetician per excellence, Prof. Dhal set a common standard among the Indian Languages in pronouncing them rightly taking the International Phonetic Alphabet (IPA) as its background. His famous book *'Dhwani Vigyān'* (Science of Phonetics) published both in Hindi and Odia is a precious treasure in the history of linguistics. Prof. Dhal was also a prolific prose writer and an astounding biographer. His travelogues are enjoyable, moving and interesting.

Prof. Golak Bihari Dhal was born on 3rd March 1919 at a small village 'Ganjeidiha' of Dhenkanal district. His father, Bholeswar Dhal and Mother Janha Devi had a great hope on him from his childhood. Golak Dhal had his primary education at his own village school. He passed matriculation from Dhenkanal Garh High School (now B.B. High School) in first division and studied B.A. (Hons.) at Ravenshaw College. He did his M.A. (Sanskrit) from Patna University. He was a successful lecturer and his fame spreaded throughout Odisha. He went to England, America and France to obtain a deep knowledge in comparative linguistics. He was awarded by the Orissa Sahitya Academy and Central Govt. for his translation literature and literature on children. He was a nominated member of the Oriya Script Reformation Committee Board of Primary Education too.

To know the heart of a nation is to know the heart of a language. ' A real language is speech'. The great intellectuals of India had delved deep into linguistics thousand years back. The influence of 'Mantras' (Sacred Chantations) has not faded away. Even once Hitler pointed out that the influence of speech is more powerful than that of the written language. All the revolutions that took place at different phases of time were source of powerful speeches not written books.

The great grammarians Pānini and Patanjali identified the different organs of speech from their own experiences. The pronounciation of Odia and Sanskrit alphabets Ka, Kha, Ga, etc. has been scientifically and specifically evolved by them. Leonard Bloomfield has rightly told on Pānini : *"This grammar which dates from somewhere round 350-250 B.C. is out of the greatest monuments of humane intelligence. No other language to this day has been so perfectly described."*

But it is a matter of regret that after Pānini and Patanjali nobody has taken sincere effort in the field of comparative linguistics. In western countries remarkable achievements have been done although in India a little efforts have been undertaken. Prof. Dhal was one among such genius in India who has done some remarkale works in comparative linguistics.

Prof. Golak Bihar Dhal through his book *'Dhwani Vigyān'* (Science on Phonetics) brought about a revolutionary change in Odia language as well as other

Indian languages. The international Phonetic Symbols have been used in this book. The first two chapters have been devoted on philology and linguistics. The third chapter described on 'phonemes' and their use. In the rest chapters the descriptions on various organs on speech are vividly given and the phonetic symbols on vowels and sonsonant sounds are highlighted.

His book '*Odia Keve*' (when will odias rise up) gives a glimpse on the future of the odia language. It is a collection of essays written at different times on Odia language, National language, Government language (official language) versus English language. What is the contribution of English language to India and what role should regional language play are the bone of content of this book. He emphasized on the use of Hindi, Odia and English language in primary, high school and at college level.

Besides books on Phonetics, Prof. Dhal to his credit contributed some travelogues to Odia Literature. His works e.g. '*London Chithi*' (Letters from London), *America Abubhuti* (Experience at America), *Manisara Bhāsā* (The language of Man) *Tajamahalara Desa* (In the domain of Tajamahal), *Gangāru Godāvari* (From Ganga to Godavari) created lasting impressions on the readers. His work '*Amar Jiban*' is a powerful biography. In this book he has written about the lives of great men like Gandhi, Fakir Mohan Senapati, Florence Nightengel, Netaji Subhas Bose etc. His translation '*Godān*' and '*Goban*' from Premchand's original works has impressed the indelible feeling among the readers.

He had a great pleasure in teaching linguistics to the students all over India. Even from the movement to tongue he could recognize the nationality of the student. While writing his book on linguistics he was greatly influenced by Prof. Glecan, Prof. Fair Bass, Prof. Hoeni Gwasalad etc.

He retired as Professor and Head of the Department of Odia Language and Literature from Ravenshaw College on 21st June 1974. He died leaving behind his great contribution to Odia language and its phonetics. As Bernard Shaw donated all his wealth for the reformation of English language and script, Prof. Dhal in the same way contributed all his labour and talent for the development of Odia phonetics.

Sri Abhirām Paramahamsa: Life and Message (1904-1963)

Niranjan Mohanty

In the beginning of twentieth century, Odisha was fortunate to have given birth to a divine person– Sri Abhirām Paramahamsa. His advent was long before prophesised in palm-leaf-manuscripts by enlightened saints, like Mahāpuruṣha Achyutānanda Dās and Saint Shiva Dās, which contained details as to his life, philosophy and religion he preached later.

Childhood: On the 18th January, 1904 Sri Abhirām was born to the parents Satyabādi Pattanaik and Radhā Devi in the village Karamala of Puri district. The day after his birth, a saint from North India visited the parents and asked them to christen the child as Abhirām. The child Abhirām was later adopted by a childless couple, namely, Arjun Pattanaik and Subrata Devi. But after a few years, the foster parents passed away and the child came back to his parents. In the childhood, Abhirām was committing countless frolics and mischief like looting the fruits from orchards, and the milk, curd and sweets from the houses of many, of course leaving some coins towards the cost of the

151

things in some cases. The parents left the child under the tutelage of his eldest brother, a school teacher at Ganjam where Abhiram got his primary education.

Sādhanā: From his childhood Abhirām had shown a keen interest in spending time in meditation and composing devotional songs which was so unbecoming of a child of his age. Once he kept himself shut inside a room and got engrossed in meditation. When a long time elapsed, and there was no response from the child, the panic-stricken parents along with some neighbours opened the thatched roof. They saw their son sitting cross-legged with his body raised from the floor and stationed in the air.

In his teens, he used to abruptly disappear into the nearby forest Khāndabavana and get himself lost in meditation. Once after meditative trance, he woke up to find that seasons have changed and the body covered with sand and leaves. Here the Goddess Banadurgā revealed Herself and taught him the secrets of spiritual wisdom asking him to propagate *Ekāshara Ajapā Mantra Sādhanā* as mentioned in his writings. Thus, the young Abhirām exalted to the state of Sri Abhirām Paramahamsa.

Itinerary: Sri Abhirām opted to remain celibate and wandered through the hills and forests of Odisha with minimal possession of an ascetic, only with a Kaupina and Angi (long shirt). During his itinerary he came to interact with the realised saint Siddha Hādidas of Siddhagiri in Cuttack district and had enlightened discussion on Odishi Vaishnavism. He also came to Sankrail of West Bengal where some Odias working in a Jute Mill got initiated by him to the spiritual path and became his disciples. His mission took a definite shape with his mysterious meeting with Baikuntha who was about to end his life and miraculously escaped because of Sri Abhirām. Baikuntha had accompanied Sri Abhirām when the latter came back to his village from Sankrail. On the way, at Puri, Sri Abhirām initiated Baikuntha into Sannyāsa. In the village Karamalā, Sri Abhirām established his monastery called 'Shanti Ānandāshram'. Later, some of the disciples from Sankrail, namely, Kanduri, Bharata, Jagannātha, Prabhākara and Purnānanda came to Karamalā and joined the monastery taking initiation to sannyāsa.

Preaching: Along with these sannyāsins Sri Abhirām started his mission to disseminate the spiritual knowledge he had among the common mass and to initiate the spiritually thirsty people into his way of spiritual practice leading to the realisation of the Supreme Reality. He travelled far and wide for almost seven years from 1927 to 1933 in preaching *Ekāshara Mantra* and *Ajapā Sādhanā*. The first centre of his preaching was the village Ichhāpur to Āul in the then Cuttack district. While giving discourses at different places he had to face the invitation for arguments from the Pandits. But he could successfully establish his views that one can realise the self by an easy method without entering into severe penance of Yoga, only by *Hetu-sādhanā*, the constant watching of breath with devotion to God. His sweet and lucid discourses in colloquial language, simple and affectionate behaviour attracted millions of men and women to have their shelter in him and fulfil their spiritual cravings. He was more in a close relation than a Guru for the devotees and disciples. He was lovingly called by them as 'Thākur'.

Patriotism and Imprisonment: As a spiritual stalwart,

Thākur Sri Abhirām Paramahamsa not only gave direction to the spiritually thirsty people but codified his thoughts through his writings, especially through his *magnum opus* '*Kali Bhāgavata*' for the posterity to find direction and inspiration to trade the path of truth and rectitude. Written in verses the '*Kali Bhāgavata*' is full of metaphysical thoughts allegorically written with a reference at some places to the contemporary political condition. At that time people in India at large were trying to be free out of political slavery and economic exploitation of the British rulers. This political condition was reflected in the writings of Sri Abhiram Paramahamsa. He tried to arouse the human psyche against the alien rulers. He wrote in *Kali Bhāgavata*,

"*Pancha manati jāku kahi, Panchamajarja ate sehi.*
Gorā palatana jāku kahi, Pachisha prakrutiti sehi.
Ehiti bideshi atanti, Svarājya ujādina dyanti."

It means, "What we call the '*pancha* (five) *manas*' is the same as the Fifth George. The white forces are the 'twenty five prakritis'. These are the foreigners, the destroyers of our home land." Many stanzas in *Kali Bhāgavata* had the predictions about the death of King George-V and Quit India Movement, and also that Mahātmā by leading the Satyāgrahis would force the Europeans to leave this country. Such caustic observations about the British Rule made him the object of political wrath. He was impeached of treason by the British Rulers and was arrested in 1933 and was released on bail. The charges against him was that the book *Kali Bhāgavata* contained several passages of seditious matter intended to bring into hatred and contempt against His Majesty The King Emperor and the Government established by law in British India. The trial went on for months at Chhatrapur in the Court of Mr. A. F. Dixon. Witnessing the trial Pandit Nilakantha Das wrote in his '*Gitā Prabesh*', "The young ascetic stood in the court room day after day. He knew that he would serve a long jail sentence. But there was always a natural smile on his lips, ..." Sri Abhiram Paramahamsa was sentenced to rigorous imprisonment for one year by the judgement of the Court dated 13.12.1934. Accordingly he was sent to Rajmuhendry Jail. On account of his magnanimity and spiritual fervour, he won the heart of inmates and officers of the Jail and his jail term was reduced by one and half month. Although he did not directly participate in the freedom struggle, his allegorical writings regarding Satyāgraha, Svadeshi and Svarājya had immense effect on the freedom fighters and the Congressmen in the freedom struggle in Odisha.

Social Reformation: Through his writings Sri Abhiram Paramahamsa tried not only to arouse patriotism, but also to bring reformation in the society. He raised voice against the fundamentalism, fanaticism, casteism and untouchability prevalent in full swing in the society. He was against the division of human beings on the basis of caste, creed and religion. Also he advised not to differentiate between Nārāyaṇa, Allah and Christ as one Brahman is present everywhere. Lord Hari is present in every being, and everyone is a son of Hari. So there should be no fight between man and man based on religion. He tried to bring equality and harmony among all religions and all human beings.

He was against the social discrimination and exploitation in the form of untouchability. The practice of untouchability was well-marked in the human behaviour during his time. But his spiritual vision, the vision of the presence of the same Reality within all human beings led him to raise voice against such wrong practices through his strong universal message to bring a change in human psyche and behaviour to treat the human as human and not as inhuman. He himself practised what he said, and visited the houses of the persons belonging to the lower castes to initiate them into the way of spiritual practice propagated by him.

Institutions: Sri Abhirām Paramahamsa had established many institutions which acted as the centres of propagation and practice of his spiritual teachings. The principal institution was Shānti Ānandāshram at Shāntidhām in the village Karamalā. He continued to stay in this Ashram after being released from Rajmuhendry Jail till he left his mortal frame on 27th November 1963. He did not travel anymore, but engaged the sannyāsins belonging to his cult to travel different places of Odisha and outside to propagate his spiritual messages and teachings. Hundreds of sub-āshramas were instituted with his permission by his sannyāsins and disciples for their spiritual practices and progress throughout Odisha and a few places in Andhra Pradesh, West Bengal and Delhi. Millions of people, devotees and disciples used to come to Shānti Ānandāshram to have a glimpse of Sri Abhirām Paramahamsa as well as to have his blessings.

Besides imparting teachings to the devotees, he engaged himself in writing books, mostly in verses, in simple, lucid and heart-touching language. So far fifty three books and booklets have been published outof which some are full of prayers and devotional songs, some deal with religious code of conduct and some others deal with religion, spiritualism and philosophy.

Philosophy: Sri Abhirām Paramahamsa did not have any will to give an academic philosophy in the sense of a consistently worked out conceptual system, but a well-knit metaphysics and ethics can hardly be missed in his writings. The writings of Sri Abhirām not only disclose the originality of his spiritual vision, but bear the stamp of different thought-currents that have shaped the life and culture of the people of Odisha from time to time. The different traditions which had significant influence on Sri Abhirām are chiefly the six distinct traditions, namely, *Nagānti, Vedānti, Yogānti, Siddhānti, Srichaitanya's Prema-bhakti and Panchasakhā* tradition. The *Nagānti* tradition owes its formulation to Nāgārjuna, the founder of Mādhyamika philosophy and Shunyavāda. The *Vedāntic* tradition continued to shape the social and intellectual life of Odisha by the great stalwarts like Shankara, Rāmānuja and disciples of Mādhva. The *Yogānti* tradition relates to the Nātha-yogis who propagated yoga cult in Odisha. The Bouddha-siddhāchāryas are the exponents of *Siddhānti* tradition. The *prema-bhakti* as propagated by Srichaitanya had deeply influenced the people of Odisha. The Panchasakhā tradition started with the propagation of the indigenous thoughts by the five great luminaries, namely, Balarām Dās, Ananta Dās, Yashobanta Dās, Jagannāth Dās and Achyutānanda Dās that greatly appealed to the heart and soul of the people of Odisha. These different currents of thought are found to be assimilated and synthesised into a unique thought system by Sri Abhirām.

Sri Abhirām Paramahamsa accepts the Reality as Absolute. Every system of philosophy that propounds absolutism admits two strains of thought. One strain is that the Reality as absolute must be beyond the transitory nature of the world and at the same time it must be the Reality of the world either as its support or substratum or the cause. Attempts have been made in every system of absolutism to meet these demands of Absolute in its own way. Sri Abhirām Paramahamsa describes the first demand as *Laya* and the second demand as *Lilā*. Accordingly, one can find two modes of statements in his writings. The statement of *Laya* is negative and the statement of *Lilā* is affirmative. The negative statements express the transcendence of Reality and the affirmative statements express the immanence of It. In negative statements Sri Abhiram asserts that the Reality is *Akaitava* (non-falsifiable), *Avyakta* (unmanifested), *Nirguṇa* (non-qualified), *Ajāta* (unborn), *Asima* (unlimited), *Advaita* (non-dual) etc. In affirmative statements, Sri Abhiram describes the Reality as *Satyanārāyaṇa, Brāhman, Ishvara, Bhagavāna, Paramātman, Jagannāth, Purushottama,* etc. The transcendence and immanence of Reality, the *Laya* and the *Lilā* may form a duality. There is a tendency in Sri Abhirām's writings to overcome this duality as well.

In his writings Sri Abhirām Paramahamsa has depicted an elaborate cosmology in the pattern of *Sāmkhya* and *Vedānta*. He has extensively dealt with the concepts of *Prakriti* and *Purusha, Aparā* and *Parā Prakriti, Jiva* and *Brahman, Bhakta* and *Bhagavāna, Piṇḍa* (microcosm) and *Brahmāṇḍa* (macrocosm), and so on. An attempt has been made in his writings to overcome the apparent duality posed by these concepts.

Ways of Realisation: Sri Abhirām Paramahamsa's writings also include the instructions on spiritual practices that lead to the realisation of the Reality. He has accepted different *Yogas* like *Jñāna, Karma, Bhakti* and *Rāja Yoga* as depicted in the Bhagavad Gitā and other Indian philosophical systems. He has shown that the beginning of all these *yogas* is the *anurāga*, the liking or inclination towards the Supreme Reality and the end is the realisation of *abhinnatā*, the non-difference with the Reality. Also all these Yogas agree in their inner identity on a principle called *Samarpaṇa-sūtra*, the principle of total offering. In each of the *yogas*, there is an inner urge to offer or surrender the sense of 'I' and 'mine', the *ahaṃkāra* to the Reality. Due to this egotism, the individual self fails to realise the Absolute Reality. The *Samarpaṇa* of egotism can easily be done by *Hetu-sādhanā*, the practice of ceaseless awareness of the Supreme Reality. The *Samarpaṇa-sūtra* and *Hetu-sādhanā* are to be learnt from the adept teachers of his cult. These two may be regarded as the unique contributions of Sri Abhirām Paramahamsa to the ways of realisation of the Reality.

Moreover, Sri Abhirām Paramahamsa has introduced a yogic method of the practice of *karma-samarpaṇa*, the offering of actions through the breathing processes of *Puraka, Rechaka* and *Kumbhaka*, the inhalation, exhalation and restoration of breathe. According to him, whatever is offered to God through this technique of offerings or the yogic method of *karma-samarpaṇa* taught by him, the Lord verily accepts it. This has been realised by many of his disciples in their progressive stages of *sādhanā*. This technique of *Karmayoga* is a solace and comfort for the busy man under the pressure of stress and strain in the modern society.

Thus, to conclude, it can be asserted that Sri Abhirām Paramahamsa was a great spiritual leader of

Odisha, an ardent lover of the motherland and a patriot par excellence, a great lover of the distressed man and woman in the society, and a noted social reformer. He was an advocate of *Samatā*, the sameness or the equality. Through his philosophical writings, he has made an attempt to view the inner sameness (*Samatā*) between *Laya* and *Lilā*, between bhakta and Bhagavāna, between *Jiva* and *Brahman*, between *Piṇḍa* and *Br̥ahmāṇḍa*, between *Jñāna*, *Karma*, *Bhakti* and *Rājayoga*. He has made an attempt to overcome all sorts of duality in his philosophy.

Paramahamsa Prajñānānanda: Life and Message

Harischandra Sahoo

Triloki Dash alias Paramahamsa Prajñānānanda Giri was born in Pattamundai (Cuttack) in the year 1960 in a brāhmin family. Since the very childhood, he was found to be thoughtful and spiritual-minded and having interest in prayer, meditation and social service. During his school days, in an excursion trip to Puri, Triloki entered into the premises of Karār Āshram. He saw the photographs of some *yogis* on the wall of the āshram and came to know them to be the masters of *Kriyā Yoga*. He came back home and his craze and attachment for spiritual *gurus* was stored in his memory. He had learned the stories of life and teachings of Ramakrishna Paramahamsa and his disciple Swami Vivekananda. Tales of great sādhus and monks inspired him to lead the life of a monk and he was in the mission of searching for a true *guru* who could be his guide and mentor in the path of spiritual journey, a journey to godhead. One day during his M.A. career in Ravenshaw College, Cuttack he got the news that a great spiritual *guru* (Swami Hariharānanda Giri) is coming to Cuttack town and he planned to meet him in the house of a devotee Dr.

Niranjan Pradhan. This meeting with Guru Hariharānandaji was a turning point in the life of Brahmachāri Triloki Dash. It was like a *maṇikānchan sanjog*. The very blessings and touch of Guruji had created tremendous impact on him. Since then, Triloki had many a times met Guruvdev in different places of his visit and in Karār Āshram, Puri. He set his mind to accept Swāmi Hariharānanda to be his master and spiritual guide.

On the Guru Prunimā day Swāmi Hariharananda initiated Triloki Dash in Bhubaneswar *Kriyā Yoga* Ashram in the year 1924. A new chapter was added in the life of Triloki who was initiated for the monkhood. Very often he described his *guru* to be his friend, philosopher and guide who moulded his life at each step by love, self–discipline and yogic practice. He says that his guru, his master, his preceptor and spiritual guide is an embodiment of truth, love and compassion. He is a true embodiment of Master Paramahaṃsa Yogānanda and an ocean of practical knowledge, devotion and power. In the meantime, Govt. of Odisha appointed Triloki Dash as a Lecturer in Economics in Rourkela and subsequently, he was posted to Ravenshaw College, Cuttack on transfer. It goes without saying that he gained popularity among his students and colleagues but ultimately he resigned from the teaching post because he had a long cherished goal to march ahead in the path of spirituality. It was just like young Naren (Vivekananda) who was blessed by Ramakrishna and instructed not to be worried about material needs. Even Triloki could not complete his Ph.D. but *Gurudev* homourously called him D.M. (Doctorate of Meditation). What a faith of *Gurudev* on young rising monk! He had a passion to delve deep into the ocean of *Kriyā Yoga*. At the age of 39 years, he received the highest order Paramahaṃsa Prajñānānanda by his *Guru* on 10.8.98.

What is *Kriyā Yoga*? What is about the past masters who accelerated the *Kriyā Yoga* to see a better world of tomorrow? In India, we come across so many spiritual *gurus*, starting from Swami Vivekananda, Sri Aurovindo to the modern gurus like Sri Sri Rabi Shankar and Ram Dev Baba. Swāmi Vivekananda followed *Rāja Yoga*, Sri Aurobindo propagated *Integral yoga*, Sri Sri Ravi Shankar is famous for *"Sudarshan Kriyā"* and Sri Ram Dev for breathing exercise of *"Anuloma and Viloma"* etc. It must be kept in mind that all the propagators of *Yoga* owe their origin to the *Prasthāna Trayee"* i.e. the Vedas, the Upanisads and the Bhagabat Gitā and especially Patanjali's *Yogasutra* speaking of control of mind or consciousness (*Citta Vṛitti Nirodha*).

What is the etymological meaning of *Yoga*? *Yoga* is union of individual self (soul) with the highest self (God). *Kriyā Yoga* (*Kri-* means work and *ya* (Soul); work while watching the soul. Breath is vital. Watch the breath in every step of your life. Every inhalation is your birth and every exhalation is death. One has to realize that he is the living power of God. Therefore, one has to control his breathing. Breath control is self–control. It is through meditation, one can have control over one's own breath. *Kriyā Yoga* stimulates the brain. *Kriyā Yoga* is a means to reach the formless stage; motionless stage by transcending all forms. It is a state of *Samādhi*, i.e. the highest state of *Nirvikalpa Samādhi*. No ordinary prayer will do – a lasting calmness is required for which a *Kriyābān* has to transcend all forms. That is what the upanisads call *"Turiya State"* It is called as transcendental meditation since sense-organs can not grasp it. Thus *Kriyā Yoga* is a breathing technique (breath – control and spinal exercise where one elevates himself. He goes above the body, mind and intellect. *Kriyā Yoga* is a synthesis of action, knowledge and love where there is a real communication with the God. One merges with the God. The Indian treasure of *yoga* was revived by Mahāvatāra Bābāji, Lāhiri Mahāsaya. Following the path of Vivekānanda and Swami Rāma Tirtha, Swami Yogānanda went to propagate *yoga* to the Western world.

Let us know very briefly about the veterans and spiritual masters of *Kriyā Yoga*. Mahāvatāra Bābāji revived the *Kriyā Yoga*. It is said that Babaji Maharaj initiated great spiritual teachers and saints like Sankara, Kabir etc. He was the spiritual preceptor of Shri Lāhiri Mahāsaya, who is considered to be the torch-bearer of *Kriyā Yoga*. Lāhiri following the footprints of his *guru* Mahābatara Babaji demonstrated how to practice *Kriyā Yoga* to enter into a higher plane of consciousness; so that a man becomes a balanced person : a *Shitaprajñana*. Mahāvatāra Bābāji is considered to be a "Supreme Yogi".

Lāhiri Mahāsaya was a *gruhi* who gave initiation to *brahmachāris* and *sanyāsis*. There was no barrier of caste, creed and religion to get initiation. Thus Lāhiri Mahāsaya had Muslims (*fakirs*) as his disciples. He was advising his disciples to have self-analysis and self–reflection. The ultimate goal of life is to have liberation from this worldly bondage and the *guru* (mentor) plays a vital role to guide one to find the spiritual treasure. Lāhiri Mahāsaya is called *"Father of Kriyā Yoga"* Shriyukteswar Giri, a great *guru* got intiation form Lāhiri Mahāsaya and achieved realization and further guided many disciples and emphasized for regular practice of *Kriyā Yoga* in the day to day life. Three important services like *'tapas'*, *'Svādhyāya*' and *Iswara Praṇidhān* are necessary in every step of life. By meditation, the mind (*Citta*) can be controlled. Practice of *Āsana* and *Prāṇāyāma* gives eternal happiness.

Shri Bhupendranath Sānyāl alias Sānyāl Mahāsaya was initiated to *Kriyā Yoga* at the age of 16 years in Benaras in the house of Lahiri Mahāsaya. He was born in a brāhmin family and he was a *Gṛuhi-Sannyāsi*. He established *'Gurudhām"* in Puri (1923) and Bhagalpur (1924) and initiated many disciples including Swāmi Hariharānanda. In order to gain spiritual growth, one should have control over tongue and by practice of *prāṇāyāma*, inner impurities are removed.

Mukuṇda alias Paramahaṃsa Yogānanda was born on 5th Jan. 1983 in Gorakhpur. The year 1983 is famous in history for Swāmi Vivekandnda's delegation to World Parliament of Religion, Chicago. He was blessed by Lāhiri Mahāsaya, the *guru* of his father Bhagabati Charan Ghosh. He was given the title "Paramahaṃsa" by Shriyuketswar Giri. He was popular in the Western world (next to Swami Vivekananda) and authored many books like : *Autobiography of a Yogi, Whispers from Eternity, The Science of Religion, The Divine Romance and Metaphysical Meditations* etc. His book, *"Autobiography of a Yogi"* is a master-piece and a best seller. His physical death was miraculous like that of Sri Aurobindo's leaving the mortal body at Pondichery Ashram.

Manmohan Mazumdar alias Swāmi Satyānanda Giri (born in 1896) was a multifaceted personality. He was a profound thinker, a singer, a musician, a poet and above all a good social worker and a lover of mankind.

In the year 1911, he had the chance to meet Swāmiyukteswar and was impressed by his personality and surrendered before him for being a disciple of *Kriyā Yoga*. Mahātmā Gandhi hearing about Satyānanda invited him to Sābaramati Āshram where he was a guest for some days. Prior to that Satyānanda had established an āshram in Ranchi and was in constant touch with Karār Āshram at Puri.

Rabindranath Bhattāchārya alias Swāmi Hariharānanda Giri was born in 1905 in a Brāhmin family of Habibpur (Nadiā, West Bengal) near the birth place of Sri Chaitanya. Father Haripada was well-versed in ayurveda, astrology and palmistry. His father was very much excited in watching the extra-ordinary qualities in Rabi and took initiatives for his allround growth. In course of time, Rabi took a vow to lead the life of *Brahmachāri* and he was given advanced knowledge of *Kriyā Yoga* form Bābāji Mahārāj, Sri Bijoy Krishna, Swāmi Sriyukteswara Giri, Sri Sanyal Mahāsaya, Swāmi Satyananda Giri and Swāmi Sivānanda etc. He was initiated by Sri Jagadaguru Bhārati Krishna Tirtha on 27.05.1959 and on direction of Shriyukteswar Giri he came to Karār Āshram at Puri to look into the day to day management of the āshram. He was an Indian Yogi and a spiritual humanist. He visited many western countries like Paris, Switzerland, Belgium, England, Holland, France, Austria, South America, United States, Canada, Florida and progagated *Kriyā Yoga* and established Āshrams and meditation halls. He was influenced by the *Bhgabat Gitā*, *Upanisads*, and Indian Mythology. He has authored many books. To name a few; *Kriyā Yoga Daṛsana (Odia), Philosophy of Kriyā Yoga, Kriyā Yoga : The Essence of All religions and scientific process of soul culture, The Bhagabat Gitā (3 Vols) On Isā Upanisads, Spiritual Significance of Hindu worship, Kriyā Yoga Sādahnā (Odia) Each Human body is a Bhagabat Gitā, Kriyā Sādhanā Tattva (Oida), Vaijñānika Kriyā Yoga Paddhati (Odia) etc.*

Human life is the most precious one on the earth. Man's life must be a life of action. While doing our own work, we should devote ourselves for the betterment of others like the poor, the needy and the deprived. In the words of Utkalmani Pandit Gopabandhu Das;

"Nija swārtha pāin jāta nuhe Hindu
Biswa Prāṇa Pāin tāra rakta bindu".

It means a Hindu's life is not meant for his own sake but for the sake of others; every drop of blood should be dedicated for the betterment of the universe. Gopabandhu was considering the universe as a family. (*Basudhaiva Kutumbakam*) Swāmi Prajñānānanda was influenced by Pandit Gopabandhu and goes one step further when he says that a man should be compassionate. It is easy to speak of compassion but difficult to practice it in day to day life. A life of sympathy, empathy, compassion involves loving and caring for others. We all are the children of God. How can a man be compassionate? It is only when a man sees himself in others, he feels sympathy for others.

When one looks from a close quarter, Swāmi Prajñānānanda is found to have love and compassion not only for the flora and fauna but also for the animals like cow. Cow is the symbol of purity in holy scriptures of the Hindus. Swāmiji lays emphasis on cows for which he has organized several camps to create awareness for the protection of cows and cattle (*Go Pujan Samiti*). The environment of the āshram at Bālighai is a symbol of his love for making orchards and gardens for the protection of the environment.

Human life should be a life of values. What does it mean when Swāmiji gives emphasis on values? It is the moral values for which he is advocating. Whenever we speak of what one ought to do and what one ought not to do, it comes within the ambit of personal morality. One ought to improve upon his personal morality by doing good things and avoiding bad habits. *Dhyāna* and *Yoga* help us for inculcating good habits. Personal moralities are reflected in one's life-style i.e. his daily behavior, his activities, his concern for others etc.

The religious scriptures of the world like the *Bhagabat Gitā*, the *Bible, Torah* and *Yoga-sūtra* of *Patanjali* speak of universal value–system. A man's love sympathy, compassion, forgiveness for others are social values and are necessary to maintain the cultural values or cultural ethos. Here Swāmiji wants to speak of a man who follows the principle of love in action. he becomes ideal for others. People love him and follow him. Sri Rama in the *Rāmāyana* is symbol of an ideal person (Maryādā Puruṣha – Puruṣottam). Sri Krishna in *Mahābhārat* is an ideal person.

Swāmi Hariharananda, the preceptor and *Guru* of Swāmi Prajñānānanda attained *"Nirviklpa Samādhi"*, the highest level of consciousness by meditation. As regards to Swāmi Hariharānanda, Prajñānānanda in *Divine Bloosoms* writes :

"A unique world teacher, proficient in many languages, free from religious dogmas and sectarican beliefs, he has been described as the embodiment of the love of Jesus, the clear sightedness of Sankara, the devotion of Sri Chaitanya and the compassion of the Buddha."

Guruji instructed Prajñānānanda for constructing an āshram in Cuttack by the side of the river Mahānadi. Consequently on a small piece of land, an āshram was set up in Jagatpur in May 1993, which was named as "Prajñāna Mission". It is functioning for the services of humanity and as a meditation centre of *Kriyā Yoga*.

Prajñānānanda is very good in oratory. He had the chance to visit different places of western countries along with Gurudev. Places like Florida, Sterksel (Holland), Miami, Vienna, Germany and Switzerland where *Kriyā Yoga* āshrams were established. *Guruji* had in his mind to make him his successor for which he guided and molded his activites at ever step. Apart form *Kriyā Yoga* āshram, Swami Prajñānānanda established Harihārananda Gurukulam Āshram at Bālighai (Puri) in 2000. A charitable dispensary named "Harihārananda Charitable Health Centre" was set up in Bālighai (Puri) and a residential school named "Harihārananda Residential School" was established near Kendrapara.

Paramahaṃsa Prajñānānanda is a prolific writer. Most of his books are based on life histories of past-masters of *Kriyā Yoga*, about the science of *Kriyā Yoga* and Indian philosophy and culture. To name a few : *Mahavātāra Bābāji, Lāhiri Mahāsaya, Swāmi Sriyuketswar, My Time with Master, The Life and Teachings of Paramahaṃsa Hariharānanda. A Life of Compassion, Who are you?, East meets West, Divine Blossoms, The Path of Love, Know your mind, The Mahābhārat* etc. and many more.

Swāmi Hariharānanda, the illumined master had his *Mahāsamādhi* on 3.12.2002 in Homestead Āshram. He was an ocean of Spiritual knowledge, spreading endless love to the mankind. It was no doubt a great shock to his ardent disciple Prajñānanda who tried to overcome the absence of *Gurudev* by following the footprints of the loving master at each and every step of his spiritual mission.

Pranakrushna Parija: A Veteran Scientist

Siba Prasad Adhikary

Pranakrushna Parija was born on 1st April 1891 in a middle class family in Icchapur village under Ballikuda area, 36 miles from Cuttack in Odisha. He lost his father BiswanathParija at the age of 12 and soon after mother Jayanti Devi passed away. Hence he was dependent on other members of his extended family. After initial education in a vernacular school in the village, he joined the minor school in April 1901 at Ballikuda at a distance of about two miles for which he had to walk 4 miles each day. As he was very good in studies got double promotion thrice and completed middle school in 1904, stood first in Odisha, got fellowship of monthly four rupees and free ship and joined Ravenshaw Collegiate School at Cuttack for further studies. He stood 1st from Odisha in the Entrance examination (called Matriculation from 1910 onwards) and then joined Ravenshaw College and secured 4th position in 2011 under Calcutta University which covered Bengal, Bihar, Odisha and Assam at that time. For B.Sc. course he joined Presidency college, Calcutta and studied Physics, Chemistry and Mathematics. His classmates were the famous scientists Satyendra Nath Bose and Meghanad Saha and teachers Acharya Jagdish Chandra Bose and Acharya Prafulla Chandra Ray. He passed with Mathematics Honours in 1913 and also received Joynarayan Prize for standing 1st in Sanskrit in the University. While as a Post-graduate student in Mathematics the Govt. of Bihar and Odisha decided to send three students to England for higher education in which Pranakrushna Parija was selected. He proceeded for England in a ship from Bombay on 14th August 1914, reached after 20 days of voyage and joined Christ College under Cambridge University with subject in Natural Science in the 1stTripos. He took Botany Honours in the 2ndTripos course in 1916 and joined under the guidance of Prof. F. F. Blackman, the famous Professor of Botany of international repute. He secured 1st class in 2ndTripos and received Frank-Smart prize and fellowship and joined as a research student at Cambridge school of Botany. He worked there on the mechanism of respiration in the leaves of evergreen plants which continue to exist in a state of maturity for very long periods of time. Subsequently, he studied the drift in respiration of apples maintained in refrigerator for storage. The objective was to find out the senescence mechanism, the dominant stage of ontogeny in the ripening fleshy fruits so that those can be stored for longer periods to meet the food requirement during 1st world war in which England was involved at that time. The research was also intended to find out the whether the two types of organs, the ever green leaves and ripening fruits, so strikingly different from each other, manifest the same fundamental principles of respiration. The findings of this study was published in 1928.

During the period as researcher at Cambridge he was selected for Indian Education Service, returned to India in 1921 and joined Ravenshaw College, Cuttack as Professor of Botany on 4th August 1921. He devoted fully to strengthen Botany teaching and research at Ravenshaw and opened Botany at B.Sc. pass level in 1924 and Botany Honours in 1930. Soon after Ravenshaw became an active center for Research in Botany and became well-known in India. Prof. Parija worked on problems both of fundamental and applied nature as Odisha state was encountering those days particularly in the field of physiology of rice during salinity, drought and waterlogging. These are as follows:

(i) Water hyacinth and other aquatic weeds : During the beginning of twentieth century the water hyacinth, *Eicchorniacrassipes* brought to India due to its beautiful violet flowers could establish quickly and went on spreading in a fast pace in water bodies posing threat due to their water-clogging behavior. An expert committee was setup all over India to study its life-history, cause of rapid establishment and method of control of this obnoxious aquatic weed. Prof. Parija received grant from Imperial Council of Agricultural Research to study this problem in Odisha. A team of research scholars from various parts of India joined the project and carried out the work. They reported that seeds of water hyacinth remain dormant at least for one season and retain their viability for seven years. The weed is able to flourish in a wide range of pH with optimum growth at 6 to 8 pH. It also has the capability to resist drought to a considerable extent. Coppersulphate was found as the most effective weedicide to the water hyacinth.

(ii) Experimental morphology of angiospermic plants: Prof. Parija along with his students, P. Mishra, P.Mallick, K. Samal and B. N. Misra worked on experimental morphology of several species of angiospermic plants like *Brideliapubescens, Impatiens balsamina, Tecomacapensis, Momordicadioica, Ipomoea crassicaulis, Cucurbita maxima, Scirpus articulates,Daturaalba, Helianthus annus, Ixora undulate* and *Amarenthus*specis.They established that the thorns that arise on the stem of *Brideliapubescens* are morphologically roots. Prof. B.N. Mishra, former Professor at Berhampur University worked for Ph.D. on the topic "Autecology of *Ipomoea crassicaulis* (Benth). Robinson under the supervision of Prof. Parija and obtained Ph.D. from Utkal University in 1965.

(iii) Research on algae : While working on the life history of aquatic weeds of Chilika lake, the largest brackish water lagoon of Asia located in Odisha state, in connection with prevalence of malaria around the lake, Parija studied the algal succession on a Charāiguha rocky island on the way to Kālijāi. Diatoms were found dominant and appear maximally twice a year. Diatoms and red algae grow in the deeper waters of the lake even at feeble light due to their capability of chromatic adaptation. In addition, the green algae *Chaetomorpha* and *Enteromorpha* also occur in the lake. Indian Council of Agricultural research funded a project on "Mass culture of Algae" in 1968 in which Prof. Parija along with Prof. H. Pattnaik, former Professor of Botany and Vice-Chancellor of Berhampur University surveyed blue green algae in soils of Cuttack and also studied effect of growth and change of pigmentation in few blue green algae in different light intensities and temperature.

(iv) **Plant physiology, especially on rice :** Government of Odisha, under the Department of Agriculture sanctioned a Rice Research Scheme from April 1937 in which Prof. Parija was entrusted to work on physiological aspects of rice plant in Ravenshaw college. The project continued further after it was completed in 1941 with fresh funding from the Imperial Council of Agricultural Research and was continued till March 1945. Prof. Parija and the team had worked on this rice project for eight continuous years and contributed several new findings to science. They reported that the quality of flood resistance was induced in rice plants by pre-sowing treatments of the seeds by (i) low temperature at 2-5 degree C for 6 days, (ii) anaerobiosis for 3 days or anaerobiosis for 3 days plus low temperature for 3 days. The treated plants survived submersion under water better than the control plants and yielded higher. Further drought resistance quality was induced into the rice plants by pre-sowing treatment to the seeds at high temperature of 40 to 42 degree C. Also saline resistance quality was induced into the rice plants by pre-sowing seed treatments with 1.7% of common salt solution.. Breaking of dormancy in winter paddies with a view to growing them was achieved by him through various seed treatments such as smoking, drying, de-husking and soaking with juice of germinated grains.

Due to all these work carried out at Ravenshaw College, Cuttack, and Odisha being a centre for origin of rice, Govt. of India established a Central Rice Research Institute (CRRI) at Cuttack, during the pre-independence period, (later named as National Rice Research Institute, NRRI) in which Prof. Parija played a key role. In recognition of his contribution on developing drought, flood and saline resistant paddy seeds, one of the high yielding strains of paddy later developed at CRRI was named after him. Further, Odisha being an agriculture based state, prone to frequent flood and drought, his research triggered the state Govt. to establish the Odisha University of Agriculture and Technology in Bhubaneswar, the third oldest agriculture University of India.

Prof. Parija was the President of Indian Botanical society held at Allahabad University in 1930. Also was the General President of Indian Science Congress held at Bombay in 1960. In the 47th Indian Science Congress, he delivered the lecture titled *"Impact of Science on Society"*. He had also written several popular science articles, one of which published in *Everyman's Science* and the others mostly in Odia language. In 1960 he was awarded the Birbal Sahani Gold medal by Indian Botanical Society who was his close friend since Cambridge days. On one joint expedition near Nagpur, he picked up a fossil fruit not known earlier which Prof. Sahani later named as *Enigmocarponparijae* in his honour. With later discoveries of the flowers and seeds of this fruit Prof. Sahani changed the name as *Sahianthusparijae* which links both of them, Prof. Parija was a member of the Governing body of Birbal Sahani Institute of Paleobotany at Lucknow founded by Prof. Sahani.

Educator, Academic Legacy and Achievements: Selected for Indian Education Service while working at Cambridge, England and joined Ravenshaw College, Cuttack, India as Professor of Botany in August 1921 and worked for 24 years until 1945. He served as the Principal of Ravenshaw College, Cuttack (1936-1945),

Vice-Chancellor, Utkal University (1943-48) and (1955-65) for three terms of 15 years, Pro-Chancellor of Utkal University (1951-55) and Pro-Vice-Chancellor, Benaras Hindu University for 3 years (1948-51). He was Vice-President of International Botanical Society twice in 1959 and 1964 and Served as the Editor of the *Journal of Indian Botanical Society* (1935-42). He was the Founder Fellow of the National Academy of Sciences, Allahabad and National Institute of Science of India, 1935; Fellow of Royal Asiatic Society, Calcutta with Berkely Memorial Gold Medal, 1966; Awarded Order of the British Empire, 1943; Received BirbalSahani Gold Medal by Indian Botanical Society, 1960; Doctor of Science (Honoris Causa) from Patna University (1944), Utkal University (1949), Sri Venkateswara University (1962) and Sambalpur University (1972).

External Services and Social Life: Prof. Parija was appointed as Director of Agriculture, Govt of Orissa in 1945; Member of Central Advisory Board of Forest Utilization by Government of India, 1949; Chairman of the Expert Committee of Ministry of Food and Agriculture by Govt of India in 1953; Member of the official language Commission (1955-56) by Govt. of India; Chairman of the Geological Education Committee of Govt. of India, 1946; Member of the University formation Committee, 1938 by Govt. of Odisha which lead to the formation of Utkal University as 17th University of India in 1942; Chairman of General Education Committee of the University Grants Commission,1963; Chairman of the Inter-Universities Board comprising Vice-Chancellors of India and Ceylon, 1961; President of Utkal Sahitya Samaj (1934-38); Elected as M.L.A. as an independent candidate from

Balikuda Constituency of Odisha in 1952; Awarded *Padma Bhusan* by Government of India, 1955.

In addition while at Cambridge, he served as the President of the Indian Majilis Society and also of "Unit League", a forum of Indian students whose aim was the unity and integrity of India. The wellknown Indian students in these societies were: Srikrushna Memon, George Mathai, RabindraNath Banerjee, Subhas Chandra Bose (Netaji), Y. J. Taraporabala, R.S. Inamdar, Kamta Prasad, C.V. HanumataRao, K.M. Khadiae, BirbalSahani, T. Ekambaram, K.C. Meheta, C.D. Deshmukh, D.M. Bose, S. P.Agharkar and many others who later established themselves as Professors, Scientists, ICS officers, Lawyers, Ministers and Patriots back in India working for Independence of our country. When the British Govt. formed the Lord Lytton Committee in 1918 to examine the difficulties and problems of Indian students in England, three persons selected by the Indian Majlis to speak on their behalf were Khadia, Subhas and Pranakrushna. While Lokamanya Bal Gangadhar Tilak visited Cambridge, stayed with Pranakrushna Parija in his lodging, and addressed Indian Majlis.

Throughout India, Burma and Ceylon services of Prof. Parija were asked for as an examiner. Contemporary Botanists Like Prof. Sriranjan, Prof. Panchanan Maheswari, Prof. Birbal Sahani, Prof. M.O.P. Iyangar, Prof. S.P. Agharkar, Prof. JanakiAmmal and Prof. Amarchand Joshi assisted any student who was recommended by him for higher studies. All of them, and in addition, Sir C.V. Raman, Prof. Satyen Bose, Prof. Santi Swarup Bhatnagar, Prof. C.D. Deshmukh and even political figures like Netaji Subhas Chandra

Bose (born in Cuttack and studied at Ravenshaw Collegiate school), Chakrabarty Raj Gopalchari, Smt.Sarojini Naidu were the guests while he was the Principal of Ravenshaw College. Although he was in Government service, he was a passionate patriot. The freedom fighters of that era have recorded how Prof. Parija's house was a safe meeting place for Congress party meetings even when British rules declared the Party as an illegal organization. He used to give monetary assistance to many impoverished freedom fighters which shows his commitment to the cause of the Nation. This is the brief profile of our revered Prof PranakrushnaParija, the most respected Founder Professor of Botany, first researcher/scientist in the field of plant science in Odisha state, and the first Vice-Chancellor of Utkal University.

Hrudananda Ray :
The Paradigm of Philosophising
(1930 – 2015)

Sarat Chandra Panigrahi

Professor Hrudananda Ray was born in Cuttack (Odisha). His father was an eminent lawyer of Odisha. He studied in Ravenshaw Collegiate School where he was a close friend of Nandini Satapathy, the former Chief Minister of Odisha. He passed I.A. from Christ College, Cuttack and B.A. Philosophy Honours from Ravenshaw College. Then he went to Benaras Hindu University to pursue his M.A. in Philosophy. In his student days he was initiated and influenced by Bichhanda Charana Patnaik whom he accepted as his *guru*. Bichhanda Charana Patnaik established Kalinga Bhārati, the purpose of this institution was to propagate the cultural heritage of Odisha mainly focussing on the illustrious writings of Kabi Samrat Upendra Bhanja which was ignored. Following the instructions of his *guru*, Hrudananda Ray travelled nook and corner of Odisha and delivered talks before the public regarding Bhanja Sāhitya and other related issues concerning Odishan Culture. His oratory style was simple and unique which appeals common man. He lived what he beliveved.

Professor Hrudananda Ray has authored many books in English and Odia. In English his books are *Dialectic, Sankara as a Romantic Philosopher* and *Immanuel Kant*. Among his Odia books most worth mentioning are *Pāschātya Darsanara Itihāsa* (co-author), *Advaita Vedānta Parichaya, Nabajātaka Tattwatha Khanda, Brahma Sutra : Sankara Bhāsya* (in four volumes), *Jā ṇe Anubhabi Anubhavare* (autobiography) and *Kalibhāgavata Samikhyā* where he has pointed out the philosophical implication of *Kalibhāgavata* written by Thakur Sri Abhirām Paramahaṃsa.

During his study in B.H.U. he was the most favourite student of great teachers like S.K. Maitra, Ramakanta Tripathy, Bhikanlal Artreya, Professor J.L.Mehta who praised him and said that they were proud to get a student like him. He passed M.A. being first class first. Then he started his work for Ph.D. and got Gaekward fellowship for this. His supervisor was eminent international philosopher T.R.V. Murti. Tittle of his thesis was "Role of Negation in Dialectic". He submitted his thesis and it was informed to him that the examiner wanted to revise two chapters of the thesis. Professor Ray said that he cannot revise the thesis as per the choice of the examiner as he was convinced that the justification he has given was appropriate. So he did not resubmit the thesis and was complacent with his decision. This kind of attitude is not found in any research scholars as everyone wants to get their Ph.D. at any cost. But Prof. Ray wanted to be committed to his existential faith at the cost of Ph.D. degree.

He had such intellectual acumen that he was awarded Fulbright scholarship and Smith Mund travel grant to go to America but he refused by saying the he has to do again A.M. (M.A.) in America which he has done in prestigious B.H.U. Hrudananda Ray was different from others by refusing to resubmit his thesis whereby he could get his Ph.D. and his rejection of going to America when at that time everyone was aspiring for Fulbright scholarship.

After coming to Odisha, he joined Odisha Education Service and taught philosophy in different colleges of Odisha for more than three decades and was the principal of S.C.S. College, Puri and Deputy Director of Tourism of Govt. of Odisha. His commitment for philosophy was not confined to classrooms but was widened to the public for inspiring them to live with freedom and elevate them to the status of self-awareness. One of the most important task he has done was to create an association called 'Philosophic Meet' for interaction among people interested in philosophy. As finance was required, he printed a ticket with the following words of George Sāntāyana;

"*Heart has a logic, which head knows not, Columbus discovered America without a chart.*"

The Philosophic Meet became very popular in Odisha. In one of the meetings, Professor S.K. Chhattopadhya said that the "Philosophic Meet" is the first meet of Philosophy Sammilana which is first in history of philosophy circle of Odisha which should be given proper dignity as this shows that philosophy is not a luxury for intellectuals but a way of life that is connected with all *shāstras*. This shows how Professor Ray was committed to the cause and popularisation of philosophy. His scholarship shines equally well both in Indian and Western Philosophy which shall be discussed in the exposition of his books in English.

In the book *Dialectic,* Ray has made an attempt to emphasise the nature of critical phase of philosophical consciounsness which is not criticism of this or that school of philosophy. Dialectic is the critique of philosophy, itself. It is philosophising made self-consciousness, i.e. it is philosophy of philosophy. This has been accepted both in eastern and western philosophy not as a way of thought but as a way of life. In every discourse dialectic is implicit, which consists in the systematic enlargement of its structure. There is no growth without negation. Every act of self-assertion is prompted by the implicit source of challenge of different persons interested in mutual polemic. Ray cites Sāntāyana's view regarding dialectic and says,

"Dialectic is the conscience of discourse and has the same function as morality everywhere, namely to endow the soul with integrity and to perfect it into a monument to its own radical impulse".[1]

Ray points out that Plato expresses deep indebtedness to the Eleatic tradition for initiating dialectical methodology. In the *Statesman*, 266, an Eleatic stranger teaches about the dialectic attitude by saying, *"the dialectical method is no respect for persons, and cares not for great and small, but always arrives in her own way at the truest result. Dialectic aims at truth not caring for personal praise or blame."*

The advaita dialectic is fully alive to the question of transcendence, and therefore is more reflective than Platonic tradition of form. The Platonic tradition, inspite of the full-blooded dialectic, fell a victim to dogmatism for its inattention to formulate a satisfactory view of negation. According to Socrates as found in *Republic*

532-533 power of dialectic can reveal the truth. Diaecticconsciousness is *prius* of dialectical understanding.

The life-blood of dialectic is opposition. In a dialectical purusuit resolution of conflict is finally achieved when a more inclusive discourse renders mutual translation possible. This procedure can be seen in Hegelian Dialectic where the generic discourse may be confronted with its opposite in a still higher synthesis which moves towards the apex of an all-inclusive universalized discourse or the Absolute Idea.

Ray discusses about the nature of dialectic in both Indian and Western philosophy. In Indian philosophy dialectic is termed as *anviksisi* as found in Kautitya's *Arthasāstra* which means the science of reviewing or critical examination. It is not a science of acquisition or manipulation but a science of reflection, classification or correction. In *Purāṇas*, the *anviksiki* is treated as *Tarka-Vidyā* or *vādavidyā*, the art of discussion. Plato speaks of dialectic as "the soul's conversation with herself". (*Theatetus*, 189 e ff). In Mādhyamika Buddhism, dialectic is identified with critique of all philosophy.

The value of dialectic was recognised by Nāgārjuna and his disciples. The leading texts on dialectic of Mādhyamikas can be seen in *Múla Madhyamā Kārikā* of Nāgārjuna and *Chatuhsatakam* of Āryadeva. Āryadeva puts a word of caution against the indiscriminate use of dialectic. It should be pursued by persons having the ideal of self-culture.

"A person intent upon self-purification is only to be acquainted with dialectic, but not any body or every body. For the medicine administered in inappropriate case results in poison".[2]

The Advaitins and the *vijñānavādins* have

appropriated the Mādhyamika dialectic. The dialectic treatise of the Advaita school like *Khandana Khanda Khādya* of Sri Harsa and *Tattvapradipika* of Citsukhāchārya are great contribution in understanding dialectic of Advaitins where dialectic is recognised as a path of spiritual realisation. The dialectic as employed in Advaita consists in criticising the modal view of reality. The substance-view by the rigour of its own logic passes into the no-view of reality in the hands of the advaitins. The dialectic of advaita, like that of the Mādhyamika discovers the spiritual ultimate as the ground of dialectical negation.

According to Ray, dialectic is intimately connected with communicative translation of concepts in active conversation making the meaning clear which implies transmission and reception, suggestion and response. The dialectical operation raises the mind to the summit of intelligibility rendering all the modes transparent to each other engaged in the pursuit, J. Adler in his book *Dialectic* says *"The history of philosophy is a sustained conversation prolongd through milenia; it has been continuously dialectical or controversial"*. These conflicts arise at a particular stage and grows up to the highest pitch of reflection where each of the systems realise its dogmatism in its own way and the conflict is resolved in dialectical translation. Therefore, the conflicts of discourses are resolved by gaining insight into the nature as discourses.

Plato says that the corruption of dialectic in undeserving hands lead to *"the lawlessness of which the professors of art are full"*. Unworthy man in possession of dialectic, instead of being *"an observer of law"* is converted into a lawless person, flattered by name, fame and money". So Plato tried to distinguish between the right application of dialectic and wrong application of it. The use of dialectic is the common vocation and prerogative of both the right philosopher and wrong philosopher. But the direction and the intent of the vocation distinguish a philosopher from a philosopher in inversion. Plato made a relentless effort to restore dialectic to fulfil its most ennobling spiritual role.

In his book *Samkara as a Romantic Philosopher* Ray tries to expain Sankara's Vedānta in the light of romanticism. Sankara was fighting to establish Advaitism and with all humility he styled himself as a commentator not a founder of Advaita philosophy. The eminent philosopher Radhakrishnan declares about Sankara that,

"*Sankara stands out as a heroic figure of the first rank in the somewhat motely crowd of the religious thinkers of mediaeval India. His philosophy standsforth complete, needing neither a before nor an after*".[3]

According to Professor Ray, the romanticism and advaitism are mutually compatible. For him, romanticism is the feeling of impulse and the demand that reality is with in us. A romantic person feels that he can never be satisfied unless he realizes the infinite to be no other than his own self. The identification of infinite with the self is the height of romanticism in Advaitism. The absolute choice for the Advaitin is either self-infinite or nothing else.

Prof. Ray admits that it is very difficult to define romanticism. While attempting this he has quoted Professor S.K. Maitra who says that in a sense all art and philosophy are romantic.[4]

According to Ray, romanticism laid great stress on the total personality of the man which is more than mere rationality. Epistemology of romanticism is exclusively emotional. Where ever there is spiritual unrest the individual feels the necessity of revaluation of values and all this happens due to romanticism.

Ray is of the view that romanticism preserves what is best in intellectualism and rejects onesided view of the reality. Romanticism instils in us to think and feel more deeply and intensely to recognise the fundamental values of life which confers freedom. In otherwords deeper concern of life is preserved against deterministic and atomic attitude of intellectualism era. The epistemology of empiricism is based on sesnsation while for rationalism reason is the only source of knowledge. But romanticism discarded both these isolated faculties and accepted "the active commerce of the whole mind with the world" as the proper foundation of knowledge. Ray points out that for Sankara the ultimate reality is *truth, beauty* and *good (Satyam Sivam and Sundaram)*. For the conservation and integration of all values of life, the experience of the self as a whole should be brought to focus of our attention.

Intellectualism stressess upon abstract ratiocination and positive description but romanticism was not satisfied with this factual poverty and advocated the cause of concrete living. He substantiates his view of considering the view of Sankara regarding knowledge. Sankara says that for practical purposes the subject and object of knowledge is admissible but the full knowledge of reality consists in transcending this duality. Sankara does not discard reason but truth by its very nature transcends reason. So there is a possibility of a higher kind of knowledge which is called as intuition and that is the culmination and the fulfilmentn of reason. Ray offers a broad definition of romanticism which may be quoted as follows,

"*The romanticist's love for the whole results in the love of freedom, because the whole is freedom. ...It exists by it-self, in itself and for itself. It is at once the supreme existence and value*".[5]

Man is the vital focus in romantic philosophy. Man is the meeting point of the infinite and finite. Man is the architect of his own destiny. Man bears within himself the immense cosmic energy and if he disciplines himself can realise the pinnacle of perfection. In this sense romanticism is a form of idealism which aims at an apex of summit of values that inspires human existence to realise perfection.

REFERENCES :

1. Sāntāyana, *The Realm of Essence*, p. 100
2. Āryadeva, *Chatuhsatakam*, VII, 18
3. Radhakrishnan, *Indian Philosopy*, Vol.II, p.446.
4. *The Neo-Romantic Movement in Contemporary Philosopy*, p.5.
5. H.Ray, *Sankara as a Romantic Philosopher*, Cuttack, Akash Publication, 1931, p.44.

Philosopher of Excellence : Jitendranath Mohanty (1928 - 2023)

Harischandra Sahoo

Prof. Jitendranath Mohanty, an internationally acclaimed philosopher was born on 26th Sept' 1928 in a remote village named Nilakanthapur in Chaudakulat of Kendrapara district. His father Jagannath Mohanty working in Judicial service had to move from one district to the other on transfer. For the education of his children he shifted his family to Cuttack city. During the vacation, Jitendranath used to go to his village with his father. Jitendranath enjoyed the village lifestyle amidst the joint family. The rituals, festivals, temple (Bansi Gopinath), natural surroundings including flora and fauna and peaceful and simple village-life had left an indelible mark in his memory. The village-life is many a times better than the self-centered city life. He expressed grave concern to see the fast detorioration of village-life in course of time. Jitendranath completed his schooling and stood first in first class merit list of the Board examination jointly conducted by Bihar, West-Bengal and Odisha province. Noted personalities like Janakiballav Pattnaik (Chief Minister of Odisha) and

Justice Ranganath Mishra (Chief Justice of Supreme Court of India) were his batch-mates who occupied third and tenth position respectively in the merit list. He passed I.A. Exam. from Ravenshaw College, Cuttack and was graduated from Presidency College, Calcutta in the year 1945. In the year 1952, he completed P.G. Degree in Philosophy and obtained law degree from Calcutta University. In all these examinations, he secured first position. For his Doctoral degree, he joined in Gottingen University and worked under the supervision of Herman Wein. He came back to India and joined in Hoogly Mahsin College as a lecturer. He recollects sweet memories of the ferry in double decker boat while going to Mahsin College. Later on, during 1955 – 1960 and 1960- 1962, he was in teaching job in Calcutta University. Upto 1970, he was working as B.N. Seal Professor of Calcutta University, the chair which was once upon a time occupied by Prof. S. Radhakrishnan. He was visiting professor in Burdwan and Viswa-Bharati University and visiting fellow in All Souls College, Oxford (1982). He was also Professor in Temple University, Philadelphia, Wodruff Professor of Emory University, Georgia. He was awarded Ph.D. from Gottingen University. In the year 1985, he was conferred with Honorary D.Litt. Degree from Burdwan University and in the year 1995, Doctorate Honoraris Causa from Jadavpur University. In 1997, he was elected as President of Indian Philosophical Congress. In the year 1998 Utkal University honoured him. On 19th February 2009 he was given Civic Award in Jaydev Bhawan, Bhubaneswar, the function being presided over by Janakiballav Pattnaik which was organized by Sambad Groups. In 2010, at Choudwar College, Choudwar All Odisha Philosophy Association honoured him for his

Life-time Achievement in Philosophy and in 2017, Ravenshaw University conferred Ph.D. Honoraris Causa. He had received prestigious Hombolt Prize in 1992 for best research work in German language and he was occupying the post of Director in Husserl's Archive.

During his early youth, he had some dilemmas in mind; whether to accept Marx or Gandhi; whether Sri Aurobindo or Sankara? Gradually the dilemma was resolved, he became an ardent follower of Gandhi and Gandhian Philosophy. He spent some time with Vinoba Bhave, the exponent of "Bhudān Yajña" during his trip to Odisha. He changed his mind and accepted Advaita Vedānta of Sankara. He was expert in languages like Sanskrit, Bengali, Odia and German. He had command over philosophy and mathematics.

He got married to a Bengali Lady (Bani) and the marriage was performed in Baji Rout Ashram (Angul) in the presence of Nabakrishna Choudhury and Malati Choudhury. He had one son (Babuni) and one daughter (Mitti) who are well settled in America. Some consider him to be an Atheist but he remains silent when there is a discussion on God. In the words of his grand daughter, he was a *semantic agnostic*. He loved his mother very much and had a promise which he fulfilled nine years after her death. He had '*Asthi Visarjan*' (burial ashes) of his mother in the holy Ganges as promised to her. Much before his death he donated his property for the development of educational institutions of his village. He was a man of simple living and free thinking.

Jitendranath was interested in Indian Philosophy. Especially Advaita Vedānta of Sankara, Navya Nyāya and Mimāmsa. From among the contemporary thinkers R.N. Tagore, Swami Vivekananda and Philosophy of Sri

Aurobindo attracted him. He was intimately connected with Sri Ramakrishna Āshram at Belur Math and used to spend his time there during his trip to India. He wanted to master Navya Nyāya; Gangesha's Theory of Meaning for which he had to study Sanskrit for seven years with a classical Sanskrit pandit. Mahāmahopādhyāya Pandit Yogendranath Tarkavedāntatirtha and Pandit Ananta Kumar Tarkatirtha taught him the details of Indian Philosophy: Vedānta and Navya-Nyāya respectively based on Sanskrit text. During his stay in Calcutta, he recollects his sweet memories of the College street and veteran teachers like Gopinath Bhattacharya, Krushnachandra Bhattacharya, Kalidas Bhattacharya, Nalini Brahma and Rasbihari Das. As collegues, he always remembered his interaction with philosophers like Pranab Sen, Sibjivan Bhattacharya, Sankari Banerjee and Bimal Krishna Matilal etc. whose philosophical insights enriched his thought. He acknowledged that he had leant form his students like Tārā Chatterjee, Arindam Chakraborty, Lawrence Davis and Anindita Balslev. Thus his educational career was initiated from Cuttack and ended in Calcutta.

Jitendranath was out and out a phenomenologist. He was influenced by the German Philospher Edmund Husserl (1859-1938) who was considered to be the father of phenomenology. Husserl brought the notion of phenomenology from Franz Brentano. Phenomenology as a school of thought is considered to be influential philosophical current in Continental philosophy. It is described as a rigorous science dealing with phenomena in which objects are directly presented to our experience as they are. As a methodology or a process, it aims at an open-ended system instead of a closed system. It starts with a radical beginning (*radix*) since its goal is to reach at the root of philosophical questioning. From phenomenology, as the foundation we find the development of existential interpretation of Heideggar, J.P. Sartre and Ponty, Gadamar and Reicour's hermeneutics and Derrida's deconstruction are based on Husserlian Phenomenology. As a process, Phenomenology is concerned with description (it is a descriptive science) which is free form prejudices and biases. Prof J.N. Mohanty elaborately and critically analyses the view of Husserl in his book *"Edmund Husserl's Theory of Meaning"*.

J. N. Mohanty's book *"Concept of Intentionality"* is the most celebrated work. Intentionality is one of the core concepts of Phenomenology, the science of consciousness; "When I perceive, imagine an object, my consciousness is already there. When I am conscious, I am conscious of something as the objects. Consciousness cannot be blank or vacuum. The world is accepted by me in my consciousness. The object presented to the consciousness is called *noema*. The process of knowing is called *noemata* and the intending consciousness is called *noesis*. It is intuition which helps me to be conscious of the world". Phenomenology provides us the knowledge bereft of presuppositions which can be obtained by bracketing (suspending) empirical or metaphysical presuppositions. Our experience constitutes what he calls as "Life-world" (*Lebenswelt*) that validates the idea of subjectivity. Life-world is all-inclusive horizon i.e. possibility of world so given and experienced. In his book entitled *"The Possibility of Transcendental Philosophy"* he deals with nature of philosophy and the notion of transcendental subjectivity which is a medium to access the real source of complete meaning of the world.

His book, *"Theory and Practice"* shows how theory and practice (*Praxis*) are interwoven by the concept of intentionality. There is nothing called purely theoretical or purely practical. Practical intentionality is intentionality in action. It is consciousness in action. His works on Indian Philosophy includes *"Gangesha's Theory of Truth"*, *"Reason and Traditions in Indian Thought"* and *"Essays in Indian Philosophy"*. In the book *"Reason and Tradition"*, he describes Indian Philosophy in the context of tradition and modernity, the nature of Indian logic and the nature of Indian philosophical thinking.

Indian Philosophy is generally emphasized as practical whereas Western philosophy is theoretical. It has the practical goal of removing suffering and achieving a state of bliss (*Mokṣa*). *Mokṣa* is not a theoretical enquiry for its own sake. This notion has given rise to certain misunderstanding.

Edmund Husserl says that Indian and Chinese philosophy are placed on a plane with Greek Philosophy but Greeks have a theoretical attitude. As Indian philosophy has a mythical – practical world-view, therefore, it does not have a theoretical attitude, so cannot be termed as philosophy. Prof. Mohanty says that a large portion of Indian Philosophy have theory. Argument of Husserl is due to misconstruction of theory and practice or due to the relation between theory and practice. Right attitude is to provide possibility of theoretical thinking and connecting theory and practice in an intimate manner.

In this connection Prof. Mohanty quotes form Vātsāyan's *Commentary on Nyāya Sūtra* –

"*Without valid cognition, these is no knowledge of object*

– without knowledge of object – there is no success in practical response – Depending on the nature of the object, either he desires it (to give pleasure) or shuns it (to give pain)."

Knowledge leads to desire, desire to effort, effort to action, action to success or failure. Success if the object is correctly determined by knowledge. This is recognized in all classical philosophy of India. Gangesha in *Tattva Chintāmaṇi* says that the attainment of higher good comes from right knowledge. No person shall study a text if it does not serve the worthwhileness of the individual. These two works reflect the attitude of Gangesha regarding the relation between theory and practice.

Classification of the disciplines :

To clearly understand the relation, discipline or vidyā is classified into four kinds : (1) *trayi (Vedas)*, (2) *Varta* (agriculture, trade and commerce), (3) *Dandaniti* (Politics and punishment) and (4) *Anvikṣiki* (that illumines and clarifies all sciences by application of *pramāṇas*) Above three has both theoretical and practical use. Kautilya says that it has a practical use, does good to mankind, *buddhi* is settled in pleasure and pain, makes one expert (*visārada*) in wisdom, speech and action – All the four have practical consequences.

Practicality of theory : Three Arguments : Object, Meaning & Truth :

(1) Object : Gangesa and Vātsāyana use the word *artha* either as the objects known or which satisfies or frustrates one's pleasure. But there are objects which do not give pleasure or pain when the authors were talking about the objects, they mean those true cognitions which give rise to the widest good. No object is worth enquiry

unless it gives rise to attainment of pleasure and avoidance of pain. So the arguments from objects implies a condition of enquiry not of object. *Artha* is to be replaced by *Visaya*.

(2) *Meaning* : The *Upanisads* or *Vedic* scriptures do not contain descriptive statements about reality but contain only statements which ought to be done or ought not to be done. Prabhakar Mishra argued that no sentence is meaningful if it deals with some course of action either acceptable or unacceptable. If such a theory is accepted then seemingly theoretical discourse becomes practical. A distinction is made between *dharma* and *Brahman, Karma* and *Jñāna*. Sankara says that *dharma* depends on efforts of a person but *Brahman* is independent of personal efforts. Sankara says that a person can be made to act through imperative but knowledge arises when certain conditions are satisfied.

Experience is not the source of knowledge of what is to be done but verbal instructions are whether an action is to be done or not depends on one's choice not upon knowledge because due to dullness of mind one may mistake unreal to be real. Does it mean that reducing all discourse to practical discourse must be rejected? Suppose some one says that 'There is a snake over there" – It is an utterance for future course of action. We should distinguish between the utterance of sentence and meaning of a sentence. Utterance leads to a course of action but what the sentence means is not practical but theoretical

(3) *Truth* : According to some like Karl Potter who says that truth is the property leading to successful practice. J. N. Mohanty rejects this view and says that successful practice is a test of truth not its nature. Only

Buddhists say that such a distinction between truth and falsity is pragmatic, not ontologcical. According to Prof. J.N. Mohanty, knowledge of truth must be practically beneficial but this does not imply that there is no theoretical cognition.

Almost all Indian philosophies hold the view that knowledge of reality by dispelling ignorance can remove suffering. But such knowledge is not theoretical knowledge but intuitive, then it is wrong.

Theory of Practice :

Indian philosophy is constantly engaged with theorizing about practice. Indian philosophy beginning from *Mahābhārat* pursued four goals *purusārtha*. Hindu authors theorized about them and compared scientific treatises on each. Vātsāyana's *Kāma Sūtra*, Kautilya's *Artha Sāstra*, Jaimini's *Brahma Sūtra* and Bādarayana's *Brahma Sūtra*. In these works, appropriate theme was defined, means to achieve the goal were laid down and theoretical justification was provided for the entire project.

There are two kinds of thinking about practical matters (1) dogmatic and (2) critical. Dogmatic practice provided a list of duties and virtues one ought or ought not to do. It may be in the form of *Varnāshrama Dharma*.

Critical thinking about practice asks questions like – how are the words referring to duties and virtues are interpreted? It gives rise to hermeneutic issues about principles of interpretation – priority of word-meaning or sentence-meaning, the role of context, the intention of the author etc. These epistemological questions are not the only theoretical questions that are to be settled. Practically, the more important the question is, is it enough from a moral point view to do one's duty – with a certain attitude or spirit? Is *dharma* a necessary means to *Mokṣa* and if so why? Answers to these questions are based both on epistemological and ontological grounds.

Nyāya, for e.g. holds that all actions are motivated to acquire happiness and decrease pain. Badari in antiquity and Srikrishna of the Gitā holds the view that duty is to be performed for its own sake. Prabhakara appeals to hermeneutic principles. The psychological view is, can a person be incited to act simply by linguistic form of an imperative or does he need to be motivated by desire for happiness?

The metaphysical issue is : is the self subject to natural attractions and repulsions or a pure spirit transcends mechanism of nature? Ethics is to be grounded on :

(a) Hermeneutic of conjunctive sentences
(b) a psychological theory, how a mind works
(c) a metaphysical self.

A person, according to Prof. Mohanty, who abides by *dharma*, acts in a spirit of selflessness and is satisfied with reasons why he should do so is engaged not in dogmatic practice but critical practice. He is acting in accordance with a theoretical belief. Critical thinking is an attitude who abides by rules in a spirit of detachment and he also examines the presuppositions of the rules and if needed rejects some, amends others. This is not a wholesale rejection – as you can not reject a leaking ship in mid-ocean but have to repair in plank by plank. Indian thinkers did it by adding or deleting or amending the given rules in the texts. In the *Gita*, *Yajña* finds a reinterpretative and Gandhi's distinction between Varna and Caste.

Theory and Practice : Indian philosophy says that philosophy is not merely a theory but also an application of theory in practical life. Indian philosophical systems did not ask questions about their own beginning – historical or conceptual. Each is from a distinctive interpretive of the historical tradition beginning with dogmatic ontology but developed into a critical, epistemologically self-reflective theory. They never asked the question, what is conceptually first proposition of the theory? Is this first proposition of a self-evident truth or is it to be validated in the same ways as the rest of the theory. While the philosophies are theories, they are neither intuitive nor axiomatic, nor empirical but hermeneutic and critical in method : irrespective of their content and subject matter.

How can such a theory be realized in practice? Application of a theory to nature and application to and relevance for human practice are completely different. Each Indian philosophy gives its own version of the ultimate end such is to be pursued and also gives an account of the path to be followed – in terms of its own metaphysics or epistemology.

Indian philosophical systems claimed a total and radical transformation of one's ordinary being, freedom from the bondage of *Karma* and *rebirth*. Now the question is, can theoretical knowledge give rise to such consequences? Parts of every system is indifferent to the grand goal, there are many logical, epistemological and semantic thesis which every theory defends in different ways to the great claim made in the system.

Prof. Mohanty is aware of the fact that relevance of philosopy was neglected in the past but with the advancement of science and technology, he points out that there is a special relevance of philosophy today. In this connection, he raises a lot of allied problems regarding the nature of scientific objectivity, value / culture neutrality of the sciences and the meaning of life which can be solved by philosophical enquiry. While discussing about culture, he insists that the dichotomy between 'my culture' and 'culture of others' can be overcome not through science and technology but through mutual understanding and intersubjective sharing and participation. He refutes the view that cultures are self-contained units and proposes that cultural identity is a higher order construction which destroys the internal differences.

The most valuable contribution of J.N. Mohanty lies in showing the primacy of man's *Lived Experience* (lebenswelt) in which the narrow superficial dualism of subjectiveity and objectivity, fact and value, science and religion, realism and idealism fade awary and all that is lost by these distinctions are restored.

In his autobiography *"Between the Two Worlds : East and West"* (Oxford – 2002) Prof. Mohanty writes that he has spent maximum period of his life time in India, Germany and USA. But he admits that the Indian City-life and village-life is full of brotherly love and affection. He says, *"How one person, an Indian by birth, a Hindu by faith, a philosopher by profession, living in USA for three decades – never forgetting the Indian heritage?"* From this it is clear that when he compares between East and the West, he prefers to the East. In Sri Aurobindo's Philosophy we see a synthesis of East and West. But Jitendranath Mohanty advocates in favour of Indian Culture. He advocates that a culture is a sedimentation. A culture grows and develops over a period of time. Indian Culture is neither an Odia Culture, nor a Bengali Culture, not even a Punjabi Culture, it is something above the narrow geographical boundaries what he calls "Transculturality." He quotes R.N. Tagore who writes; *"Hethaya Arya, Hethaya Anarjya, Ek dehe helo lin."* The Sakas, the Hunas, the Pathānas, the Moghuls contribute to what we call Indian Culture. Languages are many, religions are many, the way of living is different, but, we call ourselves belonging to Indian Culture.

At the age of 95 he left for heavenly abode on 7.3.2023 in America. It is no doubt an irreparable loss to philosophy fraternity. He said that a successful life is an aesthetic project. Our search for completeness amidst the incompleteness continues for all time to come. The author is fortunate to have a live discussion with this great personality in World Philosophy Conference at New Delhi and International Conference of Society for Asian & Comparative Philosophy held in Utkal University, Bhubaneswar.

REFERENCE : (Works of Jitendranath Mohanty)

1. *The Concept of Intentionality*, Warren H. Green. Inc (1972).
2. *Theory and Practice*, Jadavpur Studies Series.
3. *Reasons and Tradition in Indian Thoughts*, Clarendon Press, Oxford (1992).
4. *Between Two worlds : East and West*, Oxford (2002).
5. *Gangesa's Theory of Truth*, ViswaBharati (1966).
6. *The Self & Its others*, Oxford University Press, New York. (2000).
7. *Ja ṇe Prabāsi Odiāra Ātmakathā* (O), *The Samaj* (29.12.2012).
8. *The Philosophy of J.N. Mohanty* edited by Dayakrishna and K.L. Sharma, ICPR Series, New Delhi.

Ganeswar Misra: Placing Philosophy on the Logical Track

Ganesh Prasad Das

I

Ganeswar Misra was born in 1918 in Bira Purusottampur Sasan of Puri district. He passed Matriculation in 1937 from Puri Zilla School, completed I.A. (1939) and B.A. (1941) from Ravenshaw College, Cuttack. He was declared the best graduate of Ravenshaw College for the year 1941. In the year 1943, he completed his M.A. from Patna College (under Patna University) and in 1944, he joined as a lecturer in Philosophy in Ravenshaw College. He went to London availing overseas fellowship in 1953 (selected for Ph.D. for education, psychology and Philosophy, under the supervison of Prof. A.J. Ayer and completed Ph.D. in Philosophy. He came back to India in 1955 and in the year 1958 he joined as a Reader in Philosophy in Utkal University, Bhubaneswar. He retired from Utkal University on superannuation as a Senior Professor of Philosophy in the year 1977. He died of cancer in 1985.

Ganeswar Misra is recognised in the philosophical circles all over India for his seminal and unconventional contribution to the study and research of Indian philosophy in general and Advaita Vedānta in particular. In one of the ICPR seminar, Professor D.P. Chattopadhyaya said that Misra undertook with 'courage, originality and creative impulse' the 'painstaking and insightful reconstruction' of Samkara's views about the empirical world. The distinctive marks of his outlook are analytical, rational, anti-metaphysical and anti-speculative.

His contributions can be put under two categories: (1) contributions to Indian philosophy and culture, and (2) contributions to Odishan philosophy and culture. He produced three books in English on Indian philosophy and a number of articles and one book in Odia on Indian culture - the Vedic culture to be exact. The entry in English captioned "Philosophy in Oriya" composed by him for the *Marāthi Encyclopaedia*, a preface in Odia to *Alekha Parambrahma Darsanam* (*Uttarārdha*), the book *Vaidika Dharma Cetanā: Eka Dārsanika Vichāra*.

II

Ganeswar Misra struck roots in his maiden work of the mid-fifties of the last century done at London University under the supervision of A.J. Ayer and published posthumously in 1986 under the title, *Sources of Monism: Bradley and Samkara*.[1] Non-dualism of Āchārya Samkara of India and Absolute Monism of F.H. Bradley of England are two great and highly respected systems astonishingly similar in respect of their doctrines and arguments.

This might appear to be a work in comparative philosophy bringing out the similarities and the differences between philosophical frameworks of Bradley and Samkara. But this is a critical work in philosophical logic. As H.H. Price testifies, there is always progress in philosophic scholarship. Misra tries to give a clear exposition of the logical framework of these two philosophical systems, whose conclusions are found to be similar; yet the principles leading to them quite dissimilar. He then tries to pointout in the contemporary idiom the shortcomings of both the systems, meet the misdirected objections against them and place them in their proper perspective.

The cardinal principles of Bradley's logic are that existence is a system, knowledge is a system, thinking is a system and discourse is a system. This means that any element in the universe is a necessary element. In the matter of thinking and judgment, the terms and relations imply one another and form an indivisible whole. According to Bradley, reality as a whole is the subject of every judgment. In seeking to apply a predicate to reality, a judgment involves itself in self-contradiction. This can be avoided only by expanding it to a system of mutually implicative elements. Hence the theory of internal relations and the coherence theory of truth are the necessary features of thinking.

Misra points out in this connection that no contradiction is involved in a judgment and thinks that Bradley has suggested implicitly a re-definition of self-contradiction, as a result of which he regards all empirical judgments as self-contradictory. According to Misra, a contradiction is due to linguistic habits and that it does not mystically intimate us about the ultimate structure of knowledge or the inner structure of reality. Bradley's contention for the unreality of relations is rejected by Misra. He points out that Bradley's proof is *a priori* and very vague; it fails to prove anything about the actual constituents of the world.

According to Bradley, relations are attributes, but, according to Misra, to say that relations are or are not attributes is to commit the error of type-crossing. Bradley is of the view that all the properties of a particular, including its relational properties, are constitutive of the particular in question. Misra regards this as a recommendation offered by Bradley, which, if accepted, would paralyse speech. Bradley advocates the coherence theory of truth in order to establish the unity of all knowledge and existence. He regards coherence as both the nature and the criterion of truth. This implies that there are no truths, but one Truth. What are ordinarily regarded as true are but approximations in various degrees of Truth in the absolute sense. Misra points out against Bradley that coherence is very often employed as a test. But it cannot be regarded as the fundamental test. The fundamental or the ultimate test of empirical knowledge is observation, Misra contends.

In this way, Misra gives an exposition of the sources, that is, logical foundations of Bradley's monism. They are embedded in a theory, or, rather in several theories regarding the nature of language. Misra, following Russell and others, tries to show that nothing about the world can be inferred from the nature of language. It is wrong to suppose that the structure of language and the structure of reality are congruent.

III

Coming to Samkara's non-dualism, Misra discovers in it a philosophy of language, which is far more profound than that of any of the analytical philosophers of the twentieth century and that his views about language lead to his metaphysical view that duality is unreal. Samkara seeks to examine critically the views of the grammarians about the nature of meaningful sentences. He finds that a grammatically complete sentence is not absolutely complete in sense. Like Bradley, Samkara also supposes that meaning is a whole and discourse is a system.

Misra asserts that according to Samkara, all sentences are not of the S-P type. Coming to the interpretation of a subject-predicate sentence, both the subject and the predicate can be interpreted either in denotation or in connotation. The latter course is adopted by Samkara and supported by Misra. Bradley's view is that they can be interpreted in either way. If it is interpreted in the denotative way, it becomes tautological and if it is interpreted in the connotative way, it becomes self-contradictory.

The sentences, which are not amenable to S-P analysis, are the sentences, which are called identity-sentences or identification-sentences (*akhandārthaka vākya*s). These are the sentences, which do not assert relations. They are known as non-relational sentences as distinguished from S-P sentences (to which all sentences are reducible, according to Bradley) as well as from the relational ones (which cannot be reduced to S-P form, according to Russell). A non-relational sentence is not regarded as an identity-sentence in Bradley's sense. In this sense, it is tautological. But an identity-sentence in Samkara's sense is significant, whereas a tautological sentence is not regarded as similarly significant.

Inspite of the excellence of Samkara in pointing out distinctions that are important for philosophy of language, this entire question of sentential form is an ill-formulated question, according to Misra. The reason is that nothing about the form of reality follows from the logical form of sentences. Russell's bold statement that the Absolutistic metaphysics of Advaita Vedānta is due to the belief in the universality of subject-predicate propositions is shown to be wrong. "It is the repudiation of subject-predicate logic rather than its acceptance which lays the foundation of Samkara's absolutism; what Russell says is true of Bradley but not of Samkara."[2]

After a critical examination of the views of both Bradley and Samkara, Misra concludes that both are playing a verbal game. They try to re-write the language in such a manner that in their new language system the word 'reality' does not apply to the phenomena in question. It is a game, which almost all philosophers have played and they play the game with all seriousness in the make-belief that they are trying to discover what is true and to know what is real. Both Bradley and Samkara use language, which is strongly suggestive and full of vivid imagery. They often use such phrases as 'meaning in the absolute sense', 'absolutely speaking about the qualities of the real', etc., in such a way that the words 'absolute' and 'absolutely', which are grammatically different, appear to be semantically different too. But in spite of their grammatical difference, they are identical in meaning. Moreover, whatever one says about meaning in absolute sense or identifying an object in absolute way, one does not prove the existence of anything. Misra calls these philosophers 'verbal magicians' as they try to re-write language creating their own problems in the sequel and push their revisions under the veil of advocating factual theories by making use of the language of assertion instead of language of suggestion. The metaphysician dwells upon the lack of a sharp criterion or rule for the application of certain expressions. He uses such facts about language as a justification for changing the language. All this is not for practical everyday use, but for the pleasure of contemplation.

IV

There appears to be certain confusions giving rise to misunderstanding of Misra's point of view. Firstly, the confusion is between linguistic philosophy and philosophy of language. What was Samkara doing according to Misra – linguistic philosophy or philosophy of language? One is regarded as a linguistic philosopher, if one proclaims that problems of philosophy are but problems due to linguistic confusions, whereas one is regarded as a philosopher of language, if one systematically reflects upon the concepts and categories pertaining to science of language. Samkara, according to Misra, is a linguistic philosopher who is not, however, a full-fledged philosopher of language, except that he has important reflections on problems of meaning of words and sentences. Secondly, there is the confusion that analysis of language must result in intimations about reality, which is 'language-transcendent', and that it is not there in Misra's analysis. It is a fact that language is used and understood in a linguistic community, i.e., it is intentional. The philosophical problem lies in explaining how exactly language is related to reality. Some philosophers try to explain that the form of language and the form of reality are identical. They contend that there is one fundamental form of assertion and there is one fundamental form of reality. Misra finds fault with Samkara for advocating this view and takes him to task for being a revisionary metaphysician. Lack of intentionality in Misra's analysis as alleged by some scholars like J.N. Mohanty is no threat to his point of view. However, I think that there is a problem in Misra's characterisation of Samkara as a revisionary metaphysician. But this does not belittle the originality of Misra's approach.

V

In his later writings, Ganeswar Misra went on to explore how far the presentations of Samkara and other Vedāntins could be enlightening in the contemporary idiom. The thrust of his explorations lies mainly on the following points:

(1) The account of the concept of *adhyāsa* that Samkara gives is logical, not psychological. This point involves a wider one.

(2) Philosophy is concerned with the analysis of language, not discovery and description of facts. These two points involve a third one.

(3) *Sabda* as a *pramāṇa* or source of knowledge signifies a critique of language, not scriptural revelation and authority.

The first and the second point could be taken together. Philosophy does not enquire about physical facts in the way in which physics and chemistry, history and politics, psychology and cybernetics do. The framework that a philosopher presents may, of course, serve as a model for enquiries in other areas of knowledge and there is no bar on the philosopher to pursue enquiries other than philosophy and he might engage his own framework as a model in those other enquiries. But, then, the distinction between the philosophical enquiry and non-philosophical enquiry should not be lost sight of. Particular matters of fact do not go to corroborate or controvert a philosophical doctrine. "They are neutral with respect to matters of fact," as Ayer puts it. The task of Samkara is not to explain why and how perceptual illusions occur and to suggest means of release from them. *Adhyāsa* is his technical term for the logical unsoundness of judgements. Misra interprets Samkara as propounding a 'critique of language' with the conclusion that 'language necessarily falsifies reality it purports to represent.' It is, therefore, an entirely logical point and the situations of rope-snake or shell-silver illusions are merely illustrations of that point. Samkara proceeds with the discussion of *adhyāsa* with the premise that the ideas of 'you' and 'I' or the ideas of 'object' and 'subject' are opposed to each other like light and darkness. It is important to notice that light and darkness as matters of fact may combine and co-exist. We may then get baffled trying to describe the situation as one of light or of darkness. But as concepts they cannot be combined without violation of principles of logic. The expression 'light and dark' is self-contradictory. In any propositional symbolism *visayi* and *visaya* are two distinct and opposite ideas. Misra takes *visayi* and *visaya* to be logical subject and logical predicate respectively. According to him, *visayi* is *svayamtistha* (self-existent) and *svayamprakasa* (self-expressing) and *visaya* is *aparatistha* (existent by other's help and *aparaprakasa* (expressed by other's help). This is a distinction of fundamental sort that the logical subject and the logical predicate or their attributes are distinct and asymmetrical in respect of the roles they play in a propositional symbolism, which is a logical entity. It would not be proper to suppose that they are articles of furniture in the world.

VI

Ganeswar Misra contributed a paper entitled "Metaphysical Models and Conflicting Cultural Patterns" to the volume *Indian Philosophy Today* edited by Professor Nanda Kishore Devaraja.[3] This was and continues to be widely read, discussed and appreciated by his peers, researchers and students. Misra seeks to show here that there are two opposing metaphysical world-views, the one of pure thought and the other of pure action. There is a sense in which the concepts 'pure thought' and 'pure action' apply only to God as He thinks of doing something and the thing is done. "Let there be light." And there was light.[4] Similarly, *"tadaiksata bahu syam prajayeya iti."*[5] And there was the world of multiplicity. In the context of the human person, the concepts 'pure thought' and 'pure action' have to be understood differently. According to Misra, a thought is pure "if a self-conscious being performs it in his own private sphere of self-consciousness", and an action is pure "if it happens to the body, uncontrolled by the mind, in a public world of physical objects in accordance with purely mechanical laws."

A life of pure thought can be taken in this context as a life of self-knowledge, life by self-realisation and life for self-liberation. This is popularly known as the spiritual culture. It belongs to the East or to India, to be more specific. This intends to insure moral life for human individuals and the human society at large. Peace, non-violence, amity and removal of strife and war, exploitation and subjugation are the ideals of this cultural model. But transcendentalism and seclusion, lack of initiative for ambitious developmental work are some of its undesirable facets. On the other extreme, a life of pure action can be taken as a life of relentless activity or persistent labour with clock-like regulation and accuracy. Man is, as it were, a mini-machine fitted as a component to a big machine called the society or the world. This is popularly known as the mechanical culture. It belongs to the West. The outcome of this model would be fulfilment of some of human wants. But it would lead to escalation of those wants and the resultant frustration due to their non-satisfaction. Further, there are certain higher-order aspirations, which would be ignored leading to incomplete growth of the human being. Both the patterns appear to have certain worthy features and yet both suffer from grave logical errors.

Misra contends that there is a third model, which absorbs the worthy features of the opposing models and avoids the errors they are infected with. The human being is not a spirit, nor a mechanical gadget. The human being is a person. He is not simply a mind, nor simply a body; he is a mind-body-integration. If the man is conceived in this model, then a culture of humanism would flourish ushering in human amity, unity, equity, brotherhood, peaceful co-existence, international understanding, free from dogmas, confusions and hidden agenda and purged of racial, religious and colour discriminations.

Misra observes, "The philosophy which points out the logical errors in the philosophical pictures of the past is the critical and analytical philosophy of the modern age...Clarity is the aim of this modern philosophy; logical analysis is its method; clearing away of the misunderstanding is the result which it achieves." He adds, "helping to see the baselessness of clashing cultures is the role of modern philosophy" as it "has brought man to his original home and the man at his own home is engaged in a constructive programme of work..."

VII

Misra throws new light on the no-substance view of Buddhism and its apparent opposition to the Vedantic view. He says that it is language that creates the illusion of identity, substantiality and changeless permanent ground. "This is the same alarm clock that I am using for the last fifty-five years" creates the illusion that there is an internal core of the clock, which has not undergone any change and on account of which it has been identified as the same clock. This is an illusion created by language," he asserts in his characteristic way.[6] What is there in reality is ceaseless continuous flow of successive events. The clock might have changed totally imperceptibly over the years and yet it is identified as the 'same' clock. This is 'overclouded by language'. It is *ajñāna* not to know this and *tathatā* to know this. This wisdom is struck by Buddha. He, therefore, determined that as everything and being change, sorrow too could change.

This does not contradict the Vedāntic doctrine that the world is an illusion according to Misra. The Advaitin merely points out that what the Buddhist is saying might create another illusion, i.e., the illusion has no basis in the structure of our understanding. Because of the structure of language, I am obliged to take that the world has one substantial character. The Buddhist suggests that this take could be avoided, whereas the Advaitin suggests that it could not be. "The illusion consists in transferring the logico-linguistic character to the phenomenal order, to use the form as if it were the content."[7] To say that it is an illusion of language implies that our understanding could get rid of the same. This is the illusion. The Buddhist is a victim to it in his denial of a substantial basis. The Advaitin points out that the Buddhist in talking of *svalakṣana* makes an impossible claim that we can jump out of our conceptual system and know reality as it is in its own nature (*svalakṣana*).

Misra has another important paper on Buddhism to his credit, namely, "Buddhist Logic and Its Doctrine of Apoha", included in the volume entitled *Language, Reality and Analysis: Essays on Indian Philosophy* published with J.N. Mohanty as editor.[8] Misra claims here that Buddhist logicians like Dignaga, Dharmakirti and others "were logicians in the sense in which the contemporary logical analysts are logicians"; they "were not interested in exhibiting the rules of different logical patterns."[9] "They were a kind of descriptive metaphysicians," who "were engaged in exhibiting pervasive features of underlying linguistic structures. According to the Buddhist logician, a cognitively meaningful judgment is made up of two components. One of them is referring and the other describing. A referring word merely refers; neither affirmation nor negation in respect of it makes sense. 'This' and 'I' are referring words *par excellence*. "This is" is a redundant and "This is not" is a contradictory statement. The referent is always an existent thing (*bhavavastu*). It is a *svalakṣana* as it does not carry the supposition of its negation; it is a bare particular, but not a point-instant as Stcherbatsky translates it. It does not have spatio-temporal determination, which is due to intellect. It is just out of point to say that the logical particular is constant flux or it does not undergo change, Becoming or Being. As such, the differentiation theory of meaning (*apohavāda*) that the Buddhist advocates seeks to catch this *svalakṣana* by shedding the determinations, according to Misra.

Misra contends that according to Samkara, all words are connotative including proper names.[10] A proposition is thus a complex constituted by words that are universals in signification. The reality, which we intend to talk about, "is presupposed but does not directly come within the meaning-scope of the proposition."[11] For the Buddhist, such a supposition is uncalled for. According to my understanding of Misra here, the Buddhist logician claims that a judgment has a subject that refers to something and a predicate that says something about it. What the logical subject refers to and what the logical predicate says is not the logician's cup of tea. The common man can posit this seminar as the subject and say that it is running smoothly, or the metaphysician can posit the Absolute as the subject and say, "The Absolute is such that the seminar is running smoothly." This Buddhist view is not transcendentalism, not realism, not idealism, not logicism; it is simply logic of language or logical grammar.

REFERENCE :
1. Anu Books, Meerut.
2. *Op. cit.*, p.78.
3. *Genesis* 1.3.
4. *Chhāndogya Upanisad.*
5. The Macmillan Company of India Limited, Delhi, 1975, pp. 155-168.
6. *Analytical Studies in Buddhist Philosophy*, p. 85.
7. *Op. cit.*, p. 86, Wittgenstein said in his *Tractatus*, "It (object) is both form and content".
8. E.J. Brill, 1990.
9. Chapter 7.
10. *Analytical Studies in Indian Philosophical Problems*, p. 35.
11. *Op. cit.*, p. 37.

Binode Kanungo:
The Maker of Encyclopaedia
(1912-1990)

Pabak Kanungo

(Freedom Fighter, Gandhian, author of the Popular Odia Encyclopedia Jñānamandal, initiator of encyclopaedia movement in our country, erudite scholar, journalist, Popularizer of Science, Social Reformer, crusader against illiteracy and ignorance and the architect of a remarkable movement for spreading enlightenment among the people in the post-independence era.)

Binode Kanungo was born on 6th June, 1912 in village Mallipur, Kisannagar P.S., Cuttack district of Odisha. He was the only son of Keshab Chandra Kanungo and Peera Dei. At the age of six only, he joined the family of his maternal uncle Prof. Artaballav Mohanty, an eminent Sanskrit scholar and had his primary education at Naganpur, Prof. Mohanty's village. In 1926 Kanungo came to Cuttack and studied at Ranihat High School of which he was the first student on it's establishment. On passing his middle school level examination with a scholarship, he got himself admitted into the famous Ravenshaw Collegiate School which had

Netaji Subash as a student once upon a time. In 1930, when in class X, Kanungo heard the call of the Mahatma Gandhi who, from that day, became his life's beacon. He deserted the school in April that year alongwith some of his fellow students and joined the Freedom Movement.

Between 1930–32, he was imprisoned twice. When lodged at the famous Patna Camp jail, he came in contact with some of the leading figures of the Indian Freedom Struggle. Also, he joined the 'Individual Satyagraha' after Congress was declared unlawful by the British Government. In May, 1934, Gandhiji started his, 'Harijan Padayātrā' in Odisha. It is of historic significance to record that he was appointed as a special correspondent of the Samaja to cover Mahatma Gandhi's famous Harijan Padayātrā from Puri to Bhadrak in 1934. The translation of Binode's reporting in the Samaja on the Padayātrā was being daily read out to Mahatma on day-to-day basis. Gandhiji, the best known example of a journalist in the history of mankind, guided, advised and explained to Binode the ways and means of becoming a good reporter.

While filing reports on Mahatma's progress for the Samaja, Kanungo came into close contact with him at a personal level and that continued till Mahatma's death. By that time, Gandhi's indisputable credentials for goodness had deeply influenced and dazzled millions of his fellow countrymen and others throughout the world. Kanungo observed him from very close quarters and learned the most valuable Gandhian lessons during that period. Since then, Gandhiji's guideline—one must do only that piece of work that will benefit the 'poorest of the poor' and pave the way for a society where everyone could have the minimum needs of life created impact on dominated Kanungo's thought and action. Freed from the mimicry of formal colonial education, Kanungo took the plunge to self-education. Mahatma's famous call 'no nation grows without education' was ringing incessantly in the ears of youthful Kanungo.

Years that followed till India's independence, Kanungo had to undergo various jail terms. In the brief intervals out of the jail, he spent his time doing newspaper reporting, teaching adults and children and perfecting his own agriculture techniques. Gandhiji's emphasis on social reconstruction appealed to him greatly. That universalization of education was a must; he understood it perfectly. He already had his own plan of spreading education. Till his end, the dedication was complete. From 1934-38, on Mahatmas instructions, he worked at Bari Ashram in Jajpur district with 'mother' Rama Devi and Gopabandhu Choudhuri, her husband and a close associate of Gandhi. Kanungo was also selected personally by Gandhiji to work in his all India scheme *Samagra Grām Sevā*. In between he was engaged in organizing Congress Sevā Dal Camps also. Binode had the distinction of holding the prestigious position of Assistant Editor of the Samaja during the 1940's and was entrusted with the responsibility of covering the Second World War. He was imprisoned by the British authorities for his role as a Journalist and freedom fighter. In 1939 he married Sashibala (d.1996). She chose to follow her husband's footsteps—joined the Freedom Movement and became a security prisoner (1942-44) at Cuttack Central jail during the Quit India movement.

Kanungo was last imprisoned in 1942 and was lodged at Berhampur Central jail. During his quiet detention of more than three years, he deeply pondered over definite ways on how to make people free from ignorance and poverty of knowledge. All his later landmark literary achievements had their inceptions at Berhampur jail only, where all important leaders of the state were interned as security prisoners. How to democratize knowledge became an obsession with Kanungo. By that time he had already read hundreds of books on virtually every branch of human knowledge and taken thousands of pages of copious notes. It served him in two ways —first he made good the academic loss suffered because of leaving the school and secondly, it prepared him to write for the multitude with equal ease as for the enlightened. During this period, his first book titled as *'Saptastra'*-on major weapon systems used in the second World War, was published.

He was released from Berhampur jail in 1945: Bowing to Gandhiji's wish, he retired to his village and engaged himself in constructive social work and engaged in agriculture for living. His success as a *'chāsi'* or farmer was unmatched and drew laurels from every quarter. He setup a *Khadi Centre* in his village Mallipur, which attracted national attention. During this period he was blessed with a daughter. Meanwhile, in 1952, came the first general election of India. Kanungo contested it on Socialist Party ticket and lost. Stalwarts like Achuta Patawardhan and Jaya Prakash Narayan were his poll campaigners. This short stint in election politics was his first and last. In 1954 Kanungo finally made up his mind that his priorities were lying somewhere else. He discussed it with Sashibala; left children (by then their second child, son was also born) with her at Mallipur and started for Cuttack to begin work on the monumental *Jñānamandal*, the Odia Encyclopedia. He carried from his village 'a Rupee' only and a bicycle. But, this stubborn disciple of Mahatma had already set his goals—nothing on the way could prevent him. Along with raising a reference centre for the future encyclopaedia project, he was writing excellent books for children and adults alike, was editing a children's magazine *'Sishu Sampad'* which was very popular at that time and was contributing to the social life of Odisha.

The first volume of *Jñānamandal* was released on 2nd December, 1960 by Chief Minister Dr. H. K. Mahatab. *Jñānamandal* literally means the circle of knowledge. From then on it has evoked the kind of enthusiasm which only a few other Odia masterpieces have any parallel. It is referred to as a gift for those underprivileged who are hungry for knowledge. Moreover *Jñānamandal* is recognized as one of the pioneering popular encyclopaedias among all the major India languages. But publishing an encyclopaedia set was not an easy task in his state. Even against heavy odds, Kanungo's spirit was not to budge. Acute mental strength and will-power propelled him to write volume after volume. Other than this voluminous work of his, he also authored more than 100 books on various subjects of human interest. Such diverse themes like medical science, astrophysics, nuclear physics have become so lucid in his writings that they have become everyman's guide to a vast range of subjects. Einstein's dictum that *'mother tongue should be the only medium of learning'* has been truly reflected in the success of Kanungo's 365 Days series of books. Each book in the series bears an imaginative title and attracts the young and the old alike. He was also a pioneer in adult education movement in India and worked closely with Maulana Azad. A comprehensive handbook on adult education was authored by him as far back as 1950. Some of Kanungo's books have been translated into different Indian languages.

Binode Kanungo was an institution by himself. — scholars have hailed his mission as a "national work", "fundamental work in language and literature and a valuable contribution to human society". His singlehanded contribution to democratization of knowledge has few parallel in India. The Films Division of Govt. of India made a documentary film on his life and work and ran it in all the cinema houses of the country in 14 regional languages in addition to Hindi and English versions. The national dailies and foremost periodicals of our country had extensive coverage of him and on his mission. In its Great Masters series Doordarshan has carried him twice even after his death. His rerniniscences are preserved in the All India Radio's National Voice Archives. Kanungo was a recipient of *Padmashri* and numerous literary and other awards. He was awarded twice the prestigious *Odisha Sahitya Akademi* Award. On his death on June, 1990, the House of the Odisha Legislative Assembly unanimously resolved to pay the respect of the nation to him through State Honour, although Kanungo never had during his lifetime occupied any public office or had any governmental credentials.

Shri Biju Patnaik, who was Patron-in-Chief of the National Encyclopedia Centre and an intimate friend of Kanungo had said "*Kanungo was one of the most interesting and multi-faceted personalities of our times. In his endeavour to free people from the poverty of knowledge, he undertook the stupendous task of compiling 'Jñānamandal' which is regarded as one of the best edited encyclopedias in Indian languages. Undoubtedly, his single minded devotion and* insatiable urge for knowledge enabled him to accomplish this monumental work, despite heavy odds. I have no doubt that Binode Kanungo will be remembered for all time to come for his significant contribution to the field of human knowledge."

While complementing Kanungo on the occasion of the publication of the 40th volume of the Odia Encyclopedia Shri Rajiv Gandhi had said— "In every country, we have remarkable individuals, who have done much for the enlightenment of their fellow human beings. Shri Binode Kanungo is one such outstanding scholar. The Odia people will long be beholden to him for this monumental Odia Encyclopedia."

Distinguished personalities from all walks of life, who have visited Jñānamandal Reference Centre have appreciated the stupendous effort that has gone into making it a remarkable centre for research, academic pursuit and dissemination of knowledge. Containing huge records of enduring value, this centre for research and learning had attracted scholars from all over the country. After visiting the Centre and meeting Late Shri Kanungo, Shri Pranab Mukherjee (Former President of India) had said— "No word is sufficient to express the state of mind when I entered into this hall, which is the storehouse of knowledge in the real sense of the term. Knowledge is stored here and that is way no word can express the achievements of the great organiser."

Noted Gandhian and former Governor Shri R.R.Diwakar had described the work as "Jñāna Yajña" when he visited the centre in early 1980's— He wrote;

"I have seen encyclopedias in many languages, but I had no occasion to meet an encyclopedic man, who could not only understand but write on various subjects with, ease and felicity. This is a fundamental work in language a d literature, just as there is fundamental work in science and applied science. The inspiration which is operating here is the urge to share his knowledge with his brethren and at present and with generations to come. I wish him full success in this "Jñāna Yajña"— to noble work of spreading knowledge."

This is what Prof. Hiren Mukherjee said— *"A visit to Jñānmandal today has been a remarkable experience. It is nothing short of amazing that one dedicated man, with a few equally devoted assistants can undertake and also perform a stupendous literary project. Shri Binode Kanungo has, it appears, only one aim in life and that is to bring all knowledge to every door in so far it is possible to condense the ever widening departments of knowledge. For this purpose work goes on and it is a sheer joy to see the numerous files on different subjects neatly stacked and being continuously added to and amended."*

Shri Binode Kanungo was a pioneer in field of popularization of science. His Popular Encyclopedia, 40 volumes of which have so far been published, contains hundreds of educative science articles. Besides these Kanungo has made a valuable contribution to our Children's literature and had written nearly a hundred small books for children. One is simple charmed with the treatment of very difficult subjects made intelligible to the young mind. Written with simplest Odia, the treatment of the subject is such that it grips the interest of the readers and is certainly entertaining reading for the children. Original in its technique, each book, in its own imitable way removes a longfelt need in this domain of children's literature in Odisha. Even complicated scientific facts are explained vividly and rendered intelligible to young mind with allegorical description. The style and the illustration are at once attractive and instructive. With a view to making the story simple and within the grasp of children, Kanungo has used imagery from everyday experience with great success.

Bhikari Bal: The Bhajan Samrat of Odisha*

Sunamani Rout

Every morning the atmosphere of Odisha reverberates with the heart-touching devotional numbers of Bhikari Bal. It appears as if Lord Jagannāth wakes up with the song. Bhikari Bal, a rare talent is not only pride and glory but also our national property – a spiritual experience of the mass.

Sri Bal's melodious voice pervades every nook and corner of Odisha. His popular and hearty hymns hold listeners spellbound. His efforts to propagate a pure and devotional fervor among the mass immortalise him. Though he is no more but his warbling songs are still afresh like basil leaves on Lord Jagannāth in the temple of memory.

Bhikari Bal was born on 25th May 1929 in Sobola village in the district of Kendrapra. His father's name was Rama Chandra Bal and mother Gelha Rani. He has not forgotten Lord Jagannāth in ups and downs of life. He prayed the Lord as a true devotee. He implored :

Duniāre jebe dina pare rāti
rāti pare dina sata
mo rāti emiti asarā kemiti
kuha prabhu Jagannātha ?

(In the world, when the night follows the day and vice-versa, why then my night is without a complacent feeling. Explain me my Lord (Jagannāth) why this is so?)

Sorrowful night in his life was endless. He lost his parents in his childhood. Still he struggled for survival in the face of sorrow and abject poverty, maintaining his family with music as a livelihood. Various deterrence in his life never hold him back.

He was deprived of singing before four years of his death as he was confined to bed with disease. He performed his last stage music program on 14th May 2006. There after he could not sing any more. Perhaps for this he sang in a conceited tone

Kaliā Sānta ho!
eki kala prabhu eki kala
Bhikhyā delanāhi, thāla bhāngi dela,
kala mote sāta para.

(Oh my Lord, Kalia Thakura! What you did ? It does not matter that you did not give alms but you have broken my begging bowl, kept me away from you!)

Many of his hymns reflect his sorrow, poverty, wants and helplessness. He prayed to God as his master and at times as a friend. That gave him immense peace of mind. His devotional songs reflected his eye and awakened a new vista of life.

His parents named him as Bhikari to save him from the God of Death (*Yama*) as four male children before him had died. But his nick name was "Kāliā". From childhood he mesmerized the audience by his musical talent, later on, his talent was recognized and earned laurel by coming in contact with the famous music master Balakrushna Dash.

He sang Jagannāth's hymns and prayers for the first

time through Kolkata's HMV Company's LP records. Those two records were, *'Bhakti Puspānjali'* and *'Saradhā Bāli'*. Likewise, he sang and recorded Kalicharan Patnaik's songs through L.P. record in 1976 for the first time. That helped to revive memory of Kabichandra. Many of those songs later on became household songs.

This apart INRECO Company of Kolkata recorded through LP and EP records, Upendra Bhanja's Odishi songs. Many devotional songs sung by him have created a Renaissance in the annals of Odia devotional songs.

People also know him as a successful and well-known singer. His songs in more than twenty five cinemas bear a testimony to his singing skill. That's why, he has been rewarded by Govt. of Odisha.

In his busy day life he was involved in many music institutions and won kudos. Friends' Cultural Association of Jatani, Gokul Chandra Sangita Sadan of Kendrapada, Kalavikas Kendra of Cuttack, Utkal Sangeet Bharti of Choudwar are among them. He served as a Professor in Utkal Sangita Mahavidyalaya, Odishi Vocal was his field. The retired from services in February, 1997.

Bhikari Bal popularized Odia music not only in Odisha but also beyond. He won laurels in Koklata, Delhi, Madras, Assam for his performances. He propagated devotional fervor in some of the western countries also.

Bhikari Bal is no more among us but his voice and musical dedication continue unabated. Bhikari Bal was an uncommon man, a devout devotee. He conquered the hearts of the millions though his devotional number. A man is known at the time of his death. His death has proved his greatness. People witnessing that incident on mass media on the other day need no further elucidation.

Once Gandhiji told "My life is my message". Life

of Mahatma Gandhi based on truth and non-violence was an indomitable inspiration for the world. Similarly Bhikari Bal's songs reflect every titbits of life, faced during his life time. He gave importance to thought, language and syntacticality of the hymn that was to be sung. This made his music very active and heart-touching.

He reached pinnacle of glory by singing the songs of both old and new singers. In the songs of these famed singers Bhikari Bal's life was portrayed. He also corrected some of the songs and lent voice to it. This is why his songs are very real and lifelike.

Bhikari Bal was greedfree and unselfish, did not care for wealth. He left all his property for his elder brother in his native village and came to Cuttack. His elder brother was Dhani (Dhaneswal Bal) and he was Bhikari (beggar). All through his life he prayed to the Lord Jagannāth but never asked for anything.

Jaganātha ho, kichhi māgunāhi tote
Dhana māgu nāhin, jana māgu nāhin
Māguchhi saradhā bāliru hāte.

(Oh Lord Jagannāth! I do not beg anything, neither the wealth nor family members. I simply beg a handful of blessings from Saradhā bāli (the sacred sand of the grand road).

Whatever amount he earned by singing, a large chunk of it he donated to different institutions. Donations were to Jagannāth temple of Puri, to Sobola temple at his village, to Utkal Sahitya Samaj and to an institution of Dhenkanal. This type of attitude proved his large heartedness and a penchant for divinity.

He was a staunch believer of Lord Jagannāth. He remembered to the Lord in his work and word. Even in the fag end his life, he uttered the name of the Lord.

In some of his village and modern songs, we find his juicy attitude :

Kalasa upare āmba dāliyā
Gori kaniāku bara kālia
Gāon jhiamāne ākhi tharā thari
Karāndi pakāi nelā bālia.

Bhikari's colour was black but his wife was fair in complexion. Bhikari Bal dearly loved his only daughter. After the daughter's marriage, he was feeling helpless. But by God's grace the daughter stayed near him and took care of him. His songs bear testimony to many events that happened during his life.

Almost every musician is a lover and bit of libertine in attitude. Bikari Bal is not an exception to it. Many might have realized this aspect of his life from his behavior and conversation. At times he was making serious situation light through his unique way of conversation. Many of his modern songs bear an eloquent testimony to it.

Real picture of his life has been reflected in many of his songs. This great soul is now in heaven. But the entire world is now abuz with his God-gifted voice. His melodious strain surpassed time and space and enthralled the masses from generation to generation and it will go on forever. That voice will never die down. It will continue to go on and on.

---

* Translated to English by Prof. Nikunja Bihari Mishra.

Chittaranjan Das: Writer Extraordinary
(1923-2011)

Dhaneswar Sahoo

Chittaranjan Das, well-known as Chitta Bhai in Odisha, was a great literary luminary. He was a freedom fighter, prolific writer, educationist, columnist, translator and intellectual of high order. He is well-known as a non-fictional writer and has authored more than two hundred books. He is also a widely-travelled person and well-versed in different Indian and foreign languages. He has made immense contribution to Odia literature. If his works could be translated into English language he would be internationally recognized. His writings are insightful, thought-provoking and laden with philosophical reflection.

When he was a student of Ravenshaw College, Cuttack, the most premier educational institute of Odisha, he was moved by Mahatma Gandhi's call to join the Quit India movement in 1942. He left his studies and participated in the freedom struggle and was imprisoned. After his release from the jail, he went to Shantiniketan and studied at Viswabharati which was started by Rabindranath Tagore. He studied Philosophy, Sanskrit and Comparative Literature and learnt different languages.

At that time many eminent scholars and Professors of international repute were at Viswabharati and Chittaranjan had the privilege to study under them. This university opened his eyes and gave him great exposure to the world of knowledge. He studied the original texts of Indian Philosophy in Sanskrit under the guidance of some renowned scholars. At the end he presented a dissertation on Benedict De Spinoza, a philosopher of the 17th century of the rationalist school of thought. After studying five years at Viswabharati, he was selected to go to Denmark for higher studies. He spent four years from 1950 to 1954 at Copenhagen University in Denmark and studied psychology and sociology. He learnt Danish, Finnish, Germany and French there. He returned to Odisha in 1954. During this time Nabakrushna Choudhury, the great Gandhian thinker, was the Chief Minister of Odisha who wanted to open some post-basic schools on the model of basic education of Mahatma Gandhi. Chittaranjan was requested to start the school at Champatimunda, in rural background near Angul. The school was named *Jeevan Vidyālaya* (School of Life) and functioned under the stewardship of Chittaranjan from 1954. This was a new experiment where the pupils were given the freedom to learn different subjects of their choice along with manual work and ethics. The school had the autonomy to select its syllabus, pattern of examination and method of evaluation. Later on this was not taken in good spirit by educational authorities who were in the helm of affairs. There was serious difference of opinion with the administration. Finally, Chittaranjan left the school with a heavy heart as it was built with his idea and vision during these four years. Then in 1959 he was given an offer to be a faculty in the Rural

University near Agra founded by the Government of India. After serving there for three years he went to West Germany for a higher course for one year. He continued in the Rural University for more than a decade and finally left the institute for some reason or other. On the eve of Sri Aurobindo's birth centenary some Integral Schools were opened in Odisha in accordance with Sri Aurobindo's and Sri Mother's philosophy of education. Chittaranjan was requested to join in the first Integral School that started in Bhubaneswar. He served some years there and then was given the task by Sri Aurobindo Educational Trust to be in overall charge of the Integral Schools as its number increased numerically in the state. He moved from school to school, interacted with the students and teachers and guided the teachers and prepared the curricula for Integral education in the state.

Chittaranjan had, to speak the least, two ambitions, to be a teacher and to be a writer. With his knowledge, qualification and exposure he could have been in any other job and would have gone to a high position. But he did not opt for any lucrative job but worked as a teacher in some institute or other like a rolling stone. He had some ideological conviction and had never compromised with a system against his principle.

Coming to his literary contribution, he is well known in Odisha as a non-fictional writer having more than two hundred books to his credit. He was a well-read person and versatile in many branches of learning. He was conversant with different languages and had read original works in respective languages. He had access to many disciplines like literature, philosophy, psychology, sociology, education and cultural anthropology etc.

His creative pursuit started when he was in prison.

In that young age he started writing poems and his collection of poems is published in a book under the title 'Dui Adhyāya' (Two chapters) consisting of thirty-four poems. But later on, he gave up the practice of writing poetry and confined himself to non-fictional prose writing. Basically, he was a literary critic, essayist, biographer, translator, researcher, columnist, critical analyst, reviewer and philosopher. His creative talent limits no bound. He developed a unique style of his own. His command over Odia language was commendable. He was also a brilliant orator and spells bound by his speech. His sense of humour, wit, depth and rational presentation has made him popular. He was regularly contributing columns and essays to widely circulated Odia dailies and magazines. His writings were widely acclaimed by the readers. Despite all his talent and acclamation, he prefers to live like a common man. He joins the youth camps (called Sruhrut Sibir) and does odd jobs, plays with the students in the school, renders social service organized by the Aurobindites and at the same time given intellectual deliberations. He also widely travels, goes to different places in India and outside India to join seminars and conferences, moves from school to school to teach the students and to guide the teachers of Integral schools, regularly contributes articles to newspapers and magazines and again writes voluminous books. It is really a wonder how he gets so much of time to do all those works simultaneously. Despite all his engagements he was passionately involved in writing. He lived a creative and so to say a meaningful life till he breathed his last on January 16,2011.

His intellectual horizon was expanded by his in-depth study of the thinkers, litterateurs and philosophers of both east and west. Among Indian luminaries he was greatly inspired by Mahatma Gandhi, Rabindranath and Sri Aurobindo, to mention a few. In his youth he was moved by Mahatma Gandhi's ideals of non-violence, swaraj, satyagraha, civil disobedience etc. to fight against the British colonialism for which he left his studies and joined the freedom struggle. After independence of the country, he was steeped in Rabindranath's ideals to prosecute his studies at Viswabharati. The songs and cherished ideals of the poet had a lasting impact on Chittaranjan. Being moved by the ideas and ideals of Mahatma Gandhi and Rabindranath, he translated some of their works into Odia. In his later life he was engrossed in the philosophy of Sri Aurobindo and translated his seminal works. Particularly Chittaranjan translated Sri Aurobindo's *Life Divine, Synthesis of Yoga, Human Cycle and Ideal of Human Unity* into Odia. In this stupendous task he went deep into the metaphysical world-view of Sri Aurobindo. Later on he also translated all the works of Sri Mother. In his intellectual journey Mahatma Gandhi, Rabindranath and Sri Aurobindo greatly inspired him to shape his personality.

Chittaranjan was equally inspired by the great thinkers of the western world. His intellectual awakening, erudition and critical thinking were greatly enhanced because of his western exposure and academic pursuit. He had the privilege to know and read some great minds who have made significant contribution to the world of ideas. Even he came in personal contact with some philosophers, psychologists, humanists and some illustrious thinkers of humanity of his time. He had widely travelled and gone to many universities when he was in Copenhagen. In this process he developed personal acquaintance with scholars and thinkers. As he had learnt different European languages it became easier on his part to mix with the people and to know their culture, tradition, life style etc. All these cumulatively helped Chittaranjan to develop a universal vision. He has outgrown all boundaries and has become a knowledgeable person and a unique personality.

About his intellectual contribution it can be said that he was primarily a literary critic and the best essayist of his time. He has more than thirty anthologies (each anthology is a conglomeration of various essays). Every anthology consists of thought–provoking essays. The essays in an anthology spread over various themes relating to literature, society, human situation,educational ideas, ethical issues, cultural problems and sociological issues etc. Some of his anthologies are incisive critique of civilizational progress, social tradition, cultural mores, educational system etc. of the society.

He was regularly contributing articles and essays to different leading newspaper of Odisha. On any social issue, political situation, literary theme he presents his analysis and gives his reflection. His analytical presentation and insightful observation do touch a common reader. Satire, wit, rational expression and critical analysis are the characteristic features of his assays. He is well known in nook and corner of Odisha for his regular columns in newspapers and magazines. His essays have been compiled in different volumes. As a columnist he occupies a unique place in public memory.

He has some research works to his credit which contain his in-depth study of some literary figures. His work on Mahimā Dharma is a master piece for knowing the theological doctrines, metaphysical theories, order of the cult, its literature and philosophy. Similarly, his works on the devotional poetry of Odisha known as *Panchasakhā* are so to say research treatises. Chittaranjan brought out the philosophical and metaphysical doctrines latent in the poetry of Balaram Das and AchyutanandDas. Cittaranjan has authored some books on the "Cultural progress of Odisha through Literature"; "Historical, Social and Cultural background of Odia Literature";"Literature and ... (Sahitya O...) "etc. Each of these works is a critique of literature.He analyses how Odia literature in form of poetry, down the ages, has influenced the cultural and social life of Odisha. He shows that society and culture are manifested in literature or in other words literature is the reflection of the ideas and values that people live by or adhere to.

He has authored nine travelogues. Some of them are about his experience in Denmark, Nepal, China, Israel and America the countries which he has visited on different occasions. When he was at Copenhagen in Denmark, he visited most of the European countries. Wherever he has gone he has tried to know the culture, art, social life, political history, educational system, economic progress etc of the people of the land. Each travelogue relating to a country or countries gives a vivid description of the people of the soil and their social system. He dips deep to know people and their life style, customs, academic curricular for the students and the great litterateurs of the land. He has two travelogues relating to his experience and aesthetic feelings while travelling through sea-routes for days together. One travelogue *"Silatirtha"* is about his experience in the Himalayan region, the gigantic mountains, the streams, dense forests, rivers and the natives of the land. His travelogues are interesting readings to know a people and their place with diversities.

His work *"Samāj Parivartan O Vikās"* (Society: Change and Progress) is a sociological treatise discussing at length the notion of society and the factors leading to social evolution and progress. He has analyzedthe cause of social change and how social revolution sometimes gives a leap to social progress. Why it is the case that some nations are economically developed and other nations are economically backward or languish in dire poverty? He analyses how the role of science, technology, economic planning, political stability, democratic values, socialistic welfare measures, the educational system, people's sense of moral accountability etc. play important roles to shape the progress of a notion. He has translated a voluminous book *"Methods in Social Research"* by W.J. Goods and P.K. Hatt into Odia which is an analytical exposition how to study human society and social progress. These two works (one is his own and one is his translation) are two important classics in pursuit of sociological study.

Chittaranjan is a first-rate translator. He has translated books from English, Bengali, Danish and Germany. In the early phase of his life, he translated some works of Mahatma Gandhi and Rabindranath. In later years he translated some major works of Sri Aurobindo and almost all works of Sri Mother. Apart from that he has translated more than thirty important classics relating to literature, auto-biography and educational philosophy of the West. The works of some Nobel laureates like Boris Pasternak, Ladiesl St. Raymant, FranoisMauniae, Giellerup are translated by him into Odia. He has also translated some of the works of famous Russian writer Leo Tolstoy and the works of Jawaharlal Nehru, our first prime minister. Nobel laurate Albert Scheweitzer'sautobiography and Nobel laurate Martin Luther King's work have also been translated by him. Some of the works of Bengali writers like Ashapurna Devi and Jatindra Mohan Sengupta are also translated by him. The works of some eminent educationists and philosophers of the west like Albert Luthuli, Khalil Jibran, Antoine Exupery and Barrows Dunham are also translated by Chittaranjan. Similarly, he has translated Harsh Mander's book "*Unheard Voice*". Most of the works he has translated into Odia are classics, books of Nobel laureates or insightful works. Odia literature has been greatly enriched by these translated works.

Chittaranjan has authored four biographies. They are (i) *Marco Polo* (ii) *Swami Vivekananda* (iii) *Nabakrushna Choudhury* (iv) *Christen Kold*. Marco Polo was an Italian explorer of the 13th century. He introduced Europe to China and central Asia and wrote about his adventures while going through the central part of Asia. Swāmi Vivekananda was an Indian monk, religious teacher and philosopher. He became famous after his address at Chicago, USA in the World's Parliament of Religion. Chittaranjan presents Swāmi Vivekananda as a social revolutionary and not just as a religious monk. Nabakrushna Choudhury was a freedom fighter, ardent Gandhian and the Chief Minister of Odisha. He left politics and dedicated his life for social upheaval. Christen Kold was a great educational reformer of Denmark. Chittaranjan has presented all these great figures from different perspectives while discussing their life and vision. Chittaranjan has also written his autobiography which contains his varied experiences, vision and dream. He has met many eminent personalities, scholars, literators and philosophers. It is one of the finest autobiographies written by an extraordinary writer. He titles his autobiography as *Mitrasya Chaksusa* (In the Eyes of a Friend). Besides he was regularly writing his diary expressing his ideas, thoughts and reflections on various themes. All his diaries are published in about twenty-three volumes which seem something unique. If he would have written nothing save his diaries still, he would have taken a unique position in Odia literature. All his diaries are published under the title *Rohita's Dairy*. Rohit literally means rising sun. These volumes are conglomeration of multifarious social, psychological, literary and philosophical ideas written date-wise in chronological order.

When he was teaching at *Jeevan Vidyālaya* at Champatimunda every day he was writing his thought, feeling and dream to be read in the presence of all students to inspire them. Later on, these writing are published in two volumes under the title *Jeevan Vidyālaya* (Life's University). He wants to give the message that our life can be our university to learn from our varied experiences and relationships. Listening to the inspirational words regularly from their teacher, some students wrote their own diaries expressing their dreams of life. Similarly, Chittaranjan had authored a book describing all events of the school with his own reflective remarks. The book is titled *Jangal Chithi* (Letters from the Jungle). *Jeevan Vidyālaya* and *Jangal Chithi* consist of many reflective and inspirational message to the young minds. Wherever they may be or may work in future, they must have a sense of concern for the society and humanity at large, that would add to their quality of life was his message to students.

Chittaranjan has two books titled *"Viswa Parikramā"* (Traversing the Universe) and *Grantha Manthan* (Churning

of Books) which consist the review of books. In *Viswa Parikramā* he has taken ten books of the Western world which have made significant contribution to the world of ideas. He presents the salient ideas and summary of each book and then his own observation and estimation of the work. The books that he has reviewed are :
(i) *The Impact of Science on Society*- Bertrand Russell
(ii) *The Revolt of the Masses*- Jose Ortega Gasset
(iii) *Civilization on Trial*- Arnold J. Toynbee
(iv) *The Philosophy of Civilization* – Albert Schweitzer
(v) *The Reconstruction of Humanity* – P.A. Sorokin
(vi) *I and Thou* – M.M. Bubber
(vii) *Man for Himself* – Erich Fromm
(viii) *Small is Beautiful* – E.F. Schumacher
(ix) *Towards Psychology of Being*- A.H. Maslow
(x) *The Hidden Remnant* – Gerald Sykes

Needless to say, each book is a thought-provoking work giving insightful reflection on some area of human knowledge. His review of these books is both informative and illuminating creating interest in the reader to read the whole text.

The other book – review "*Grantha Manthan*" consists of nearly fifty-eight boos. Out of 58 books reviewed by Chitaranjan fifty-three are in Odia and five are in English. He has classified the books that he has reviewed under five categories such as (i) Poetry (ii) Story and Novel (iii) Essay (iv) Biography and Autobiography (v) Research works. In the last category, there are eleven Odia dissertations and five English dissertations. While reviewing the books of all the categories he points out the important idea or message contained in the book and its drawbacks, if any. His book-reviews reveal his horizon of reading all kinds of books.

Chittaranjan has also made some important contribution to children's literature. He has more than one dozen interesting books primarily for the school children though all readers can read them. These are some story collections translated from different languages, biographies, description about some countries etc.

Though he mostly writes in Odia and translates important books into Odia, he has some English works to his credit. While he was a student of Viswabharati, Shantiniketan he had prepared a thesis on Benedict De Spinoza, a philosopher of the 17th century of continental philosophy. He analyzes Spinoza's contribution to the then emerging trend of modern philosophy and his humanistic vision of life. Chittaranjan has written on Balaram Das and Bhakta Charan Das, two noted poets of medieval Odisha. He depicts their contribution to Odia literature and analyses their ideas in their contemporary period, Chittaranjan's book *"Studies on Medieval Religion and Literature of Odisha"* is a research work which deals at length the religious trends and the devotional poetry in the medieval period. His book *"A Glimpses into Odia Literature"* is an analytical and historical study of the basic trends of Odia literature. The evolution of Odia literature and its major trends are explained and critically evaluated in this work.

Chittaranjan was affectionately called as Chitta Bhai by all in Odisha. In Odisha he has thousands of followers and admirers who express unconditional respect and love for him. One of his ardent followers Bhagyadhar Sahu has brought out some volumes on Chittaranjan taking articles from cross-section of intellectuals from Odisha on Chittaranjan. So far, he has brought out six volumes under the title *Parārtha Pathik* (Unselfish Traveler)

Before his eightieth birth anniversary a commemorative volume was prepared and published under the editorship of Prof. Gourang Charan Dash. The volume consists very illuminating articles on the various aspects of Chittaranjan's contribution. On the eve of his birth centenary in 2023 more than one hundred on-line meetings were being organized by his followers starting from his 99th birth anniversary. The talks are also compiled and sofar, two volumes are published. These volumes are named $\bar{A}u$ Eka $Sak\bar{a}l$ (Again A Dawn). Some other volumes may come out in future as it is going on.

Chittaranjan was a public intellectual of his time and one of the illustrious writers of Odisha. He has enriched Odia literature in many ways by his unparallel contribution. He was quite popular for his articulate non-fictional writing and oratory. He combines creativity and erudition. In the true sense of the term, he is a writer extraordinary.

Shreeram Chandra Dash: A Multifaceted Genius

Niranjan Barik

Professor (Dr.) Shreeram Chandra Dash is a legendary iconic personality of Odisha who was a professor, a writer, an orator, a columnist, a lawyer, a social leader, but extraordinarily superlative in true sense of the term in each and every field that he did tread ! Encyclopaedic in knowledge, he has rightly been described as a colossus, a giant among the intellectuals of the country in contemporary India. Prof. Dash was born in colonial India (pre-independent India) on 17th November 1918 in a remote village of present day Odisha named Bira Narasimhapur in the Balikuda block of Jagatsinghpur district. His father, Hadibandhu Dash and mother Bimala Devi were blessed to nurture this extraordinary wonder child.

The village Bira Narasimhapur did not have a formal school, even an equivalent of a play school or Nursery, what to speak of a primary one, by the time he was growing up in his school going age. His ancestors were rāj-purohits (priests serving royals) and therefore, his father was well-rooted in Sanskrit but not exposed to the so-called modern or western education.

But he was interested that his son Shreeram should have sahib education. With the initiative of his father a pānthasālā was started in front of their house and the teacher there or any pundit /scholar coming across this child lost no time to discover and recognise that child was of exceptional talent and must be a prodigy.

Shreeram's genius was spotted by a school sub-inspector, Kishori Charan Das visiting the Ochinda Lower Primary School ,his first formal school, and asked the teachers to take him for the entrance exam for scholarship at his Manijanga (Office of the School Sub-Inspector), near Tirtol. One student from each Lower Primary School was to be selected. Hearing this teachers prepared Shreeram for the scholarship examination. The lure was rupees three as scholarship per month availing which one will be waived off tuition fees. Shreeram naturally was selected as the best one from the school for the 1927 scholarship examination.

He took another examination at Cuttack in December 1931. Odisha was still five years away to become a separate state. The DPI (Director of Public Instructions of Bihar-Odisha) was holding this examination among minor school students in a centre in each district. To come to Cuttack, Shreeram had again to walk miles to catch a bus at Jagatsinghpur, the nearest bus station. It was the first bus ride for the young fellow. Again at Cuttack for the first time Sreeram saw train and the railway station as well as exposed to electricity light. He describes in his life history how he was enthralled to see the electric bulbs on lamp posts emitting soothing light ,on the banks of Kathajodi in the early morning when he went for bath and other routine to the river. He had then never imagined that he would own a house in Cuttack, he says with reference to his house in Kukuriapada of Cuttack city, which became a palace and paradise for him.

He got stipend after having passed the ME examinations and entered into Ravenshaw Collegiate School in 1932 as a student of Class VIII to continue up to 1936 May for four years. He did Odiyas proud by standing first in the Entrance Examination in 1935 in the entire Orissa-Bihar region which would take him to Ravenshaw College hereafter.

While still a student he wrote his first essay entitled 'Delhi Jātrā' in 1939.This was published in an important Odia monthly NabaBharata edited by Nilakantha Dash. Published in two parts, this article, describes his participation in the All India Debate Competition organized by Anglo-Arabic College (later Jamia Millia) of Delhi. He came in contact with Subhas Chandra Bose and participated in the Students Conference at Cuttack. But as he was then a career-minded student hailing from a poor background and supported by government scholarships his pecuniary conditions did not permit him to participate in the Ravenshaw College Students` strike in 1939 for which some student leaders bore grudge against him, though he had publicly explained his condition.

In his graduation stage, he had Economics honours and History (Pass) and he was well appreciated by his teachers like Artta Ballabh Mohanty, Ratnakar Pati, Nishikanta Sanyal, Ghanashyam Das, Nirmal Banerjee, Suresh Chandra Bardhan, Narayan Mohan De and Bipin Bihari Ray etc.

In 1940 he went to Patna College for his post-graduate course in Economics as in Ravenshaw College there was no M.A. class in Economics then. In Patna, he was associated with Young Men's Association (Debate branch) and there his eloquence as a speaker in English won him profuse appreciation. He was the president of the Chānakya Society which was an Economics-Association. After the completion of his M.A. course in Patna in 1942, he came to Cuttack and worked at Nababharat office for some months and then he was posted as an Inspector Accountant in the Income Tax Department. Later in 1943 he was posted as Supply Supervisor and continued till 1945 when he was posted as a lecturer in Economics at Ravenshaw College.

He was transferred from Cuttack to Puri, Balasore, and Jeypore, as it is said ,due to the pressure of H.K.Mahatab who had almost ordered his dismissal from service on grounds which Shreeram had given explanation to be false and concocted. However it was cancelled by Nabakrushna Chaudhury in 1951. Later in the 1950s, Mahatab had a deep appreciation for Shreeram Babu's scholarship and he even asked him to write essays in 'Jhankāra' (Odia monthly magazine). He came to Ravenshaw College again in 1952 but he got permission for higher study and research and went to the Free University of West Germany in December 1953. He remained there for sixteen months and completed his Doctorate on The Constitution of India: A Comparative Study and found four months from September to December of 1954 to visit some European countries. Even he also participated in the International University Teachers Conference held at Vienna on 10th September 1954 representing Utkal University.

Sreeram Babu completed his doctoral research in a record time of fourteen months. During this period he also had to complete the language course in Deutsch apart from his regular research work. Interestingly he typed his thesis as he could not afford to the cost i.e. 5000 marks demanded by the typist for typing out the thesis. He bought a typewriter in East Berlin for 300 marks and typed the whole thesis by himself working hard, twenty hours a day. He finished it in less than a month and submitted the thesis in September. These copies in German language were to be kept in the Library. Otherwise his two copies of the thesis were in English submitted to Examiners. On December 10, 1954 he was examined for the degree of D.Phil. The degree required a language test in Latin. Prof Dash was allowed to appear for an examination in Sanskrit .

As regards the language test in Sanskrit, Shreeram's story goes like this. After knowing from his guide that his thesis had been approved by the examiners, Shreeram was asked to meet the Dean for scheduling the viva voce date .Dean was History Professor Horshefeld. He had taught Shreeram for a semester in his class and had good impression of Shreeram as a bright student who had attended all his classes without missing a single one. But when Shreeram saw him, he put before Shreeram a Himalayan hurdle. Dean asked Shreeram if he was reading Latin. If he had not finished it he would not be able to take the Viva. Shreeram had Sanskrit for six years upto I.A. class. The guide advised him to plead with the Dean to allow him to take the viva in Sanskrit as it was as much a classical / an old language as Latin, Arabic or Hibru. The Senate allowed him, thanks to his Guide's efforts, to take the viva in Sanskrit. There are Sanskrit Departments in all the Universities in Germany and Free University also had one. Shreeram was asked to go to a Sanskrit professor in the University for taking examination in Sanskrit .The Professor took the examination and was impressed with his Sanskrit knowledge and chaste pronunciation. Shreeram had recited *slokas* from the *Bhagbat Gitā*. He had with him Achārya Harihar Dash's edited Geetā book written in Odiya and it was his regular habit to read a paragraph in the morning. His Sanskrit recitation from Gitā was also recorded. The Sanskrit Professor who was taking the examination took that odiya version Gitā from Shreeram and deposited in the Library. Shreeram was astonished to find that, the Library of Free University also had an Odia section.

Shreeram Dash came back to India and was posted at Ravenshaw College in 1955. While he was in Ravenshaw in 1958 Political Science as a separate subject in Hons and Pass was opened and for that, he had a great contribution. In 1962 he was posted as Reader in Political Science and joined Utkal University in 1963. While he was in Ravenshaw he had passed Law in first class as a private student in 1961.

Dr. Dash was the President of the All India Political Science Association in 1970 and 1972. He was the General Secretary of that Association in Pune in 1957. In 1966 on 28th January there was a Youth leadership training Camp in the Department of Political Science organized under the auspices of UGC at Utkal University campus. Professor Dash used that occasion which was largely attended by the Political Science teachers and arranged on 30th January, the first All Odisha Political Science Conference which was a grand success. Dr. Dash had several testing phases in his life. But he was fearless to face any adverse situation. When he lost his job in

1975 he entered into the legal profession and had great fame in that line also.

His eminence in the field of Political Science in India was recognised when he was elected General Secretary and Treasurer of Indian Political Science Association in 1957 at Pune and he organised the Annual conference of the Association at Ujjain in 1958, at Jaipur in 1959 and at Patna in 1960 .He was the Editor of the Indian Journal of Political Science in 1964, 1965, and 1966 .He became the Vice-President of the Association in 1969 and was elected as President of the Association in 1970, a seminal honour for any Political Scientist of the country .The Annual Conference of the Association under his Presidency was held in Calcutta in 1972 which was inaugurated by Smt. Indira Gandhi the then Prime Minister.

He was an eloquent speaker and a powerful writer.As Professor Satyanarayan Rath, his second in command in the Political Science Department of Utkal University would testify, "A large number of articles were published by him in different journals, magazines, and newspapers. He had powerful essays in *'Sahakāra'* from 1941, in *'Nababhārata'* from 1939, *'Satyabādi News'*, *'Dagar'* and *'Jhankāra'* from 1952. His books in English include The *Consitution of India : A Comparative Study*(1968), *Gopabandhu Das*(1976), Orissa(1970), *'Gopabandhu : A Biography'* (1964), *Problems of Higher Education* (1976), *Comparison of the Fundamental Features of the Constitution of India* (with those of the United States, Weimar Germany and West German Federal Republic(1954)), *States of our Union : Orissa* (1978)." His autobiography *Mo AkuhāKāhāṇi* is a great contribution to Odishan Studiess.

His book entitled *Europare Mo Anubhuti* (My Europe Journey) was also famous and for this, he got Odisha Sahitya Academy Award. His first book in Odia was *Mo Desha* published in 1948 which presented the administrative history of India from 1765 to 1947. His outstanding novel was *Real Romance*. According to some ,he has published 42 books in English and Odiya .At one time his books on Civics and Political Science were used as text books from M.E. Schools upto the post-graduate stage .

For his right mentoring and encouragement, during his Professorship, the Department of Political Science of Utkal produced a large number of All India Service officers, who in course of time ordained the posts of Chief Secretary, Director General of Police in several states and Secretary to Government of India. To the immediate memory of this writer, some contemporaries come to mind in Civil Service, mentored by him as R.N.Das, Sujogya Mishra, Devdas Chhotray, Ajit Kumar Tripathy, Bijaya Patnaik, Mrutunjaya Sarangi ,Ramesh Chandra Mishra in IAS, Santosh ku Sahu, Jayanta Hota in Indian Revenue Service, Kharavela Swain (Indian Railways Accounts Service and later thrice MP of Lok Sabha) Gagan Mohan Tripathy in Indian Railways Traffic Service. Innumerable students of Political Science joined Orissa Administrative Service and Banking as officers and have been quite vocal about Prof. Dash's inspiration, his personal *'mārga darshan'*, encouragement and sustained tips for competitive examinations.

Though a man of political philosophy who dealt with Socrates to Marx, he was aware of the importance of administration, especially in a developing society as ours and the need of the Weberian Bureaucracy .Therefore he mentored students to write civil service examination. In his prime of youth ,Shreeram had missed the bus. He had been qualified and selected for IAS in the Emergency Recruitment ,but a negative report from the Odisha government or its Vigilance Department stood on the way, the hurdle of which he could not surmount inspite of his running from pillar to post and even trying to see Patel, the Home Minister. It is also one of the reasons that he wanted to see his students in large numbers joining the crucial service and adorn positions in different parts of India .

But he was extremely self-respecting and very blunt too in his words that landed him in trouble at various stages in his life. After having an illustrious teaching career as the Professor and Head of the Department of the Post-Graduate Department of Political Science in Utkal University he was unceremoniously handed over a letter of Compulsory Retirement on 23rd Dec 1975 by the Chancellor. The whole country was reeling under the authoritarian rule at that time in view of the Internal Emergency declared by Mrs. Gandhi. He started practising Law after leaving the University. It is said that he had been offered a position of Professorship at Bhagalpur University, but he chose the profession of law and serve the people here in safeguarding their rights.

Bipin Behari Rath, an eminent lawyer and a Gandhian writes : "Within no time he established him to the top in the profession and in recognition of which he was declared a Senior Advocate by the High court of Odisha, even without having the usual length of practice for being considered for such distinction as per convention. His mastery over constitution law ,services and education matters ,rules and regulations among others brought unexpected results to the clients. As a spell binder ,he had a great demand in every nook and corner of the State and was known to be a crowd puller ,his talents in the legal profession attracted clients from all over the State and kept him ever busy in the profession till the last ."

B. L. Hansaria, former Chief Justice of Odisha and later a Judge in the Supreme Court of India had to say the following about Shreeram Babu :

"*Dr. Dash was basically an educationist, I of course knew him as an advocate. Having been an educationalist, he however, used to appear in those cases whose subject matter used to be education. On this branch of law, he was in complete command could even say that he was an encyclopaedia. And what is more, he knew about all the relevant statutes, case laws etc. relating to anything to do with education by heart. His memory was so sharp that he would not need to refer to the statute to find put its number or content, nor read the case law to put forward its ratio.*

In one case, we called upon Dr. Dash to assist the court to find out the meaning of the expression, "eminent educationalist". As such a person could be nominated as a member of the managing committee of a school. I thought that no advocate would be in a better position than Dr. Dash to assist the court in this regard. 'Let it be said to the credit of Dr. Dash that he assisted the court exceedingly well, and we adopted all that what was stated by him."

On his demise, *Cuttack Law Times* paid him a fitting tribute in the following words, "*On his death India lost a great political scientist, Orissa lost a great son of the soil, High Court bar lost a senior and a Member glamourously genius, the clients lost a dependable lawyer, the Orissa*

Society lost a social reformer and CLT lost one of its great patrons".

Thus Prof. Dash coming from the Academia soon illuminated another world, and earned the approbation of both the clients and judges as a competent legal luminary.

Finally his rendezvous was with real politics. The essay on Dr. Dash will not be complete if we don't take account of his forays into the muddy waters of politics in an electoral fray in the fag end of the trajectory of his chequered life. The Internal Emergency declared in 1975 was lifted in 1977 and elections to Lok Sabha were held wherein the ruling Congress party was routed. The elections to the State Assembly followed thereafter and Prof. Das decided to contest the elections on the ticket of a newly formed political party 'Utkal Janata'. He fought from Balikuda, his home constituency and his election symbol was 'Elephant'.

His family members and students campaigned for him with zeal and sincerity. His old octogenarian father Hadibandhu Dash (81), was quite joyous to campaign for him. 'I fought from our home constituency because I thought it would be convenient for my father to join in, writes Prof. Dash. *"He loved to go around the villages to canvas for me. When I offered him a lift on my car, he would politely refuse, because my father loved to cover the distances on foot."*

Because Prof. Dash was a household name and a very popular orator, people thronged his meetings in large numbers to listen to his speeches. Going by the attendance and public response to his meetings, compared to those of his rivals, it would seem that Dash was going to win hands down. But that did not happen. There was a huge electoral swing in favour of the Janata Party all over the country and Balikuda was no exception. Umesh Swain from that party won the Balikuda seat by polling 28,736 votes. His nearest rival Basudev Mahapatra from Congress Party bagged 19,727 votes and to the surprise of many Prof. Dash got a meager 2,458 votes.

It was truly a frustrating experience for Professor Dash who put all his resources into this election. He describes his feelings after the defeat in the following words, "I was very confident from my childhood because I fared exceedingly well in every examination I sat for. I used to speak very well too, which gave me a feeling that I would be able to influence my voters with my thoughts and ideas..... But the elections proved that I was grossly mistaken."

Coming from a Professor of Political Science of his stature and experience, his other statement was very profound and poignant. He said, "I found out during my election campaign that no real election is being conducted here. Votes are merely being bought and sold like any other commodity in the market..... I realised during this time that, as a teacher of Political Science, I have not told my students the whole truth about the elections." Was he vindicating Machiavelli, the Italian realist of 13th Century when he said," For a man who wants to make a profession of good in all regards must come to ruin among so many who are not good."?

Dr. Mahatab who understood Professor Dash quite late, made a profound statement, *"Sreeram babu will remain eternally a member of the opposition party. Who ever may form the Government, he will criticise them."* Shreeram Babu was a victim of jealousy and misunderstanding though he was always empathetic to his friends and foes alike. He held Pandit Nilakantha Dash, Dr. Pranakrushna Parija and Godabarish Mishra as his ideals. Making compromise with injustice was not in his blood. Professor Dash never flattered anybody for self-interest, rather always called a spade a spade. Governments never gave him the recognition and the award that his exceptional merit and democratic spirit so well deserved.

Professor Ashok Acharay, an illustrious scholar and Professor of Political Science, Delhi University pays tribute to Dr. Dash in glowing terms :

"Professor Dash, inspite of the few detractors he had, came across to me as a very generous person who would offer advice or help to anyone who went to him.Everyone knows how he has shaped many many student's careers and encouraged generations of students to successfully write the Civil Services examinations. But his biggest achievement lay in building up the popularity of Political Science as a discipline and his scholarly contribution to studies in comparative constitutionalism."

Professor Dash, a liberal democrat was not a narrow nationalist. He harmonised nationalism and internationalism in his ideas. In fact he was a Cosmopolitan thinker, as somebody who felt like a global citizen as evident in his IPSA Journal 1960 paper which Professor Acharay quotes to emphasise the political philosophy of Professor Dash and branding his nationalism as sublimated nationalism :

"India while subscribing to democracy, harps on the dignity of the individual and this humanism has enriched the dignity of the individual and this humanism has enriched the character and content of her democratic institutions. She has also sublimated her nationalism to the cause of

internationalism which is another name for humanism or cosmopolitanism and this has been possible merely because of her attachment to the individual who irrespective of his place of residence and natal and natural status ,faces common problems of life all over the world." (S. C. Dash, 1960).

Professor Harihar Das, former Vice-Chancellor of Berhampur University and another eminent scholar of Political Science vindicates the feelings of many others as he says : *"People like Prof S.C. Dash will remain immortal even after their mundane remains are consigned to flames.Such great people shall never remain die in the true sense of the term, because their memory remains in the heart of the people and provides inspiration to the society and the coming generations to be truth seekers and truth speakers and fight against injustices, oppression, falsehood and exploitation of all kinds"*. (Harihar Das)

I had the privilege of being his direct student at the PG level in Vani Vihar, Utkal University. His immaculate way of teaching is unparallel having been in academia for long and being exposed to the professors and speakers of many countries. With a photographic memory with statistics on his lips, words under command and the canvas of cognition being as large as the universe, the charismatic person was a much sought after speaker in the nook and corner of Odisha. The mention that a meeting will be graced by Prof Dash was enough to add value to the meeting and attract large number of people to his audience. He took the trouble of travelling far and wide in Odisha to educate the public through his lecture and through his brilliant oratory and mesmerising talk on political issues in a Nehruvian way. Thus he took strains till his last days to travel even to distant places in a failing health to politically socialise people face-to-face on issues ranging from local to global. As a critical thinker he wanted to sensitise people and raise debates through his columns in the widely circulated dailies of Odisha as the Samaj, Prajatantra and in later part the Sambad.

A great mind, a great soul, a rare personality of wit, wisdom and humor to have set an example of human excellence while coming from adversarial circumstances, trying conditions and humble background, to make us wonder if such a prodigy was ever born and walked on the soil of Odisha ! it is said that only a few people have the mettle to change mundane into extraordinary and make sure their names go into books for posterity to remember and Dr. Dash was one of those privileged few. Political Science is not only the science of 'what is', but what it 'ought to be'. Professor Dash pursued the latter, his route being through Gandhi and Constitutionalism, if I am not wrong ! A physician diagnoses a disease and prescribes a cure, but a patient may not be healed for many factors while he or she succeeds in similar cases. Dr. Dash as a social scientist diagnosed the ills of society, raised alarms, and prescribed remedial measures but it is for the people to follow his prescription. He continuously reminded us the importance of ours being political animals and that the price of our liberty being eternal vigilance.

REFERENCES :

1. Dr Shreeram Chandra Dash, *Mo Akuhā Kāhāni*, Cuttack Students' Store, 4th Edn, 2023.
2. Kailash Chandra Dash, *Dr. Sriram Chandra Dash- A Tribute.*

Professor Baidyanath Misra:
A Great Teacher and Institution Builder
(1920 – 2019)

Rabi N. Patra

If Odisha has a pride of place in the Indian academia, it is because of the contributions made by a number of luminaries of the State to their respective domains. A prominent name among these intellectuals of pan-India recognition is Professor Baidyanath Misra. Baidyanath Misra was born on 22 November 1920 in Dibyasinghpur Sasan of Bolagarh block in Khordha district (erstwhile Puri district). His parents were Mahadeb Misra, an orthodox Brāhmin struggling very hard to fend for his family with the meagre income of his priestly activities, and Manika Debi. An early loss of his father at age 3-4 years was traumatic and increased his problems of inadequate child care, worsened the family's penury and augmented the uncertainty of continuity of studies. However, he overcame all stress and adversity by his exemplary punctuality, hard work, sharp intelligence and strong will power.

Family

On 10th March 1950, he married Basanti Misra, a

master's holder choosing to remain a homemaker. The couple had a very harmonious life and have four children, a daughter, Bijayalaxmi, who is married to Ajatsatru Tripathy, an ophthalmologist; and three sons, Basant, who is the Chief of Surgery and the Chairman of Neurosurgery at Hinduja Hospitals, Mumbai; Jayant, who is Director and Chief Operating Officer of Indian Metals and Ferro Alloys; and Sukant, who is Dean and Vice-Provost at Texas Technical University. The son-in-law and the three sons have made their marks in their respective fields.

Education

Prof. Misra completed Class-V in his village school and Class-VII in Bolagarh Minor School. With the patronage of the great visionary and veteran leader Dr. Harekrushna Mahatab, he moved to Agarpada High School in far off Balasore district where he successfully passed the Matriculation examination in the First Division in 1942, a rare achievement in those days. He passed his B.A. from the prestigious Ravenshaw College (now University) securing the First Class First position in Economics Honours of Utkal University in 1946. He pursued M. A. Economics studies in Allahabad University with a Government of Orissa scholarship and topped in both Economics and the faculty of Arts in the University. He was awarded two gold medals by the University for his astounding performance and received the medals from Sarojini Naidu, then Governor of the United Provinces and Chancellor of the University, in the Convocation with the humoristic appreciation *'the shortest and the brightest of all'*.

He obtained another master's degree (A.M.) in Economics in 1953 from Wharton School of Finance of

Pennsylvania University, Philadelphia studying there on two scholarships - Fulbright and Smith-Mundt Scholarships - of America for one year (1952-53), and was very close to his teacher Simon Kuznets there who later won the SverigesRiksbank Prize in Economic Sciences in Memory of Alfred Nobel in 1971. Based on his performance at the A.M. examination at Wharton, he was selected to write his Ph. D. thesis straightaway without any course work which he couldnot do because he had no money to sustain for two years. He also completed a three-month summer course at the London School of Economics. After returning to Odisha, he did his Ph. D. on the theme 'Fiscal Policy in the Context of Planning: An Analysis of Keynesian Economics in Relation to Economic Development' under the supervision of his teacher Prof. Sadashiv Mishra and was awarded Ph.D. Degree in Economics by Utkal University in 1963. His Ph.D. thesis was published by The World Press, Calcutta (1966) and remains a seminal contribution in the field of Public Finance.

Stint in Politics and Journalism

Because of his closeness to staunch Congressmen like Harekrushna Mahatab, Biren Mitra, Nilamani Routray, and a great socialist leader Nabakrushna Choudhury and others, Baidyanath Misra was involved in politics right from his student days and wanted to be a politician even on his return from Allahabad when he was not very much sure about his future livelihood. On one occasion, Mahatab babu cautioned him that he wouldn't succeed in politics as he was very conscientious and instead advised him to take up the job of Editor of 'The Eastern Times', the English daily which he wanted to publish. It is another story that he was made the Associate Editor and worked in that capacity unwillingly with all sincerity for some time to earn a living but decided to leave the job and left it too. Gradually, he developed distaste and reservations towards active politics and declined the offer to contest the Bolagarh-Begunia M.L.A. seat in 1980. However, he was convinced by the then Chief Minister of Orissa Sri Janaki Ballabh Patnaik to contest the 1985 by-election from Khurda as the Congress candidate to which he agreed, contested and suffered defeat from Sri Prasanna Patashani who, it is learnt, accompanied him to help him file nomination papers but himself filed as an independent. As the results of his defeat by about 3000 votes were being announced, Prof. Bhabani Prasad Dash, one of his close associates, reached his house and congratulated him on his defeat as did his teacher Prof. Sadasiv Mishra telephonically little later. In fact, contesting Khurda by-election was the biggest mistake in his life and it was a good thing that he lost the election. It is worth noting that Prof. Misra remained a strong Congress supporter and a close confidant of a highly learned veteran Congressman Sri Janaki Ballav Patnaik and loyal to Mahatab babu throughout his life. During the end years of his life, Prof. Misra became very critical of contemporary corrupt and power hungry politicians in all political parties.

A Titanic Teacher-Researcher

Prof. Misra had a strong passion for reading and his dissatisfaction with politics as well as journalism instilled in his mind the idea of taking up a teaching job. While working with The Eastern Times he applied to the Orissa Public Service Commission for the post of Lecturer in Economics, topped the merit list and joined Ravenshaw College in 1949. He continued at Ravenshaw till 1961 with a one year leave for studying in America and London. From Ravenshaw he moved to the Orissa University of Agriculture and Technology (OUAT) as Professor of Agricultural Economics in 1961 and little later as Dean of Faculty of Agriculture of the University and the Director of Farm Management Studies, Orissa under the Economics and Statistics Department of Government of India. He served Utkal University as Visiting Professor and Head of the Department of Analytical and Applied Economics (A&A Economics) during 1977-1981 and, while working there, was appointed as the Vice-Chancellor (VC) of OUAT, a position he held from 1981 to 1985. He had a brilliant teaching career spanning over three decades (1949-1981).

Prof. Misra's appointment in Utkal University has become a part of the lore at Vani Vihar. Once he was addressing the annual conference of the Eastern Geographical Society at Vani Vihar as the chief speaker with Prof. Goutam Mathur, VC of the University as the chief guest.While listening to Prof. Misra's speech, the VC was so impressed that he was suddenly reminded of having reviewed Prof. Misra's epoch-making book *'Capitalism, Socialism and Planning'*. Recognising the great author in the speaker, he literally offered in platter Professorship at the department of A and A Economics, Utkal University to Prof. Misra. What followed has been a glorious era in the annals of the department.

Prof. Misra enjoyed two things in life- reading and teaching and is greatly adored for his scholarship, erudition and excellent teaching abilities. He is honoured for his skill in explaining complex themes in a lucid style and his ability to convey intricate economic issues in simple small sentences. His deliberations in seminars and debates at Ravenshaw with him on one side taking a socialistic stand and Prof. K.M.Patnaik on the other with a capitalistic bent were something students, scholars and teachers of Economics could relish for life. He was an eloquent public speaker who could keep his audience engaged and spell bound for a long time.

He has successfully guided a record number of 25 Ph.D. Scholars in Agricultural Economics and Economics at OUAT and Utkal University who have established themselves in the society.

Architect of Institutions

Professor Baidyanath Misra was a visionary and institution-builder with a perfect understanding of the role of education and research in human capital formation in shaping and augmenting economic behaviour and development. He played an important role in establishing 'Odisha Economic Association' way back in 1968 and nurturing it for over five decades. He was the founder secretary of the Association and became its President in 1971. The Association provides a platform to the teachers and students of economics to discuss contemporary economic issues, stimulate research and publish papers. It publishes a half yearly peer reviewed UGC Care listed journal *'Odisha Economic journal'* of which Prof. Misra was the editor for four decades (1978-2017).

As Professor and Head of the Department of A&A Economics, Utkal University during 1977-1981, he was instrumental in instituting two academic chairs, funded by the Reserve Bank of India and the State Bank of India, and operationalising the empirical research firmament in Economics. He also enlivened the Dr. Sadasiv Lecture Series in the Department and invited learned scholars like Prof. VKRV Rao, Prof. Rajkrishna, and Prof. Raja J Chelliah for delivering lectures on important topics which helped igniting the minds of young students.

As the Vice-Chancellor, Prof. Misra wanted to provide leading-edge education in research, extension and outreach in agriculture and allied sciences in India, and envisioned that OUAT should meet the bulk need of the trained manpower of the State in agriculture and allied sectors.With active support from Government of Orissa and ICAR, he could help establish four collegesduring the very first year of his tenure to realize this objective. These are: the College of Engineering and Technology (CET), and the College of Home Science(CHS) both in the OUAT campus itself, the College of Agriculture (CoA) at Chipilima, Sambalpur, and the College of Fisheries (CoF) at Rangeilunda, Ganjam. Through CET, he wished to advance knowledge in major paradigms of technology, create a culture of research and innovation among the budding engineers, promote entrepreneurship development, and generating a pool of professional technocrats; and through the CHS he wanted to build skilled manpower in the fields of nutrition and food science, communication management, consumer science, textile and apparel designing, and family resource management. The broad objectives behind establishingCoA were enhancing sustainable use of agricultural resources, soil and water conservation and management, and plant breeding. He was keen about generating technical man power and improved technology in fisheries sector, promotion of rural fisheries.

Through his innovative ideas, creative efforts and hard work Prof. Misra could take OUAT to the status of a Premier Farm University in India.

His contribution to establishing in 1988, the Nabakrushna Choudhury Centre for Development Studies (NCDS), Bhubaneswar jointly funded by the Indian Council of Social Science Research (ICSSR), Government of India, and the Government of Odishawhich laid a solid foundation for promoting fundamental inter-disciplinary research in the State. He served NCDS as the founder Director, later as Chairman-cum-Director, project advisor, and played a pivotal role in its upbringing, growth and development. His efforts and success in leading and directing research at the Centre by creating academic chairs funded by NALCO, TISCO, OMC, MCL, IDC and other sources bear testimony to his creative thinking, vision and action.

Professor Misra shouldered key responsibilities in rejuvenating various institutions and instilling outcome orientation in them such as Secretary of Odisha State Welfare Board, Deputy-Chairman of Odisha State Planning Board, Chairman of Odisha's First State Finance Commission, and member of the panel of economists of the Planning Commission of India and the Odisha Pay Commission.In all these roles, he performed with impeccable acumen and helped promote good governance. He was also a member of the Banking Services Recruitment Board for the eastern region for some time. His dedicated and committed involvement in the deliberations and in drafting Committee reports were simply extraordinary as was his assertive views in the report of the First State Finance Commission pressing for reforms for improving the State Finances which are well appreciated in academic and policy circles.

With the help from a few of his friends, he established the 'Nandighosh', a cultural club at Bolagarh and spearheaded a cultural revolution in the region as its founder president. He also did a commendable job as Chairman of 'Jan Sikhyā Sansthān', a cultural organisation at Angul, in promoting literacy, preserving cultural heritage thereby accelerating local development. As Secretary, Orissa Government College Teachers Association and Secretary of Ravenshaw Old Boys' Association, he made theorganisationslively through debate, deliberations and resolution.

Publications

Professor Baidyanath Misra's writings are well acknowledged by the readers. He has authored about three dozen books in both English and Odia languages covering various fields mostly on Development Economics, Polity and Society; Text Books for B.A. and M.A. classes; 60 Research Papers, 10 Research Reports and so on. He was also an essayist in several leading Odia journals and a columnist in newspapers. He regularly wrote thought provoking articles in Odia magazines like 'Jhankara', 'NabaJibana', and 'Paurusa' and in Odia newspapers such as 'The Samaja', 'The Prajatantra', and 'the Pragatibadi'. He had a unique model of presenting issues affecting the contemporary society-economy-politywhich bear testimony to how an economist can effectively communicate with the common men.Some of the books written by him are:

English

- *Economic Profile of India* (APH)
- *Economics of Public Finance* (MacMillan)

- *Capitalism, Socialism and Planning* (Oxford & IBH)
- Fiscal Policy in the Context of Planning: *An Analysis of Keynesian Economics in Relation to Economic Development* (The World Press)
- *Political Economy of Development* (Ajanta)
- *Sustainable Development Administration* (Saujanya Books)
- *Pursuit of Destiny* (Autobiography) (Har-Anand)

Odia
- *Ādhunika Sabhyatāra Jantranā*
- *Anucintā*
- *Punjibāda, Sāmyabāda, O Gāndhibāda*
- *Rāmarājya re Asānti*
- *Rājanitira Sukha-dukha*
- *Smruti-tirtha*
- *Samāja O Sabhyatā*
- *Sāmājika Mulyabodha*

Awards, Honours and Recognition

Professor Baidyanath Misra received numerous awards and honours. For his masterly work '*Ādhunika Sabhyatāra Jantraṇā*' and contributions to Odia literature, he was conferred the Odisha Sahitya Academy Award in 1996. The Orissa University of Agriculture and Technology conferred on him the Degree of Doctor of Science (Honoris Causa) in 2009 for his valued contributions to the field of technical education. He received the Think Odisha Leadership Award in 2010, jointly with the AICTE Chairman and the Director of IIT Kharagpur, Dr. Damodar Acharya, from the Chief Minister of Odisha, Sri Naveen Patnaik for having made path-breaking contributions in the field of education.

The KIIT deemed-to-be University honoured him by awarding the Degree of Doctor of Letters (Honoris Causa) in 2012 for being an outstanding economist and an excellent academician. Prof. Misra was felicitated by the Hon'ble Governor of Odisha, His Highness S. C. Jamir at the 49th Annual Conference 2017 of the Orissa Economics Association organised by Rama Devi Women's University. In addition to these, The PrajatantraVishub Milan award and the Nandighosh award were also conferred on Prof. Misra.

The Odisha Economic Association organises an Annual Lecture on his birthday in November every year since 2009 in fond memory of his immense contributions to the Association and the Post-Graduate Department of Economics, Ravenshaw University awards the Professor Baidyanath Misra Gold Medal to the Student having held the First Class First position in M.A. Economics Examinations of the University every year.

His eldest son and a noted neurosurgeon, Dr. Basant Kumar Misra has started the Baidyanath Neurosurgery Charitable Trust, in his honour to fund travelling fellowships of youngneurosurgeons (below 40 years) from both government and private sectors, and of senior neurosurgeons from only the public sector, seeking advanced training abroad.

Nonagenarian Youth

Professor Baidyanath Misra was somebody who started with nothing, struggled hard to pursue studies, never neglected any assignment, had a passion to ensure that none is inconvenienced due to him, and never left anything halfway in his life. A strong believer in the principle and practice of *'work is worship'*,Prof. Misra spent most of his time in reading and writing even while he was sitting at his ailing wife's bed side at a ripe age. *Pen and books are mightier than everything else* remained the basic philosophy of his life. He died old by age at 99 but young at mind and heart. He was a successful, complete man, a public figure known for his commitment, sincerity, punctuality, honesty and self esteem.Professor Baidyanath Misra's life remains a testament to the idea that *one's destiny is what one is passionate about.*

REFERENCES :
1. Misra, B. (2013). *Pursuit of Destiny* (Autobiography). Har-Anand Publications Pvt Ltd, New Delhi.
2. Discussions with Prof. Bhabani Prasad Dash, a close associate of Prof. Misra.
3. Stories told and narrations of incidents by Prof. Misra to the author during 1998-2019.

Prof. Radhanath Rath: The Man & The Image
(1920-2014)

Udaynath Das | Sayantani Behura

Prof. Radhanath Rath was an illustrious personality of modern India, who distinguished himself as a pioneering researcher and professor of psychology in our country. As an educationist, researcher and literateur unmatched by many of his contemporaries, he earned laurels for his state and the country from international circles of excellence in education. His tall erect frame, bald pate, gold-rimmed glasses and intellectual exuberance very well fitted into the image of a distinguished professor. A nationally and internationally renowned professor of Psychology, Prof. Radhanath Rath left for his heavenly abode on 29''' September, 2014 at the age of 96 at his residence in Cuttack, Odisha leaving behind a fully blossomed family and a host of students and ardent followers of his philosophy towards life.

Hailing from Talarampalli, a small village from Ganjam District of Odisha, Prof. Rath studied in Patna University for his Masters Degree in Philosophy in 1943 and took up the position of a Lecturer in Philosophy in Ravenshaw College in 1944. As in those days

Psychology was taught as a separate subject only in Calcutta University, he availed leave for four months and joined as an external student in the Psychology Department of Calcutta University. He attended all classes in Psychology under the guidance of scholarly and renowned teachers like Dr. Girindra Sekhar Bose as the Head of the Department. Following the World War in 1945, when Indian students started going to British Universities, Prof. Rath wrote a letter to the Head of the Department of Psychology, London University requesting for opportunity to pursue his studies, and was successful in securing a seat for himself. The UPSC, recognizing his merit, sent him on a scholarship to London. At that time, even an MA degree from the Indian universities was not considered equivalent to a BA degree, from the London University. Driven by his extraordinary intellect and passion for Psychology, he qualified in an examination of the London University meant for doing Doctoral research, and was admitted for Ph.D. in Psychology. He completed his Ph.D. in Experimental Psychology from the London University in 1949 under the supervision of Sir Cyril Burt, an intelligence theorist, who is even now known to researchers in Psychology all across the globe.

Following his return from London in 1949, he dreamt of starting a separate Psychology Department in Ravenshaw College much to the objections of several Heads of Humanities Division. And his vision materialized when an Honours course in Psychology was created in Odisha in Ravenshaw College (now Ravenshaw University) in 1953 followed by the creation of a P. G. Department of Psychology in 1958 after obtaining the approval of visiting team of the UGC. The opposition from and jealousy of many of his contemporaries did not deter him and he relentlessly pursued his vision with a very basic conviction "People are jealous of kings, not of beggars."

Prof. Rath did not look back and continued to strengthen and reinforce the discipline harnessing much needed resources from the national bodies such as UGC, NCERT and ICSSR so much so that by the time he retired in 1981, the Department of Psychology at Utkal University held the status of the UGC's first Center of Advanced Study in Psychology in India and first such center in Odisha. His trend-setting effort in founding a separate Department of Psychology created a new and distinct identity for the subject which was earlier a part and parcel of the discipline of Philosophy. His academic and organizational leadership earned him country-wide respect and admiration.

A distinguished academic and institution-builder, he is hailed as the founder of the first Department of Psychology both at the undergraduate and post-graduate level in Odisha. The Post-Graduate Department established by him in Ravenshaw College later moved to Utkal University Campus at Vanivihar, Bhubaneswar. He continued to head the Post-Graduate Department of Psychology at Utkal all through, from its inception till he retired from his formal teaching job in 1981. For his long standing contributions to Psychology he was soon honoured as the ICSSR National Fellow. His relentless pursuit for creating a space for his newly founded Department of Psychology in national and international horizons yielded, highly-acclaimed positive results. The recognition of the Department of Psychology of Utkal University by the UGC as the Center of Advanced Study in Psychology in 1980 constituted his crowning achievement which attracted academics and professors of Psychology from across the world, who regarded the center as a nucleus of research and study on Psychology in India. Professors from UK, USA, USSR, Germany, the Netherlands, Canada, Sweden, Denmark and other countries believed that the discipline of Psychology as pursued at Utkal University represented Indian ethos and thoughts on psychology with the regional-knowledge bases serving to strengthen the Indian psychology. Such was the tone and tenor of the Center that students from the northern and the southern parts of the country rushed to Utkal University in the 80's and 90's to complete their doctoral and post-doctoral research under the supervision of the faculty members who grew to positions of eminence under the leadership of Prof. Rath. When he left Utkal University on his retirement in 1981, the Department of Psychology had 18 teaching staff, 44 senior scholars from different Indian Universities for Ph.D. and D. Litt. degrees, three visiting professors and about 40 non-teaching staff.

Prof Rath's early researches on attitudes towards various socio-cultural, political-economic and national-international issues, inter-caste and inter-group tensions, stereotypes and prejudices prevailing in Indian societies earned him international reputation. His monograph on *'Psycho-Social Problems of Social Change'* published by the Allied Publishers on behalf of A. N. Sinha Institute of Social Studies, Patna (Rath, 1973) deliberated on the consequences of societal changes towards modernity and globalization. By then, the Department of Psychology at the University of Allahabad was vigorously pursuing research on socio-psychological issues under the leadership of Prof. D. Sinha, who was a very close personal friend and a professional colleague of Prof. Rath. For having a distinct identity and also taking cognizance of the expertise of his younger student-colleagues, Prof. Rath oriented the research focus of the department to cognitive, developmental and educational issues. His emphasis on nationally as well as internationally relevant, socio-culturally meaningful and indigenous psychological studies in subsequent research projects from national and international bodies shaped the research focus of the Center of Advanced Study in Psychology at Utkal. A classic and pioneering research on cognitive and academic characteristics of the marginalized children published as a monograph titled *"Cognitive Abilities and School Achievement of Socially Disadvantaged Children in Primary Schools"* by the Allied Publishers in the late seventies (Rath, Dash & Dash, 1979) was a significant research contribution in furthering the Department's research focus on cognitive and educational Psychology. Acknowledging the academic and research excellence of the Department, the UGC granted special assistance in 1972 to develop an Educational Psychology wing in the Department of Psychology, which was later declared as the Department of Special Assistance in 1977, and subsequently as the Center of Advanced Study in Psychology in 1980. A model preschool in the form of a psychological laboratory for Master's students was opened in 1980, emphasizing the importance of early childhood care and education for the disadvantaged children. A journey from research on social issues to the field of cognition with an indigenous tone marked the successive progression of research focus under the leadership of Prof. Rath supported by an excellent faculty trained in the scientific temper of hard-core Psychology and the social relevance of the discipline in the field of applied Psychology. During the post-retirement years, besides writing novels, he practised Psychology by teaching young children and teachers in a pre-school nurtured by him and through social and literary activism on furthering the causes of universalization of elementary education. During these years, he started a movement called *Prāthamika Sikshā Vikās Āndolana* which aimed at reforming and enhancing pedagogy in primary schools. He went on a mission to strengthen elementary education in the State following an integrated developmental approach that called for participation of doctors, teachers, social reformers and administrators. He was able to successfully enrich the quality of teaching-learning climate in more than 300 primary schools of the State. He donated the land and the house of his ancestral village to build a residential school encompassing classes from I to X, which currently has strength of about 500 students.

His visiting professorship assignment at several universities including Concordia University (Canada), Birmingham University (UK) and Malmo University (Sweden) in 70's and 80's brought together the Eastern and the Western thoughts on Psychology, sensitizing Western scholars to the unique parameters of Indian and indigenous Psychology. As early as 1957, he was honored as a member of the India Government visiting team to the USA for a six-month period to study the general western education programme. During his visit, he spent two working days with one of the greatest psychologists of the contemporary era, B. F. Skinner who presented him his book '*Walden Two*' published in 1955 and signed by him. In his personal discussions with Prof. Rath, Carl

Jung, the famous psychoanalytic thinker, expected him to appreciate and carry forward the concept of 'collective unconscious' as he represented Eastern cultural thinking because Jung's concept was at that time not well accepted in the Western, world. Having been recognized by the Indian Government for his outstanding thoughts on social issues and culture, he visited the USSR in 1966 and 1968 as a member of lndo-Russian cultural delegation. In every such visit, Prof. Rath assertively placed the Indian orientation to philosophy and psychology as a much necessary complement to Western views to understand humans and society, and was honoured with the Lenin Gold Medal for his book on Soviet Union.

The multifaceted experiences in national and international circles distinguished him as having an enviable position in his discipline in lndia and he was looked upon as a nurturing and transformational leader by teachers and researchers in psychology for attaining personal, professional and organizational excellence. ln early 1970's, he led Psychology in India as the President of the Psychology Session of the Indian Science Congress and as the President of Indian Association of Applied Psychology, and monitored the spread and the progress of the discipline in the country as the Chairman of the UGC Panel in Psychology. In his own state too he pioneered the universalization of science in everyday life as one of the founders of *Vigyāna Prachāra Samiti* in 1949.

During the retirement years, he pressed into service the experiences gathered from international and national platforms to state level missions. From the university to pre-schools, from the academic settings to government advisory bodies and from hard-core psychology to an applied focus in the world of media and entertainment, he traversed all roads in multifarious ways to leave in the minds of the public the overwhelming influence of psychology in human life. Not only did he lead university teachers as their president for a long span, he also led a mission to enrich the quality of learning experiences of young children in primary schools and pre-schools. As a psychologist and a member of the Board of Secondary Education, Odisha for a long span over one decade and a half, he brought positive changes to the course of secondary education in the state and was instrumental in the nationalization of school textbooks. Not only did he contribute immensely to the course of teaching and research in psychology, he also used his psychological intuitions in shaping the architectural plan of Cuttack as a member of the Cuttack Development Authority for many years. It is not that he studied, professed and preached psychology only in his life and academic circles; he brought Psychology closer to the common man through his articles and writings on psychological issues in Odia newspapers as an invited popular columnist for a long span and also by acting as a member of the state's Film Censor Board to evaluate films on the criteria of human psychological parameters. Known for his social and psychological activism, he advocated all along for human rights and adorned the Chair of Odisha State Child Protection Society until 2010. A many-splendoured personality, he blended in his distinctive and uncommon personal profile, a philosopher, an educationist, a researcher, a writer, a social reformer, an activist and a visionary.

His manifold research and study of Psychology paved the way for generation of scholars to explore new frontiers of the discipline. His original insights on psychology earned him laurels from reputed institutions of the world and he travelled more than 20 countries to deliver lectures, guide research on the subject and teach as a visiting professor. Prof. Rath had said many times that he had the knack of jumping into unknown waters without knowing swimming and deriving satisfaction on arrival at the destinations. Through perseverance and broad-based visions, he relentlessly served the institution and people and shaped their destiny and retired from the university job in 1981 leaving all his colleagues and ardent followers with memories to be proud of. Following his retirement, he whole-heartedly devoted himself, to writing novels as a means for understanding and portraying human mind and characters.

The culture of science and technology in the State of Odisha got a boost, when Prof. Rath organized the Annual meet of' the apex and the most prestigious association of Indian Scientists, the Indian Science Congress in 1962 and then also in 1977 as its Local Secretary, functioning on behalf of the University and the Government. Inspired by his academic and organizational leadership skills, the International Association of Cross-Cultural Psychology organized its annual conference at the Utkal Department of Psychology in 1980 with Prof. Rath leading the Conference as its Chairman. The conference, attended by more than 150 world-known cross cultural researchers from abroad and about 200 delegates representing Indian thoughts on psychology, created a platform for sharing international perspectives by analyzing social and cultural issues governing human cognition and behaviour.

Starting from the traditional to the contemporary era in history of Psychology, both psychologists and Psychology have been preoccupied with the challenge to establish Psychology as a science and with analyzing the kind of science it is. Methodologies are thoroughly divided by the boundaries between the quantitative and the qualitative, sometimes one being dominant over the other, and sometimes one being less objective than the other. The goal is to go above the dilemma where a psychologist acts keeping in view the mainstream as well as indigenous perspectives. Prof. Rath was one of the very few Indian Psychologists who rose above these ambiguities, and in an interdisciplinary manner contributed immensely to the fields of Psychology and Literature. With his eclectic orientation, he emerged as a hardcore academic and channelised his energy towards psychological activism. Great medical professionals of the state turned to him for psychological help for themselves as well as for their patients. He was a missionary with a vision of a better world and to realize his visions, he constantly strove hard to make things better than what they were.

The 'discursive turn' and the rigorous ongoing focus on narratives in human and social sciences (Bruner, 1986; Harre, 2002; Polkinghorne, 1988; Spence, 1982) afford new opportunities to expand the debate about the relationship between psychology and literature. Literature in its various forms, particularly novels, plays and poetry may be considered as a source of psychological data (Doyle, 1998). Literary works could help psychologists gain a better understanding of long-term psychological processes and changes, and in this way fill an important gap in psychological knowledge (Moghaddam, 2002).

Fiction or non-fiction, autobiography or travelogues, Prof. Rath's literary genius was equally strong and intense as is his contribution to Psychology. A recipient of the Odisha Sahitya Academy Award (1993) for his inspiring autobiography *Mo Swapna Mo Jivana*, Prof. Rath wrote 27 novels, 12 books on psychological issues, 4 travelogues, 2 anthologies of stories, 4 essays and an autobiography with most of the novels being written during his post-retirement years (1981-2014). A few of his novels namely, *Palita Kanya, Swagara Separe, Nagara Badhu, Pai Napaibaara Swapna* (translated as 'A Dream Beyond' in English and 'Pakar Napaneka Sapnā' in Hindi) have received wide acclaim. A much travelled man, Prof. Rath was noted for his travelogues such as *Bilāta Diary* (1950), *Navya Sabhyatāra Desha* (1965), *America Diary* (1975) etc. His illustrious essays include *Pragati* (1973) and *Agradrusti* (1995).

That he, at the ripe age of seventy, could complete more-than two dozen novels speaks volumes of his abounding enthusiasm. Jnanapitha awardee Prativa Ray writes *"insight, farsight and foresight are the true essence of a successful creator, and Prof. Rath possessed all these qualities in abundant measures"* (*Patha O Sapatha*, pg-324). She gave this comment after reading *Sāgara Sepāre*, a novel-cum-travelogue written by him. His novels are as much about developing intricate plots as about creating immortal characters that go on to stay with him for life. About his characters he says, *"The accomplishment of my doctorate degree pales in comparison with the immense humanistic gratification I derive from the simple people like Nita, Harry Cooper, Nina and Mami at London"* (*Sāgara Sepāre*, p. 95).

His revolutionary ideas, assertive personality,

progressive thinking, leftist orientation were all encapsulated in his novels. His world-view and his cosmopolitan being were evident in many of his travelogues. And his essays revealed the real man — socialistic, visionary, rationalistic, and above all humanistic.

Prof. Rath's views on literature and creativity underlined the essence of his dynamic personality independence, romance and universalism. In his opinion, *"the more creative a person, the more pained and sensitive he is. Creativity remains his most cherished object. He feels the omnipresence of beauty. He accepts this imaginary world of happiness as real. Such independent thoughts need some serious honing. Writings which amalgam spontaneous creative expressions, and are well-honed and felt creations turn out to be world literature."* (Atithi Uvācha, p. 97). As in his personal life, so in literature, his outlook was always progressive. He denounced social practices that are devoid of rationalism. Prof. Rath wrote, *"I don't subscribe to religious communalism. For me, men and women are the only two communities. The rest is all superstition."* (Tuma Binā, p. 11). A commemorative volume on his 90th birth anniversary was published by his students and ardent followers titled 'Radhanath Rath: Patha o Sapatha' in 2010. The book of almost 500 pages is a celebration of Prof. Rath's multifaceted personality.

"... it still strikes me myself as strange that the case studies I write should read like short stories and that, as one might say, they lack the serious stamp of science." (Freud, 1895/ 1955). The statement aptly describes Prof. Rath's orientation to science and life. His entire career as a psychologist was interspersed with his literary charisma. And his literary world was characterized by his immensity as a psychologist. Both these worlds did

synergize to make the man he was. It is left to his followers to brand him as a psychologist or a litterateur.

He was the editor of *"Sāmukhya"*, a prominent creative journal during 1964-69 which contained his regular writings on social issues along with the contributions of very prominent and award-winning Odia writers like Mayadhar Mansingh, Gopinath Mohanty, Radhamohan Gadanaik etc. He was a founder of Writer's Co-operative in the State, an organization committed to promoting fledgling and struggling writers. In 1966, he was bestowed with the Soviet Land Nehru Award for his book on Soviet Russia. His literary works have been compiled in nine volumes known as *Dr. Radhanath Rath Granthābalee*. in recognition of his outstanding contribution to society and knowledge, he was honored with Bharat Excellence Award Gold Medal and Personalities of India Award Gold Medal during 2005.

Deeply influenced by the Marxist ideology and the writings of Freud, he shaped his life by his sheer will power, uncommon industry and honesty and academic excellence. A man, who was very passionate about life, and adored spreading life-energy around, lived his life fully and to his heart's content.

Driven by a curiosity to know about God and a belief that the answer lies within the domain of philosophy, a man who studied philosophy for a Master's degree and did set-forth his enquiring mind to know all about Him and the religious practices, soon turned to be an avowed atheist which he continued to be, until he breathed his last. In a substantial measure as well in procedure, he proudly professed atheism and looked at the prevailing religious and ritual practices with skepticism and questioned the long held blind beliefs which were peddled as religion. Prof. Shib Kumar Mitra wrote, *"As a writer, I knew he has passionately attacked superstitions and prejudices and has worked hard to develop scientific understanding and attitude through textbooks, juvenile literature and adult writings."* (Mitra, 2010, p. 10). As against the wish for cremation at *Swargadwār* (way to Heaven) in Puri commonly held by persons of eminence, he was cremated at Cuttack with due reverence to his wishes that run counter to commonly accepted religious rituals and beliefs. His robust humanism flowed from his atheism and stood him out as an authentic secular person in the midst of an overwhelmingly religious society. His collegiate interactions with generations of students and scholars gave them not only valuable lessons on psychology but also many more valuable suggestions to shape life on the strength of humanism and human interventions as opposed to superstition-based world-view. His abiding persuasion of his students that they should worship books and knowledge instead of Gods and Goddesses of learning and idols in functions and celebrations brought out his secular credentials, which was the need of the hour to stem the rising counter-culture of religious fundamentalism.

A much regarded academic, he was an influential figure in expanding the domain and discipline of psychology. His youngest daughter Sangeeta Rath is incidentally now serving as a Professor of Psychology, and is heading the Psychology Department of Ravenshaw University which her father established 62 years back in 1953. She also served as the Head of the Department of Psychology at Utkal University which was also founded by her father in 1958.

Before he left for his heavenly abode, Prof. Rath

stamped his iconic image as a psychologist, a philosopher, an educationist, a rationalist; a social reformer, a literateur and a visionary. Though his life-span fell a little short of 100 years, he made a contribution worth more than a century, and we all proudly look at him as one among those persons who have given time and energy to accomplish something bigger than themselves. He looked bigger as he stood on a platform raised by his better-half Shanti Rath that withstood his thumping impact for seven long decades in tune with the proverbial spirit, *"Behind every successful man, there is always a woman"*. The funeral of Prof. Rath took place in Cuttack and was attended by a large number of his students, associates, friends and admirers. His legacy would endure. In person as well as in his teachings and messages, Prof. Rath would only be missed, not forgotten.

Prof. Jagannath Patnaik: A Nationalist Historian with a difference
(1933-2002)

Himansu Sekhar Patnaik

Prof. Jagannath Patnaik was born on 15th March 1933 at Radhaballavpur in Bhadrak district. His father Bholanath Pattnaik and Mother Rambha Devi were happy to see scholarly temperament of their child. He stood first in first class M.A. (History) from Utkal University in the year 1955 and started his career as a Lecturer in History in the same year in Ravenshaw College, Cuttack. He served in different colleges of the state like M.P.C., F.M., N.C., Bhadrak and B.J.B. College etc. He obtained D.Litt. Degree from Utkal University in 1988 and retired as the Professor & Head from P.G. Deptt. of History, Utkal University in the year 1993.

In modern historiographic parlance, Professor Jagannath Patnaik is a name to be conjured with. A critico-constructive historian, he is an example of relevant and cosmocentric humanism in the field of modern historiography. Like his mentor and the avant grade in contemporary historical research Prof. M.N. Das, Prof. Patnaik was a free-thinker and a fearless crusader of nationalistic ideas in historiography, especially in an age when nationalism has been the band wagon of most opportunist historians. Being traduced by admirers for a high sense of objectivity that was seldom hindered or tinctured by obnoxious notions, or being scoffed at by cynical detractors for nothing made little difference to his zeal, poise, grace, equanimity and originality. Intensely historical and seldom parodic, the self-reflexivity of his writings reveals him as no fastidious academic who delved deep into historical research not just for the sake of intellectual arrogance or polemics but as an honest mode of understanding and quest for knowledge. 'One must be a Platonist or an Aristotelian' goes the saying; he chose to be the latter so as to bask in the reflected glory of his legions of research works free from post-modernist and post-structural influences, his contributions to historiography come as a welcome break from the burgeoning hagiology of voluntarism.

No single mind in single contact with facts of nature could have created a Pallas, a Konark or a Madonna. Such conceptions are the growth of ages, the creations of the nation's spirit. Without a Copernicus or Galileo there would not have been a Newton or Einstein. It is history alone which had, although the crap and curd of evolution of civilization, held aloft for man, the mirror of what has been the genesis of intellectual growth and practical achievements. Faith in the future of society has always been through faith in history.

History is 'mankind's knowledge of itself, its self-awareness (Droysen). Our view of history reflects our view of society. Civilization is a voyage and not a harbour, a journey and not a destination. History imbibes and reflects this movement. Movement implies comparison. The historian, thus, goes by the comparative dictums of progressive and reactionary, conservative and liberal rather than in such uncompromising absolutes as good and bad. History, thus, is *"the record of what one age finds worthy of note in another"* (Burckhardt). The objective materials called facts are re-projected in and through the subjective factor of the ethos and personality of a historian. To quote Will and Ariel Durant-

"To those of us who study history not merely as a warning reminder of man's follies and crimes, but also as an encouraging remembrance of generative souls, the past ceases to be a depressing chamber of horrors. It becomes a celestial city, a spacious country of the mind where-in a thousand saints, statesmen, scientists, lovers and philosophers still live and speak, teach and crave and sing". (*Lessons of History*)

History is a processive discourse and the historian envisions the past by re-thinking and re-enacting the past in his mind. This is vital as a critical process of evaluation and a constructive process of bridging gaps. The rhetoric of history is sharply distinctive from that of natural sciences. That is why the real historian is not a plodder or compiling clerk but one who takes his raw-materials, evaluates it and organizes it in such a fashion as to illuminate our minds with respect to the nature of the past and the manner in which the past has produced the present. Indeed, *it requires a high order of mind to produce historical synthesis that to carry on historical research.* Professor Patnaik excels in this aspect of the thaumaturgic value of history. The history of a people has *"little values unless it deals with the conscious efforts of a people to achieve a civilization, to reach better standards, to live a happier and nobler life".* (Sardar K.M. Panikkar). Indeed, Professor Patnaik is the Sardar Panikkar of Odishan historiography.

Prof. Patnaik was a free thinker and fearless crusader

of nationalist ideas in historical writings. His concept of nationalism was no romantic populism. His is a top-down ethnocentric approach where people and cultures are not necessarily redundant and abstract concepts, while nationalism comes as a representative and discursive homogenization, erasing the complexity and diversity of social categories. Truth is one, not perspectival; the patterns in history are found, not made. Truth as correspondence to the reality of the past is the focus of his objective approach to nationalistic studies in general and freedom movement in Odisha in particular. He realized and played his role capably as a neutral and dispassionate judge of the objective historical truth and his conclusions, more often than not, substantiate to an everhandedness bereft of any tinge of partisanship. Nationalist studies, he believed, are no blind leaps into verbose dimensions, for those are foredosed to history. His was an attitude of incredulity towards meta-narrations on the issue of freedom-movement in Odisha. Nationalist studies are like cautions, walks in the available light for the historian's basic problem is moral in that being objective and responsible is the requirement for the health of history. One glorifies the heroes of history, but simultaneously he must not forget that the anti-heroes have also contributed equally. Prof. Patnaik's 'nationalist' discourse defines a perpetual field structured by grids of observations, mode of enquiry and registration of problems. In short, it brings into existence a space defined not so much by the ensemble of objects with which it dealt, but by a set of relations and a discursive practice that systematically produced inter-related concepts, theories, strategies and the like. He has also handled the difficult dichotomy of nationalism quite commendably in that while nationalism evokes universality and feasibility, it did not prevent the people to think autonomously and row in the own milieu and style and, consequently therefore, it did not obstruct- sedulously or otherwise – the health of indigenous alternatives. This historian knew his task pretty well, i.e. push the rubble aside to open up new ground.

Indian nationalism of the pre-independence era has grown in historical stature, posthumously though. Historians ever since have been excavating the creative dynamics of the tradition of Indian nationalism. In terms of most historical works, this tradition is not only repetition and continuation, It has involved innovation. This has primarily been necessitated by new historical outlooks. Among such outlooks, the foremost is *cognitivism*. i.e. interpretation and understanding of truth about the multifarious nature of Indian society. Consequently has come the need for a reinterpretation in the shape of historical activism in highlighting the transformation and reconstruction, through use of hitherto unavailable data, for purposive action. Concurrently naturalistic traditions of historiography emphasize the adoption of positive paradigm because the social reality is subjectivistic in nature. The processuality of the past to the present has, of late, brought to focus not only micro-analysis but also macro-analysis. Prof. Patnaik has been a master-craftsman of historiography in all these aspects. Major chunks of his numerous historical works on the freedom struggle have been micro-empirical studies on Odisha's role in it for macro-structural perspectives constituted by the national back-drop.

As a 'nationalist' historian and lexicographer, Prof. Patnaik has written numerous books, monographs and articles. All these have sanctified India's freedom struggle and canonized Odisha's role in it. While projecting a panoramic view of the process, amidst the recency and variety of a highly composite culture, two aspects are brought to the fore. In his work on *'Civil Disobedience'*, for example, the central point is that, as is recurrent in the history of India, anything progressive can be traced to the courage and ability of someone who did not feel fettered by the past. On the other hand, his commendable work on *"India in the Second World War"* reveals areas in which a break with the past *per se* seems to be its own reward. Indeed, Prof. Patnaik's platitude is commendable. His researchers galore on 'Quit India Movement', in regional and national contexts, is built on the Collingwoodian assumption that the total course of historical events is a criterion which serves to judge the individuals taking part in it. How much of it was due to popular emotion and / or economic forces and / or deliberate policy have been methodically investigated. The inter-relationship Congress ideology, political culture, socio-economic level of development and historical 'accidents' have been brought sharply into focus. His article on the role of the Indian National Congress (*Prajātantra Sāptāhiki*, Jan. 22-29, 1989) highlights the socio-economic factors as important determinants of its ideological framework. What crystallizes outof it is that the attitudes and values prevalent in society, the political culture, is of vital significance in determining the type of political party that emerges in society. Historical factors are of prime importance in the determination of party- structure. The National Congress was the creation of the post 1857 and political process in India had its echoes in Odisha after 1920. In the context of the latter, that parties arise when historical changes occur is an obvious inference. Nationalist exhortations (in reference to his article on 'Individual Civil Disobedience') are understandably the ones most stressed so as to legitimize the concept of change. Himself free from any value-bias in the use of concepts, his articles however pin-point that political actions are only comprehensible within some value-framework. It requires no operationalisation or conceptualization to reveal Gandhiji as the most common denominator among all segments of pluralistic India. Gandhiji was looked upon as an action–oriented system of positive ideas. From 1920 onwards the Congress became synonymous with him though the Swarajist or dissident factor would make such a rigid classification difficult. It was not so in the context of Odisha. Another research article "Gandhiji in Odisha" percolates down to the obvious logicality of "historical reductionism" where all propositions are reduced to either Gandhiji or the uniqueness of every event associated with him. The real distinguishing factor between mass-party or party of committee is not directly related to questions of membership; the type of allegiance is of crucial significance. What distinguished the Congress braintrust from being a set of political idealists is their acceptance of Gandhiji as the fulfillment of the need for a distinctive type of political leadership. In Prof. Patnaik's historical works both the orthodox and the heterodox get equal emphasis, the generation of unity from multiplicity is coloured by the process of accommodating the conflict that stems from diversity since diversity is the norm of every society. For him, syncretism is not merely putting things together but effecting the emergence of what is best in the apparent opposites. This he deals with the congress ideology in a three dimensional manner, i.e. the value goals it sets for the society, its action related system (like *Individual Satyāgraha* or *Quit India Movement*) of ideas, and a wider and impartial relevance to all interests in the political system it represented.

Prof. Patnaik is a capable ethno-theorist. Delving into the various aspects of the freedom struggle in Odisha, he epitomizes understanding, interpretation and construction of social reality through local, indigeneous, contextual, conceptual categories and theoretical formulations. Dealing with freedom movement in Odisha as a whole or its sporadic manifestations in different regions of Odisha, he exhibits as a specific dimensionality in micro-analysis. Whether it is in his *'Non-Cooperation Movement in Odisha* or *Civil Disobedience Movement in Odisha'*, his cognitive construction and intellectual analysis are well in evidence free from the shackles of Western paradigms, he deconstructs colonial history while grasping the core values and norms which constitute the centrality of Odishan society amidst its indigenous conceptual categories, their articulation and refinement. This leads the reader to a holistic understanding of the region as a historical civilizational entity that is identifying itself with an entire political party and taking the organized attitudes of that party towards the rest of the given social community and towards in the problems confronting the party within the given socio-political situation.

Normally, his writings on the freedom-movement in general and patriotic events and persons in particular, seldom stereotyped, are free from any tempatation to take a formulative view on the process of nationalism. For example, his monumental work. *"Odishāre Swādhinatā Sangrām"* (Cuttack, 2001) is a classic case of such a study. It has empirical validity, logical clarity, consistencey of propositions and generality of principles. From a purely historiographic point of view, one is convinced through this book that hermeneutics can focus on general validity (truth) to individual creativity. It adequately bridges gaps-social, economic and cultural to help in the holistic construction of the region, though basically this work is a theoretical cognitive exposition encompassing diverse trends, approaches and orientations in the indigenized freedom movement in Odisha. A comprehensive lexicon of the British rule in Odisha and reactions of the natives to it from 1803 to 1948, the historian has adopted a style where expression is unfettered (as in the context of the role of 'extremists', pp. 92-109), dispensation of emotions suffocated beneath the weight of objectivity (particularly chapters VIII, IX, X, XX, XXI and XXII), dimensions widex (particularly in the context of his survey of patriotic literature and on 'Odia movement") and appeal intense (a citable case is the role of women of Odisha in the freeom-movement, Chapter – III , comes as a refreshing 'selective system' (to borrow the phrase of Talcott parsons) that shows not only the cognitive and normative elaboration but also causal orientations to reality. It deals with the rise and growth of national consciousness from 1858 to 1885. This historical inquest deal with the press, education, literature, culture, political organization, communication system, the ''Odia Movement' in its infancy, and the gradual unfolding of the role of women. The historical-heritagetional is interspersed with paradigm – shift thematically, though not methodologically. Such formulation of indigenous concepts and theoretical approaches are very much necessary for analysis and understanding of social reality. This paper eleaboratively dwells on patriotic literature and traces it from Fakirmohan Senapati. One feels immense sympathy for Chandan Hazuri alias *Chākhi Khuntiā*. This valiant crusader of nationalism was the unique example of dedicated and selfless nationalism in 1857 and wrote many 'Jaṇāṇa's (devotional songs exclusively dedicated to Lord Jagannāth).

Each poem reverberated with nationslism, each stanza exposed colonical misrule in multifarious aspects and each concluded with an appeal or exhortation to the obsidian eyes to rectify the ameliorate the plight of nationalism. He wrote these 'Janāna's decades before Fakir Mohan. Similarly the role of the 'Satyabādi' school in the growth of national consciousness has been badly underplayed. The cradle of Odia nationalisms in the 20th century, this school and its galaxy of geniuses shaped the destiny of Odisha for he next two decades, won accolades from rivals at Dacca and Santiniketan and gave incentive to Gandhian zeal for setting–up national education centres. This school served as the formation of regional pride that helped dispel the colonially– generated inferiority complex. The under-projection of these simplistic but obviously significant aspect appear too true to be good.

Implicit in many historical responses to the role of women like Rama Devi, Sarala Devi, Malati Choudhury etc. is a kind of incredulity that a woman would be capable of formulating or expressing her own thought and actions. But a nationalist historian, Prof. Patnaik showed no less complicity in the selection of middle-class women as 'political actors', patriotic women of the finest and best type who have come out of their happy and comfortable homes at the call of the greatest man now (then) living (*Stri Dharma*, July, 1931, p.92). Prof Patnaik's accounts on the women-rebels of Western Odisha come as a new and added feather to the cap of Odishan historiography. Women were exempted from 'rigorous' imprisonment, but while in jail, spinning of '*Charkhā*' and weaving of 'khadi' were principal pastimes. In an ironic reversal of its previous position disallowing Khadi in jails, the cloth woven from the cotton–yarn, the prisoners spun was used to make jail-uniforms

(Kamala Visweswaran's "Small Speeches, Subaltern Gender..." in S. Amin and D. Chakravarty (ed) 'Subaltern Studies IX", 1997, New Delhi, pp. 106-107). His article of *"Women in Swaraj Movement"* (Souvenir on *Jātiya Sadbhāvanā Divas'*, Cuttack 2001) gives a comprehensive list of women participants and about women education.

The Quit India Movement, amidst all its multifarious facates, seems to have caught this historian's special fancy. Apart form many research articles like *"Massacre at Lunia : A sensational chapter in Quirt India Movement in Odisha"* (in *'Reflections on the National Movement in Odisha."* Odisha State Archives, 1997) *"Freedom Movement in Odisha"* (Odisha Review, Aug. 1989) and its Odia equivalent (in Cuttack, 2001), *"Massacre at Lunia"* (UHRJ, Vol. IV, 1993) which he supposes to be 'most eventful", and "Anti war Agitation and Individual Satyāgraha Movement in Odisha" (*Odisha Review*, Aug. 1990) and the like, each of which contains certain axiologism of this peerless historian, thre are a couple of works which can go as *magnum opus*. In the last of the above-cited articles, he has made some interesting and intriguing observationbs. He speaks of he "Right-Wing of the Congress" in Odisha that includes Mahtab, Sarala Devi, B. Dubey, Biswanath Das, Nityanand Kanungo and (hold your breath) Nabkrushna Choudhury. A pertinent observation in the same article that 'because of the united efforts of the Congress, Socialists, Foreward–Blockists and the Congress sympathizers among students" the 'anti-war' and 'individual satyāgraha' movements in Odisha were possible. Reminiscent of the Lāthi-charge on Lalaji, the British brutally lathi-charged on the octogenarian Bhubaneswar Rajguri in Nayagarh. The movement of Dhenkanal was quite popular. He also talks about the 'Unique Bravery' of the "people of that area (Lunia)". Abut the movement in the Garjāt State of Talcher, he gives an exhaustive account of the Prajāmandal movement there under the leadership of Pabitra Mohan Pradhan (*Balijatra Cuttack Utsav Souvenir*, 2002)

His book '*Landmarks of Quit India Movement in Odisha* (Odisha State Freedom Fighters' Samiti, Cuttack, 1992) deserves a detailed analysis. The author confesses that the "sole purpose of this work is to give an idea to the general readers about the landmarks of this movement in Odisha." He literally lives upto his promise. Significant is his observation at the outset, "although the Great revolt of 1857 ended in failure, it helped in the growth of national consciousness in Odisha."

His master-piece work is perhaps, the *Raktatirtha Eram* (Cuttack 1986). Eram during the Quit India Movement is the theme. Here, and 'Probably no where (else) in India were so many people killed in a single police action during the Quit India Movement, (*A Centenary History of Indian National Congress*, Vol. III, pp. 568-69). The ghastly massacre at Eram can be justifiably regarded as a mini-Jallianwalabagh'. Prof. Patnaik's this work tentatively verges on a genuflexion in historical writing. To substantiate this point, we have to refer to some canons of historical study. '*Before you study history, study the historian… Before you study the historian study his historical and social environment*'. The historian being an individual is also a product of history and of society and it is in this two fold light that the student of history must learn to regard him." (E.H. Carr, *What is History*, p. 44) "The historian before he begins to write history, is the product of history" (*Ibid*, p.40). Great history is written precisely when the historian's vision of he past is illuminated by insights into the problems of the present. History's dual and reciprocal function is to promote our understanding of the past in the light of the present and of the present in the light of the past. As Namier says, "Imagine the past and remember the future" (L.B. Namier, *Conflicts*, 1942, p.70). The mind of the historian is a field of constant interaction between the critical and the constructive. "The historian's picture of his subject ... thus appears to be a web of imaginative construction stretched between certain fixed points provided by the statements of his (sources) and if these points are frequent enough and the threads spun from each to the next are constructed" with due care, always by a priori imagination and never by merely arbitrary fancy, the whole picture is constantly verified by appeal to these data, and runs little risk of losing touch with the reality which it represents' (R.G. Collingwood, *The Idea of History*, New York, Oxford Univ. Press, 1956, p.213). Prof Patnaik's constructive outlook over the events at Eram is the cumulative result of oral history, personal interviews with the 'nearest witnesses' (to borrow from Herodotus), secret correspondences, government and press releases of the time and secret police reports (p-II).

"History ... can only be written by those who find and accept a sense of direction in History itself" (Carr, Op.cit. p.132) Prof. Patnaik epitomises this while also following the Actonian Principle that progress is the scientific hypothesis on which history is to be written. Progress in history is achieved through the interdependence and interaction of facts and values. This constitutes the central theme of his odes on 'Salt', 'Women' and other micro dimensional aspects of the freedom-movement. One such aspect is his numerous works on the martyrs and freedom-fighters. Prof. Patnaik's belief that the "role of the rebel has some analogies with that of the great man." From the pivots of journalism in Odisha like Gourishankar Ray, G.S. Das and H.K. Mahatab to individual firebrands like B.N. De, Somnath Singh, P.C. Bhanjadeo and poet Banchhanidhi Mohanty, from unsung heroes like Bhagaban Sahu, Aniruddha Mohanty, Ratnakar, Padmanav Chhotray and legions of them like Pindiki Bahubalendra to valiant tribal leaders and dedicated nationalists like Dora Bisoi, Chakra Bisoi, Birsa Munda, Kasti Dakua (of 1942 Nayagarh fame), Ratna Naik and Dharanidhar Bhuyan from dalit-leader Utsav Malik (of Nimapara, 1942) to the cavalcade of Martyrs and leaders like 'Biplabi' Chaki Khuntiā, Surendra Sāi, Bāghā Jatin, Buxi Jagabandhu, Jayee Rajguru, Laxman Naik, Khudiram Bose, Bāji Rout and Nirmal Mundā have all been dealt with, in their proper historic-individual perspectives, in individual articles. But what looms large from point of view of scientific study of nationalist historigraphy is his approach to each one of them. Each is dealt from the point of view his individual behavior, as distinct form the behavior of the groups and classes, as well as his larger contributions to the concerted shaping of group class efforts. This can be driven home with one example. "In 1907", he writes, *"when the Swadeshi Movement was losing its force, a split in the Indian National Congress was effected"*, extremists in the Congress like Bāghā Jatin believed in "driving out the British by force or fraud" (Terrorist Movement in Odisha, *Odisha Review*, Aug. 1997). This is a classic example of what Carr says 'the study of the behavior of men as individuals consists of the study of the conscious motives of their actions" (Carr, Op. Cit. p. 47). A plethora of such examples can be cited from each of Patnaik's articles on these individuals and a complilation of these articles would more than adequately serve the purpose of a who' who of the freedom movement in Odisha. From apparently insignificant issues (like coronation ceremony is the Garjat

State of Keonjhar which was more political than religious in significance) to those of immense importance like his articles on Somnath Singh (A Rebel Patriot), Annapurna Maharana, Rani Suryamani Patamahadei, "Odisha Garjat Rajyara Gahana Katha" and series of non-respective articles on creation of Odisha into a separate province. Prof. Patnaik has left no stone unturned in the lexicon of freedom movement in Odisha. His article on *"Salt Agitation in Odisha"* comes in all refreshing details about a socio-economic study of the manufacture of salt in Odisha that has continued to 'salt' the East India Company's trade in Bengal eversince the Maratha rule in Odisha; the story is stretched to its grand finale in Odisha during the 'Gandhian-era. His plausibility can seldom be doubted in his accounts of micro-movements like *'August Revolution in Bhadrak. Sub-division", "Balasore– in Freeom struggle", "Bezelgate Murder" or 'reductionistic'* articles on Bāji Rout, Barabati, H.K. Mahtab and Nirmal Mundā.

Particularly interesting are his articles on 'Keonjhar Melee', 'Ghumsur uprising, Nayagarh murder, Koraput, Tāpang, Kanikā, Kujang and Tālcher. Examples of his impeccable historical ingenuity are reflected in each such petal of his historiographical flower. To cite but one of it, in his article on Kanikā, while discussing the contextual significance of the movement there, he cites the background case of 1804-05 when the British wanted to annex Kanikā on flimsy pleas of protests from subordinate Zamindars so as to prevent the Khurda- Kujang- Kānika triumvirate against them. The rhetorical strategy adopted by the distinguished historian is not only a pleasurable experience of the 'return of cleo', but also an honest endeavour to convince those whose paradigms for understanding and comprehension may be different. Had he studied the freedom- movement in Odisha in exclusive frame-work pattens of 'elite', 'Marxist', 'Subaltern' and the like, the conclusions he would thereby have reached would have been nothing short of being ludicrous.

A scientific historian, while telling a study or analyzing a process of evolution or change must demonstrate the interpretative strengths (and limitations) of a particular concept or a medley of concepts by referring to what the evidence stands for mainstream historiography has, till date, done little or nothing to incorporate the local or indigenours perspective in the writing of the history of freedom movement in India. Prof. Patnaik's book, '*Itihāsa Prushthāre Pipili*' (Bhubaneswar, 1993), is a classic case to conscientize the role of Pipili in the history of Odisha. A virgin work of this sort was much in need, since Pipili is the hyphen among the religiousity of the Jagannāth-dharma, the artistic excellence of Konark, the seat of power at Khurda and Bhubaneswar and a vital seat of Odishan culture one of whose latent manifestations. The applique art is globally famous. A sophisticated attention to stylistic in the sense of lexicon and narrative of Pipili, its historical background with particular emphasis on its specific and immense historicity during the Afghan- Mughal rule of Odisha, the immensity of its importance during the Gandhian sojourns like the '*Harijan Yātrā*' or the week long historic 'Beraboi' session near Delang under Pipili in the post-independence era, its economic potentialities, its cultural – heritagonal treasures, and its immensely archaeological significance. Prof. Patnaik, in this immensely valuable work, makes palpable a world of experience that precedes rational knowledge including the very act of perception itself. It was, for example, at Beraboi Gandhiji had said that Odisha is the place most loved by him (1938). This statement would spring-board the people of the region to spur on the 'Quit India Movement from Ghoradia' and Beraboi to Delang and Pipili. The oratorio fire-works of women leaders like Ushamani Devi and Sunamani Devi did enough to articulate the mass-base of the Quit India Movement in the region. The book, basically, is a cognitive exposition encompassing diverse trends; but the empirically observable dimensions on freedom (or traditional patriotic) movement are tinctured by motivational and international subjectivity of human actions. A more detailed account of the Beraboi–meet would have, it is presumed, better capped a holistic construct of Pipili and its surrounding areas.

The author gains success in driving home the point that the people do shape their inherited and determined conditions of existence. The historian is all the while locating the significance of these events in the perspective of a bigger canvas. Alert to all grounds of historical enquiry, the historian is resurrecting the importance of people against the theoreticism of intellectuals. History as a process, indeed, has an objective necessity of its own.

Indeed, Prof. Patnaik exemplifies in all these works that nationalism is real thing. The total course of the nationalist history is a criterion that serves in judging the individuals taking part in it. His objectivity does not blur the vision to distinguish how much was due to popular emotion, how much to economic forces and how much to deliberate policy in the context of the resurgent or resent nationalism. This historian is, indeed, properly balanced *"between fact and interpretation, between fact and value"*, to borrow Carr's words (EH. Carr, *Op. Cit.* p.132). Interpretation is always bound up with value judgments and causality is bound up with interpretation, Historiography is a progressive science in the sense that it seeks to provide constantly expanding and depending insights into a course of events as progressive as nationalism and the freedom movement. Prof. Patnaik never, therefore, lacked a constructive outlook over the past. He was refreshing break from stereotyped nationalist historians in his capacity to rise above the limited vision of his own situation in society and in history, in a futuristic capacity that makes insight into the past crystal-clear, and in his interest not in the unique but what is general in the unique.

Human life becomes meaningful only when one understands the unity, coherence and relational aspects of events. As Prof. Patnaik presents a coherent picture of a vast panorama that was the freedom-movement in Odisha in all its isolated, sporadic or integrative elements, his presentation of a homogenous entity that was Odisha as the active recipient of leadership - efforts of the times and his documentation of historical data are among the finest examples of objectivity and realism. "The notion of unity of knowledge is the pre-requisite of any epistemic cognition" (editorial note of N.K. Singhi in Ruchi Banthiya's *From Historicity to post Modernity.*, New Delhi 1994, p.15). It is definitely related to commitment; we can well visualize the entire gamut of nationalist history, freedom movement in particular, thought the picture painted by his historicity and can thereby reach upto the truth; this commitment conforms to the dynamics in the life of the people of those particular periods of time while facing the thrust of challenges of the then times.

A historical event is more like the actual entity of Whitehead in which the whole universe, the contending forces of the past, present and the future converge In Prof. Patnaik's actual entity, we can always be in a Buddhist Universe or Bergsonian time. The actual entities move like cinematographic slides so that in the words of Heraclitus, one cannot step twice into the same river. Sometimes, though Prof. Patnaik is Napoleon to his own Robespierre or Lenin to his own Stalin and Trotsky, and quite refreshingly so.

"Cassius seldom smiles" It is Shakespeare's symbolic representation of Cassius not being a well-rounded cultural or historical personality. Prof. Patnaik was the exact opposite, like his works he was always suffused with a benign smile.

REFERENCES :
1. Jagannath Patnaik, *Feudatory States of Orissa.* 2 Vol. a (Allahabad, 1988).
2. Jagannath Patnaik, *Landmarks of Quit India Movement in Orissa* (Cuttack, 1992).
3. Jagannath Patnaik, *Raktatirtha Eram* (Cuttack, 1986).
4. Jagannath Patnaik, *Orissa, Itihāsare Ketoti Rommanchakara Kāhāni* (Cuttack, 1990).
5. Jagannath Patnaik, *Biplabi Dharanidhar* (Bhubaneswar, 1992).
6. Jagannath Patnaik, *History of Freedom Movement in India and National Integration* (Cuttack, 1986).
7. Jagannath Patnaik, *British Rule in India* (New Delhi, 1973).
8. K.S. Behera, J.N. Patnaik, H,C. Das (Ed.), *Cuttack: One Thousand Years*, 2 Vols. (Cuttack, 1990).
9. *Reflections on the National Movement in Orissa* (Bhubaneswar, 1997).

Professor Manmath Nath Das: A Renowned Historian (1924-2009)

Harish Chandra Panda

Sankhari, a little known border village in North Balasore, rose to fame in the later decades of the preceding century. Both the sons of the acknowledged philanthropist Madhusudan Das of this remote village became famous. Their reputation extends beyond the national boundaries. The elder son, Manmath Nath Das, became a well-known academician and historian, and the younger one, Manoj Das, a celebrated writer and philosopher. As their grand parents had made fortune by controlling lucrative trade and acquiring extensive tracts of fertile agricultural land, both the brothers were blessed with wealth and rural aristocracy by birth.

Manmanth Nath was born in 1924, completed matriculation from Balasore Zilla School and intermediate course from Ravenshaw College. To fulfill his father's wish, young Manmath Nath married a thirteen-year old Rajalaxmi (whose name he soon changed to Rajashree of the Mayurbhanja Pāla family). His tryst with history began when he opted for History Honours in Ravenshaw College on the advice of Professor Ghanashyam Dash. He went to

Allahabad University for his post-graduation in history during 1946-48. There he was influenced by a few history teachers like Tarachand, B.P. Saxena, Bisweswar Prasad. O.P. Bhatnagar and R.P. Tripathy, but Iswari Prasad remained his role-model. Inspite of his occasional involvement in those hectic days of the Indian freedom movement, he secured first class with distinction in his M.A. Examination.

His service career began with his joining as a Lecturer in History in Fakir Mohan College, Balasore on 17th July 1948. Possibly his stay in the old dilapidated house of Fakir Mohan Senapati here had inspired him to write a few books like *Glimpses of Kalinga History, Kalinga Itihāsa, Yuge Yuge Utkaliya Dharma O Sabhyata, Bhārat Itihāsa and Bhārat Sambidhānar Sārānsa* in early years of his career.

He served in the S.C.S. College, Puri for a short period as he left for London in December 1956 and did his Ph.D. under the guidance of Professor Cyril Henry Philips in the London University. On his return, he was posted in the Ravenshaw College during 1957-59 and soon he was selected for the post of Reader in Utkal University. By availing the Rockfeller scholarship, he went to London along with his family for higher research. During his stay at London, he got wider recognition for his book *Political Philosophy of Jawaharlal Nehru*. His return by the beginning of 1961 remained memorable for him as he was selected for the post of Professor and Head of the Department of History, Utkal University at the age of thirty-five only, and he continued to hold that position for the next 22 years.

Before availing the fellowship to join the Indian Institute of Advanced Studies at Simla in 1971, he had already obtained his D.Litt. degree in 1964 and visited the Soviet Union and Australia. With the award of the British Council Scholarship in 1976, he got an opportunity to study the archival records at London. Here his interviews with a number of British statesmen were immensely beneficial for his research projects. On his return journey, his visit to Heidelberg and meeting with Professor Hermann Kulke opened a new chapter of joint research on South Asian Studies and materialization of several joint collaborations of Heidelberg University and Utkal University. Before his London visit again in 1981, he attended the UNO's Norwich Conference and visited Canada and USA on the UGC's exchange programme. Next year he visited London and Paris as the Indian representative to the International Conference on Historical Sciences.

In 1983, Professor Das was persuaded to accept the post of the Vice-Chancellor of Utkal University which he accepted without enthusiasm. He was however successful in creating a number of new posts, introducing the Merit Promotion Scheme and taking up the badly needed works of renovation and beautification of the campus. But his disgust with the University's internal politics prompted him to refuse his second term.

His retirement from Utkal University landed him in politics. The personal wish of Rajiv Gandhi led him to contest as the Congress candidate from Bhubaneswar Parliamentary Constituency in 1991 general election which he lost narrowly. However. he was elected to the Rajya Sabha in 1998.

II

During half a century long worship of Clio, Professor Das has produced a considerable number of historical works in the form of books, monographs, research projects, theses, research papers and textbooks. He has also earned appreciation for a number of popular writings, novels, travelogues and autobiographies.

His long academic career which practically devoted to the modern Indian historiography and his impressive works on Indian history have taken him to the height of an acknowledged historian of the first order and revealed his scholastic caliber.

His Studies in the *Economic and Social Development of Modern India*; 1848-56, based on mostly primary sources, is an important analytical work on socio-economic reforms of the Dalhousie era which had witnessed breath-taking transformation of the mid 19th century Indian society and emergence of modern India, His another excellent work is *India under Morley and Minto: Politics Behind Revolution, Repression and Reform*. Based on hitherto unexplored original source materials. the book gives an insight into the official reforms during the most significant phase of the constitutional development of the British India. The book reveals the personality clashes among the British leaders connected with the Indian affairs, emergence of political parties and politics behind the constitutional reforms. The other work, *Indian National Congress Versus the British* was written with the help of primary sources preserved in the British Museum Library and quoted in C.H. Philips Evolution of India and Pakistan: 1857-1947, H.M. Hyndman's *Bankruptcy of India, An Enquiry into the Administration under the Crown Lord* and *Selected Documents on the History of India and Pakistan*. Vol.IV. The book is a factual analysis of six decades long confrontation between an all-powerful imperial authority and the most vibrant political party in India. However, the book appears monotonous and repetitive, lacking the style and co-herence for which the author is so well-known.

As a piece of excellent research, his book *Partition and Independence of India: inside Story of Mountbatten Days'* has earned international recognition. Based on rare primary sources and accounts of interviews with the key characters of the administration of the British India, the book reveals the inner story of the freedom of India and the conspiracy behind the partition. As an exposer of the British duplicity, it justifiably challenges some of the falsehood originated from the British circles and the impression created by the authors of *Freedom at Midnight*.

Another work, *End of British Indian Empire: Politics of Divide and Quit, March-August 1947"* is a factual revelation of hectic politics behind the "divide and quit policy" and a catalogue of the principal trends of the time as mirrored through the thought and action that dominated the Indian political scenario. Professor Das has also been a co-author of a three-volume work, *A Social, Cultural and Economic History of India* with other two authors, B.N. Puri and P.N. Chopra. The book portrays and evaluates different aspects of the Indian society through the ages in the framework of the usual chronological division and provides a perspective and a new outlook in viewing and understanding India's cultural heritage.

Professor Das has edited the third volume of a five-volume project. *"A Century History of Indian National Congress"'* which was published on the occasion of the Centenary Session of the Indian National Congress at Bombay in 1985. The volume, covering the most crucial phase of the Indian freedom struggle, i.e. 1935 – 1947, unfolds the intriguing and fascinating role of the Congress as well as its leadership in stewarding the country and people towards freedom.

Through exposition of historical scholarship and expansion in the range of historical investigation, Professor Das has made significant and original contribution to the modern Indian historiography. For original source materials, standard framework of research methodology, systematic presentation and charming style, his works in this field have earned alround commendation. Rise of a historian like him on the national horizon inspires the spirit of Odia people. At least someone from Odisha has reached such a height.

III

Though allured away by the Indian historiography, M.N. Das has not neglected to perform his role in the most significant phase of the Odishan historiography. Amidst all-around growth of national and regional historiography in India, Odisha had remained a *terra incognita*, a land unknown, undiscovered and unchartered in the vast ocean of history. Politically fragmented, economically under-developed and educationally backward Odisha had failed to catch up the attention of the Indologists and Orientalists. Odishan historiography had begun in the 19th century, and a few well-meaning British bureaucracts-turned historians, neighbouring scholars and local adventurists under the spell of Odia nationalism as the harbingers of Odishan historiography had drawn a hazy and haphazard outline of Odisha's history. Earlier-years of the post-independence era witnessed the growth of the badly needed research infrastructure and appearance of a galaxy of Odishan scholars whose pulsating activities of historical research signalled the leaping of Odishan historiography to its youth. Those promising scholars sincerely began to bring into light fresh source materials, unfold mysteries, bridge up the gaps, find out the missing links and apply refreshing coatings to the edifice of Odishan historiography.

M.N.Das. a solitary figure from this group of scholars, though devoted himself to the modern Indian history, clung to his roots, spent his entire career and life in Odisha and enriched the Odishan historiography in different ways. His historical writings on Odisha may be little but his attempt to promote and popularise Odisha history by founding the School of Odishan historiography cannot be ignored.

His earliest works on Odisha, such as *"Glimpses of Kalinga History, Kalinga Itihasa, Yuge Yuge Utkaliya Dharma 0 Sabhyata"* etc. are of course, informative but most of them attempt to popularise some aspects of the history of Odisha without burdening the mind of the readers with source materials. Ornamental language. out-dated style as well as emotional and patriotic prejudice negate their research value. The author himself admits, *"Glimpses of Kalinga History,* produced at the earliest period of my profession. is an immature work. It was an adventure. and it faced criticism. Many people pointed out that it was not a critical history, and it was based on emotion and patriotism.

His later writings on Odisha present a different picture. In two volumes of *The Odyssy of Emperor Ashoka Maurya; Kalinga War to World Peace,* he has attempted to present not only the saga of Ashoka but also the story of the Kalingan people who ventured the seas and neighbouring lands. The volumes, depending on the facts drawn from epigraphic and other sources, are in the structural form of a drama.

He was also the chief architect behind the publication of two outstanding works on Odisha. He edited the impressive book, *Side-lights on History and Culture of Odisha* on the eve of Bhubaneswar Session of the Indian History Congress which he had organized in 1977. The book divided into five parts and containing about sixty- six historical essays on all aspects of Odisha, continued to hold the centre-stage of Odishan historiography for many decades. A comprehensive history and culture of Odisha it was encyclopedic in character. The other one, *Odisha: A Comprehensive and Classified Bibliography* contains about 8000 entries on Odishan history culture and literature. Both the admirable compilations had the purpose of introducing Odisha to the world of scholars. In the absence of complete and comprehensive history book on Odisha, both the edited works continue to serve the scholars and readers in general who use them as principal reference books.

Professor Das has written a good number of standard textbooks in Odia as well as English. Factual details and correctness, attractive style and beautiful language which bear the influence of H.G. Wells, Vincent Smith and Iswari Prasad unmistakably have made his textbooks immensely popular among students of higher education. His books not only cater to the needs of history students but also help in popularising history all over Odisha and outside.

Besides textbooks, he has to his credit a large number of such Papers. Written during five decades of his active academic life, many of those papers are neither available nor remembered by him at present. However, from among the available ones, the worthmentioning are *Kalinga and Singhala: A Study in Ancient Relation. Suppression of Human Sacrifice among the Hill Tribes of Odisha, Odisha Through the Panorama of Indian Civilisation., Female Infanticide among the Khonds of Odisha. History of Approaches to National Integration. Contribution of Odisha to Indian Culture, Odisha : A Land of Art and Architecture Through Ages. An Introduction of Odisha. Ancient and Medieval Empires and Kingdoms. Climate and Importance of India's Kalinga Race and Their Decline.*

Professor Das nourished the school of Odishan Historiography in the post-independence era. By presiding over Utkal University's History Department for a period of over twenty two years, he has created a phalanx of Odishan scholars who have been taught and guided by him to carry on the teaching and research on the Odishan studies. And again, by founding the Odisha History Congress in 1969 and making it a vibrant academic and research body in the years to follow, he has provided a much needed intellectual forum of the historians of Odisha for deliberation and publication of their findings on the Odishan studies. The trees Professor Das planted so meticulously, have blossomed and borne fruits. Successive generations of Odishan historians during the fifties and eighties of the preceeding century have been either his students or scholars. He, therefore, rightly claims, *"I could at least inspire a number of colleagues, my students and promising researchers to take up research with a sense of devotion and bring into light something that was un-explored. Number of scholars under my guidance have simply ransacked the ancient past of Odisha. Because of their hard labour and sincere research, both at macro level and micro level, today most aspects of the history of Odisha are known.*" Expressing unbounded optimism, he confides, *"Our work is over. Whatever we have done, may be little… I believe my students and successors are doing their work, and their students and successors will continue the work."* No wounder, the Odisha History Congress, in its Silver Jubilee Year Session, felicitated him as the Patriarch of the tribe of the Odishan historians.

Professor Das has not confined himself to the complex framework of research methodology an historical profundity. He has also indulged himself in literary activities. Like this younger brother, he is gifted with artistic skill, attractive style and commendable language to flourish in the literary sphere.

Political Philosophy of Jawaharlal Nehru, published by London-based publishing house in 1961, is a book written in the earlier years of his career. It broght wider recognition and opened for him avenues of greater reward which, of course, he has shunned. Another interesting book, *Miracles of Mankind's Great Saviors; Zorosaster to Sathyasai* provides within the research framework an insight into the lives of great saviors of humanity. While the books like *Westerners in the East, Keep the Story Secret, Astaranga* etc. establish him as novelist, some travelogues and autobiographical works *like Samaya Sāgara Teere* and *Jibanara Pathaprante Digantara Drushya* speaking highly of his literacy caliber.

IV

Form his ideas, beliefs and writings on history and historians, one is inclined to call him an ideal historian under the spell of Ranke's dictum that *"strict presentation of facts is the Supreme Law of historical writing."* In his opinion amidst so many historical idealism and philosophy which are often inexplicable and unknownable, a historian's idealism should be "how to ascertain truth, the reality of the fact, not the essence, not the fictional side, not the speculation, but the bottom of truth." He firmly believes, *"History rests on truth, and a true historian's only goal is to arrive at the truth, objectivity and scientific correctness."*

He advocates for people-oriented history writing. For him history is not just for scholars and thinkers, rather it is based on people's life and their creativity an achievement. Since people have become the destiny-makers and matter in history, it is natural that the popular belief and feeling would influence historical writings, and bring the historians under different category of historical schools. Therefore, he doesn't mind if historians belong to various schools of thought. For him, it is natural and nothing wrong on the part of the British historians to belong to Colonial / Imperial School or Utilitarian School or white man's Burdern School or any other school; and the majority of Indian Historians belonging to the Nationalist School. However, he categorically disapproves the motivated and paid historians and wishes the historians not to follow any stereotype category or any particular school of thought which does not allow facts to speak for themselves.

It has been difficult for career-historians of his generation to maintain their idealism in pristine form. Professor Das is practical enough to acknowledge this when very candidly he says that a person like him with half a century's experience as a teacher and researcher was automatically influenced by many types of ideologies. He further explains, *In certain points of time under certain situation and condition, a historian may have to compromise.* However, he is not prepared to sacrifice the basic responsibility of an historian. So, he concludes, *"Majority of historians believe that let the facts speak truth for themselves, let evidences establish the truth, let us remove the idea from our mind that one belongs to left or right or center or no where. That is my opinion."*

Evaluation of the contribution of a historian of his stature and fame is a hazardous task. One must judge what and how much he has done as a historian rather than musing over what he should have done. Prof. Das has reached his academic destination in an exemplary manner. As a researcher he often sailed across the seven seas in quest of source materials and established himself as a frontline historian. He was a Vice-Chancellor who preferred honour and dignity to regard and ignominy. Without a craze for cheap popularity and publicity, and without fascination for power and regard, he has been a rare example of high value the cherished and personified. As an ideal teacher with deep erudition gifted oratory, abundant affection and impeccable integrity, he has been the role model for his countless students and admirers to many of whom he remains a living–legend and a cult-figure.

REFERENCES :
1. *Samaya Sāgar Tire*, Vidyapuri, Cuttack.
2. *Jibana Pathaprānte Digantara Drushya*, Vidyapuri, Cuttack 1996.
3. *India under Morely and Minto* (G.A. and Unwin), 1965.
4. *Indian National Congress Versus the British*, 1977, Ajanta, New Delhi.
5. *End of British Empower*, 1947, Vidyapuri, Cuttack.
6. *Glimpses of Kalinga History*, 1950, Century Publication, Calcutta.
7. *Contribution of Odisha to Indian Culture*, 1976, Cuttack.
8. *Political Philosophy of Jawaharlal Nehru*, George Allen and Unwin (1961).

Bhairab Chandra Mahanti : A Visionary and dreamer of Sports

Kharavella Mahanti

A sportsmen to the core, Shri Bhairab Chandra Mahanti, lived his life perpetuating the ideals of a sportsman. He believed in the saying – *"When the great scorer comes, do not ask him how many goals he has scored, but how he has played the game."* Of all games and sports, cricket being his first love, he would always say, *"I have played cricket with a straight bat,"* and never in his life he offered to play a cross-batted stroke. His life was an unending struggle with trials and tribulations, yet he did not dither from his convictions for the sake of convenience. His indomitable spirit was indeed the spirit of sportsman who would never hit under the belt or bowl an underarm ball. Not being blessed with a long life, his, was one of commitment, dedication and a deep concern for the depressed and the downtrodden, not to forget his stupendous achievements in the field of sports. He not only put an otherwise *'backward'* state like Odisha in the sports map of India, but also in the context of the world of sports, with the making of the grand edifice, Barabati Stadium. His humane qualities put him for above petty and mundane considerations of religion, caste, gender or any form of bigotry. Never superstitions, he was a perfect blend of healthy traditions and progressive ideas, which make him a true Gandhian and socialist. There is a huge difference between professing socialism and actually practising it. Without making any such claims, Shri Mahanti was a socialist at heart and a committed practioner of socialism. Politics was never his forte, but he remained in politics throughout his life, and was deeply disturbed, to see the turmoil and chaos that politicians of the post –Gandhian generation indulged in. The value system with which he had grown up was nowhere near with what was being furthered by almost all politicians of the latter part of the 20th century.

Those who dedicate themselves in heart and soul to the cause of the nation and make a commitment for a legacy that posterity would be proud of, leave behind an impression that can hardly be erased. Shri Mahanti was a multifaceted personality who was a front ranking Freedom Fighter, a sportsmen, a politician and Journalist, who craved not for fame, but for a harmonious social order where people could breathe freely in the true spirit of brotherhood. Born in Balisukuri under Kishorenagar block in Cuttack district, Odisha on 13th July; 1913, to a middle-class family, Shri Mahanti lost both parents when he was barely four years old. He was brought up by his uncle Shri Nishamani Mahanti who was then working in Bihar-Orissa Secretariate at Patna. Shri Mahanti passed Matriculation in First Division from Patna High School and completed I.Sc. and B.A. Courses form Muzzaffarpur, Bihar.

Shri Mahanti had an inborn talent for games and sports and an unparalled organizing capacity that made him a natural leader of the Odia boys studying in Patna before Odisha became a separate province. Jñānapitha

Awardee, Padmashri Gopinth Mohanty in his autobiography, *"Srotaswoti"*, mentions – *"Bhaira bhai is a natural sportsman, he carries a cricket ball always with him and his organizational skills have made him a leader in his own right and we all Odia boys unhesitatingly accepted him as our leader."* In all school and college competitions – be it sports or drama- Odia boys always came out champions under his guidance. In fact, a school teacher in Patna remarked, *"If you Odia boys run away with all prizes, what would be left for our Bihari boys?"*

When Odisha was declared a separate province on 1st April 1936 [it was the first province of pre-independence period created on the basis of language], Bhairab Babu returned to Odisha with hs uncle and perpetuated the joint–family tradition till his demise in 1980. he believed that joint family system was symbiotically linked with a progressive social life. He emphasized that joint family culture was intrinsic to the Indian Civilization and to its socio-cultural ethos. India, which has a continuous post for more than 5000 years owes its survival to its inherent family bonding tradition. A joint family system, he said, helps in cultivating fundamental human values like tolerance, mutual love and affection and enhances the spirit of brotherhood – which are all becoming extinct in the contemporary materialistic society.

In 1936, he joined the Development Department in Orissa Secretariat in a clerical post. To study in Ravenshaw college had been one of his cherished dreams and hence he joined the Law Course there for one year and actively took part in all sports activities. With the outbreak of the Second World War in 1939, the Odisha Secretariat was shifted to Sambalpur and when Mahatma Gandhi gave the clarion call- "Do or Die" – during the Quit India movement in 1942, Shri Mahanti quit his job and joined the Freedom struggle. He was deeply involved in the Orissa conspiracy case along with Shri Surendranath Dwivedy, Shri Banka Behari Das and Shri Nishamani Khuntia. He wrote and distributed pamphlet against British rule in India. The colonial police was on a lookout to arrest him and once while travelling from Sambalpur to Cuttack he was nabbed and put behind the bars. The trial court convicted him and he was about to be hanged. He survived the gallows because of the benefit of doubt that was given by the judge. The handwriting expert from Calcutta said the writings on the pamphlets and on other documents appeared to be written by the same person, but one cannot conclusively prove that the writings on the pamphlets and other writings were by one and the same person. The expert opined that Shri Mahanti should not be hanged. The truth is that the pamphlets were actually written by Shri Mahanti, but he wrote them with his left hand and not with his natural writing hand which was his right hand. In fact, he had the dexterity of writing proficiently with both hands. However, his reincarnation continued and he became seriously ill after constant torture by the colonial police. Upon the advice of the jail doctor he was released from prison and was admitted to S.C.B. Medical College and Hospital. Almost on the verge of death he was resuscitated and nursed back to life with the constant care and attention of his friend Dr. Feroze Ali and the lady with an indomitable spirit, Smt. Malati Choudhury. While convalascing in the hospital in 1945, Dr. H.K. Mahatab came to visit him. This meeting was as much historic as it was of crucial significance because it marked the real turning point in Bhairab Babu's life. Till now whatever he ws doing was rather tentative and he needed proper guidance and direction which only Dr. Mahatab could provide. Dr. Mahatab was the path-finder whose advice and cooperation made Bhairab babu realize his own potentialties. From being a member of the Odisha Legislative Assembly, to an efficient Administrator, to a reputed Journalist and then a veteran sports organizer, revealed the multidimentional aspect of Shri Mahanti. In 1946, he was elected to the Odisha legislative Assembly on a Congress ticket from Kishorenagar constituency and in 1947 he became the first Editor of the local daily *Prajātantra*, published by Dr. Mahatab. In 1949, he also became the first editor of the local English Daily, The Eastern Times. During this period he took initiative for the progress and spread of Children's literature with the publication of Meena Bazar section in the Prajatantra. He encouraged creativity and natured budding literary talents in Odisha.

In the General Elections of 1952, he won the Gobindpur Assembly Constituency in Cuttack district. He was appointed Deputy Minister {Independent Charge} in charge of Irrigation, P.W.D. and General Health Departments in the cabinet of Chief Minister Naba Krushna Choudhury (1952-56). Here he proved his worth as a very efficient administrator and his humble behavior was highly appreciated by all within his party and in the opposition. His statement in the Assembly that, "Majority party has to install the political apparatus to govern, but the Government is non-political", was hailed by all as a true reflection of a principled democratic spirit. Shri Gopal Chhotray in his autobiography, *"Pathika"*, has given a very apt description of the humble persona of Shri Mahanti.Shri Mahanti was again elected to the Odisha Legislative Assembly in 1971 on a Congress ticket and in

1974 he became a Member of the Rajya Sabha.

However, Shri Mahanti's identity and recognition lay not as a lay politician, but as one of the greatest sport organizers India has ever produced. Sports Culture in Odisha and the history of Barabati Stadium are inextricably linked with the the life-history of Shri Mahanti. His vision and width of imagination to place Odisha in the sports map of the country is almost unparalled. Since 1947, for thirty-three long years, he spent more than half of his entire life-span in nurturing sports culture in Odisha and he relentlessly pursued for its progressive development. His firm conviction was that it was through the medium of sports, nation-building could be enhanced because sports inculated the idea of discipline which ultimately leads to cultural progress. He would say, "If the body is healthy, the mind would be healthy and a healthy mind could only give the society and the country a disciplined and civilized citizen. To relieve society form a sick mind, the only imperative was the growth and development of sports. His untiring effort led to the construction of the famous Barabati Stadium, which was the first composite sports complex in the country. In every sense the Stadium was his brain child. Barely four months before his death when requested to write for a magazine about the Barabati Stadium, he wrote –

"I wonder where to begin and where to end. the story of the Barabati Stadium is a part of the story of my life. To me the Barabati Stadium is not merely an edifice of brick and mortar. To me, it is a movement – a movement that has placed little known Odisha in the sports map of India. Not that there were no games and sports in Odisha or that there were no good sportsmen in Odisha before the Barabati Stadium came

up. Far from it, on the contrary, the standard of the most popular games – football and cricket was very good compared to what it is today, but in a few places only, such as Cuttack, Berhampur, Parlakhimindi, Baripada and few other townships. What was wanting was that there was no organized Association for games and sports at state level and much less at the district level when I got into Odisha sports in 1947. Clubs were very few in number. With the starting of the construction of Barabati Stadium a new idea, a new spirit seized the minds of the administrations as well as the youth of the state of Odisha. Then came the Associations for different games and sports at the District level. The ideas and the spirit started spreading...."

The euphoria of Independence had hardly died when great Indian leaders were involved in Nation building and creating the largest democracy in the world. It was a generation of stalwarts, almost every leader and freedom fighter dreamt and aspired for creating a new India. This was the time too, when youthful sports lovers of Odisha were busy in Cuttack and in their own humble way were trying to give shape to the growth of sports activities in the state. It was a chance event when they organized the first big sports event in Cuttack. This was an exhibition football match between Bhawanipore Club of Calcutta and Cuttack XI combined. The match was conducted in the Odisha Police Ground at Cuttack in August 1948.

This was an ecstatic moment of delight for the people of Cuttack. Its success was immeasurable and it drew an unusually large crowd who thronged the field to cheer their home team. The Chief Minister Dr. Mahatab and several other higher officials of the State had also come to see the match. The astounding success of the event and the palpable excitement almost bordering on delirium –

of the people, left the Chief Minister in awe and admiration and the exclaimed; "*This is what the people love*". Seizing upon the opportunity, Bhairab Babu, then a Member of the Odisha Legislative Assembly mooted the idea of Stadium to Dr. Mahatab. Shri Mahanti as a representative of the youthful and dynamic generation of Indians, sought a new identity for Odiyas through the initiation of a vibrant sports culture in Odisha. Some of the people around who heard him did not even have the faintest idea of what a stadium was and they asked Bhairab Babu to explain it what it was all about. Dr. Mahatab was so charmed with the successful conduct of the football match and the people's enthusiasm that before he left Cuttack Police Ground, made a commitment that a Stadium would be built at Cuttack for the recreation of the people. The very next day the Governor of Odisha Shri Asaf Ali came to the same venue and declared that a Stadium would be built in Cuttack. This fact finds metion in an article by B.C.M. (Bhairab Chandra Mahanti) in the Souvenir Commemorating the XVIII National Games at Cuttack in 1958.

The Stadium was built with funds from common people through a raffle. The intitial cost was around one crore rupees and some people called it "the One Crore Stadium [*Eka Kotira Stadium*]". Other called it "the common Man's Stadium [*Lokankara Stadium*], since the money had come from people who contributed by buying One Rupee Lottery tickets – hence some people also called "the One Rupee Stadium [*Tankākiā Stadium*]. B.C.M. said, "Every Odia should feel that it was 'his' stadium. Since the Barabati Raffle acquired great popularity all over India, the stadium became a matter of national pride. Stadia are often named after great people. The Barabati Stadium I probably among the very few which has not been named after a person, dead or living. People close to B.C.M. wanted his name to be associated with the Stadium but he vehemently opposed the idea. In fact, very few would be knowing that when the land for construction of the stadium was allotted, the then Chief Secretary, Govt. of Orissa, Shri Nilamani Senapati granted the land in the name of Shri Mahanti in his personal capacity. But B.C.M. convinced the Chief Secretary and got the entire deed changed in the name of Secretary, Odisha Olympic Association. Crave for personal aggrandizement never vitiated his judgment and deflect him from the path of truth, justice and honour. He remains among the rarest breed of politicians and sports persons who never inducted his children either into politics or even gratifying them by making them members of any of the sports association in Odisha. He could have done it with considerable ease because he remained General Secretary of the Orissa Olympic Association for a life time. He was averse to the idea of installing images or names o any of the founder members of Barabati Stadium. He was never tired of saying that the Stadium was a creation of the combined efforts of all people of Odisha and not of an individual.

The stadium has hosted two National Games in 1958 and 1970 and many national and international tournaments for Hockey, Football, Basket Ball and Cricket. It also became a Centre for recreational, educational and cultural activities. The headquarters of Indo-Soviet Cultural Society [ISCUS] was set up here and B.C.M. became the Founder President of ISCUS.

The first cultural Relationship and Cooperation treaty between the Soviet Union and India was signed at this ISCUS office in 1966. The Lenin Peace Prize awardee and

Padma Bhusan K.P.S. Menon, India's Foreign Secretary (1948-1953) and Ambassador to the U.S.S.R., Hungary, Poland and China, signed the Cultural Cooperation treaty with the Russian Indologist Professor Chelisev, here at the Barabati Stadium. Present on this occasion were Soviet Ambassador to India Mr. Smirnov, Air Marshal Jagjit Singh Arora and Shri Bhairab Chandra Mahanti. Valentina Tereshkova the first lady cosmonant visited Barabati Stadium on the invitation of Shri Mahanti.

Seminars of national and international importance have also been held at the stadium. There have been international seminars on Buddhism and Jainism, an International Seminar on Folk Culture, International Teacher's Conference and many more. In every sense the Barabati Stadium remained the nerve centre for several socio-cultural activities for a very long time, and all due to the diligence and meticulous planning of Shri Mahanti. An article published in 1971 in the *Times of India* read, "The Barabati Stadium owes its existence to the drive and imagination of one man – Mr. Bhairab Chandra Mahanti, who built it through the proceeds of a national lottery".

Besides being the Secretary of the Orissa Olympic Association, Shri Mahanti was also Secretary of Orissa Cricket Association and later the president. He was also the President and Secretary of Orissa Football Association, President of Orissa Council of Sports apart from holding the office of President of several State level Sports Associations.

At the national level, he was Vice-President of the Indian Olympic Association for thirty long years and president of amateur Athletic Federation of India. He was the seniormost Vice-President of Board of Control for Cricket in India for seventeen years and would have been its President in September 1980, had he not expired in Moscow in July 1980 during the Moscow Olympics. He was also a member of All India Council of Sports for a very long period under Field Marshal Manekshow. In 1954, he was the Manager of the Indian Football Team to Manila and Hongkong. In 1974, Shri Mahanti was deputed by the B.C.C.I. as the Treasurer of the Indian Cricket Team visiting England. His distinctive acumen at the national level as a great sports organizer and his vast experience often brought him in close contact with retired Army Chief O.P. Mehta, the President of Indian Olympic Association and also Air Vice-Marshal C.L. Mehta, the Secretary–General of Indian Olympic Association, who often called upon Shri Mahanti for advice. Shri Mahanti also had an interaction with Lord Kilanin, the President of International Olympic Association.

Shri Mahanti's dynamism was not confined to sports alone. Social service and helping the growth of educational and cultural organizations were other areas where he made stupendous contribution. He was a member of the senate and syndicate of Utkal University and was actively involved in the activities of Utkal Rabindra Parishad, Utkal Sahitya Samaj, Kumar Utsab Samiti; Apart from ISCUS, he was intimately associated with Indo-GDR friendship and in 1976, he led the Indian Parliamentary delegation to the Germen Democratic Republic. Besides, he was patron of several other organizations.

Had the Barabati Raffle not been abruptly stopped due to petty political considerations in 1968, Shri Mahanti's dream and vision of a comprehensive development of Sports in Odisha could certainly have been realized. His scheme envisaged a seven-storied player's hostel, an air-conditioned guest House, a fully equipped Gymnasium,

Swimming pool, Cycle Velodrome, Indoor Stadium for Basketball, Vollyball and Tennis, a state of the art library, an ultra-modern Theatre Hall with world class acoustics, gardens and lawns on all sides of the Stadium and also a Planetarium within the precincts of Barabati Fort.

It would be pertinent to observe that by 1964 the grand effort to build the stadium had come to the notice of people outside Odisha and Smt. Indira Gandhi, then Union Minister for Information and Broadcasting was one of them. While speaking as Chief Guest for the Barabati Raffle Prize Award function held at Hotel Janpath, New Delhi, on 12th December 1964, she said ".... *That is why it is so refreshing to learn about this organization – The Barabati Raffle Committee, which is self-reliant and has undertaken a number of good works in the state of Orissa. I am also glad to learn that it is helping good causes in other parts of the country. This is praise-worthy.* She further added, "*Mrs. Sarojini Naidu once said that Orissa is a small state with a big heart. The activities of the Barabati Raffle Committee support this idea.*"

In the Rajya Sabha, Shri Mahanti made a scintillating speech on the quality of sports in India and what urgent steps were needed to boost the morale of sportsmen. He said sportsmen in India could improve their quality and secure a befitting place in world sports only if we could infuse advanced scientific training and coaching to them. He had spoken on several occasions in the Rajya Sabha to draw the attention of the Government on such issues, and every time his words were applauded by all members of the House. In one such speech he enquired whether the country should follow socialist countries and nationalize all sports or adopt the line of the U.S. and Western European counties and give full autonomy to all national sports federations with full financial support from the Government. Since India had no clear cut national policy for sports, all sports activities of the country were suffering and hence the pose performance. To his surprise he found that the entire House rose in support of B.C.M.'s forceful speech. He insisted that sports should find a place in National Policy. He succeeded in promoting sports into the national agenda.

The stadium today occupies a part of the ancient Barabati area. Built with modern skill and ingenuity the stadium has four covered galleries that can accommodate 45,000 spectators, a distinguished visitors-cum-high denomination ticket holder's pavilion, an up-to-date double story building as the club house with a wooden floor, a fixed stage, anterooms and boxed seats, murals depicting the highlights of Odisha history and important events in the lives of Buddha and Gandhiji. The double story Gate House has the offices of Odisha Olympic Association and provides a grandstand view of the stadium's heart the attractive oval shaped green turf, well maintained and toned to serve the diverse purposes of this composite stadium. It was on this green turf India's Flying Sikh Milkha Singh who created Athletic History in 1958 and emerged as the ace sprinter of the country. It was to this stadium that B.C.M. invited the legendary wizard of Hockey, Shri Dhyan Chand to coach the state Hockey players.

The facade at the main entrance of the Stadium has an exact replica of the famous Konark Horse, which incidentally; in the emblem of the Odisha Olympic Association. The 100 feet high seven story torch cum clock tower stands tall and stately as a symbol of Odisha's pride and glorious past. the bronze plaque of Mahatma Gandhi

– 5 feet in diameter – fixed at the top of Football - Hockey score board was inaugurated by none other than *'Frontier Gandhi'* Khan Abdul Ghaffar Khan. It is unique of its kind in the country and has a parallel only in the Lenin Plaque of the Central Lenin Stadium, Moscow.

Shri Mohanti was nominated by Prime Minister Indira Gandhi to lead a 5-member parliamentary delegation to Moscow to attend the Moscow Olympics of July 1980. The Prime Minister specifically instructed B.C.M. to observe the conduct of affairs of the Moscow Olympics Games so that India could gainfully benefit for the successful conduct of ASIAD'82, planned to be held in New Delhi. It had been decided by the Govt. of India that Shri Mahanti would be the Executive Head for conducting ASIAD'82 B.C.M. observed *"I have not seen any other previous Olympic Games, but I have no regrets since what I am seeing in Moscow is the best."*

23rd July 1980 was an unusually cold evening in Moscow. But B.C.M. met the Indian contingent in their camp to boost the morale of the Indian Hockey team. He was rather worried because the team was not performing as per expectations – it was not converting penalty corners into goals. He then had dinner with Shri I.K. Gujral, Indian Ambassador to the Soviet Union. After a hectic day-long session, he was very tired and past midnight he retired for bed. Around 1 am. at night [Moscow time] he felt a sharp, stabbing pain in the chest. He called his friends and a doctor promptly arrived, but before any treatment could begin he had a massive heart attack and that was the end of his earthly journey. His last words to his friends were *"I am having a severe pain in my chest, if anything happens to me, send my body to Cuttack."*

The entire Olympic faternity was appalled by this

catastrophe – "The Soviet leadership, the Indian Ambassador, President of the international Olympic Associational, The Indian contingent, International Journalists and officials from different countries, all rushed to Hotel Sovietskaya [where Indian diplomats were staying] to pay their last respect. 86 countries were participating in Moscow Olympics and all courtiers lowered their National Flags and as a mark of respect. Olympic Games were paused and all stood up in silence for two minutes. This was the first instance of its kind since the foundation of the International Olympic Committee in 1896. The I.O.C. wrote : *"International Olympic is now poorer due to the death of Mr. Mahanti."*

The Indian Hockey Team performed extremely well and Moscow Olympics 1980 was the last time India won a Gold Medal in Hockey. After the stunning victory, captain of the Indian Hockey team, V.Bhaskaran raised the Gold Medal to the skies and said *"This is for that greatman who gave us all the encouragement which became our strength."*

Very few indeed have had the fortune of such a glorious death. Born in an obscure village in Odisha, Shri Mahati consecrated his life for the growth and development *of "Sports Culture"* in Odisha / India and he died in the Paradise of Sports – The Olympic Games. Draped in the Tricolour, his mortal remains were consigned to the flames with full state honour on 26th July 1980. The man of sports and the Father of Barabati Stadium has gone but he has left behind a legacy that needs to be perpetuated.

Telling Stories the Indian Way: The Inimitable Manoj Das

Chittaranjan Misra

Manoj Das is one of the best story tellers of our times. A bilingual writer he has written short stories, novels, travelogues, poetry and non-fiction and has earned global reputation. His writings are discussed and adored for the humour and satire he employs and his inimitable style as a narrator. He has emerged as a reputed writer for his contribution to Odia literature and Indian writing in English. His short stories written in Odia have been published in different collections entitled *'Upakathā Sataka'*, *'Ābupurusha O Anyana Kāhāṇi'*, *'Sesa Basantara Chithi'*, *'Manoj Dāsanka Kathā O Kāhāṇi'*, *'Dhumabha Diganta O Anyana Kāhāṇi'*, *'Manoj-Panchabimsati'*, *'Āranyaka'*, *'Bhinna Manisha O Anyana Kāhāṇi'*, *'Lakshmira Abhisāra'*, *'Abolakarā Kāhāṇi'* and *'Aranya Ullāsha'*. Stories written by him in English include *'A Song for Sunday and Other Stories'* (1967), *'Short Stories by Manoj Das'*, (1969), *'The Crocodile's Lady and Other Stories'*, (1975), *'Man who lifted the Mountain and Other Stories'*, (1979), *'The vengeance and Other Stories'*, (1980), *'The Submerged Valley and Other Stories'*, (1986), *'The Dusky Horizon and Other Stories'*, (1989), *'Mystery of the Missing*

Cap and Other Stories' (1989), 'Bulldozers and Fables and Fantasies for Adults' (1990), 'The Miracle' (1993), 'Farewell to a Ghost' (1994), 'Selected Fiction' (2001), 'The Lady Who Died One and A Half Times and Other Fantasies' (2014),' The Bridge in the Moonlit Night and Other Stories- A Selection by the Author Manoj Das' (2015).

His Odia novels include 'Tandrālokara Prahari', 'Aakāshara Isārā', 'Amruta Phala', 'Prabhanjana', 'Godhulira Bāgha','Kanaka-Upatyakāra Kāhāṇi' and' Sesha Tāntrikara Sandhānare'.He has been awarded Saraswati Sammān in 2000 for his novel Amruta Phala published in 1996. His English novels are 'The Escapist' (2001), 'A Tiger at Twilight' (1991), 'Bulldozers' and 'Fables and Fantasies for Adults' (1990),'Cyclones' (1987). He has written a novelette, 'Legend of the Golden Valley' (1996).

In addition to all these he has written travelogues, poetry and non-fiction including essays on history and culture. However, the above lists of his books give an impression of his extraordinary literary output and the reason why he is popular among the readers as a fiction writer.

Graham Greene has said, *"I have read the stories of Manoj Das with great pleasure. He will certainly take a place on my shelves besides the stories of Narayan. I imagine Odisha is far from Malgudi, but there is the same quality in his stories with perhaps an added mystery."*(Web) Narayan and Manoj are equally effective in portraying rural life and landscapes of India but Green has aptly referred to the "added mystery" in Manoj Das's stories. The mystic and mythic foundation of Manoj Das's writings makes him a unique story teller. He seems to be carrying the flare of the traditional Indian narrator illuminating the inquisitive listeners/readers and signaling them the possible directions and paths they would choose in life. When Manoj Das was awarded Padmashri, P. Raja rightfully viewed it as *"a recognition of the creative mind faithful to the Indian psyche"*.

Unlike many of his contemporaries he prefers a narrator who is creative, imaginative and presents ordinary events and characters from spiritual and cosmic perspectives. Steeped in Indian sensibility he doesn't imitate realism (magical or otherwise) but combines the realistic with the other-worldly. His stories are marked by an integration of the aesthetic and the discursive. Being a true inheritor of the tradition of Indian fables developed through Panchatantra, the Jatakas, the Hitopadeasa, and folk tales Manoj Das knows how to fuse the metaphorical aspect with the narrative. His understanding of India as a land of stories and legends is like that of Raja Rao who in the Foreword of his (Rao's) novel" Kanthapura" writes: *"There is no village in India, however mean, that has not a rich sthala-puraṇa, or legendary history, of its own." Through stories, Rao says, "the past mingles with the present, and the gods mingle with men to make the repertory of your grandmother always bright."* (Rao:5) Enjoying a story of Manoj Das is sometimes a sheer delight; it's like listening to tales told by one's grandmother. But at the end of the story the listener is no more a grandchild; he finds himself mature searching for meanings in another world.

The story 'The Crocodile's Lady' can be taken as an example to show how Indian villagers live by stories. It's about the life of a woman in her nineties. She was widowed at the age of four and later in her youth dragged by a crocodile into the river. After ten years of her disappearance, she returns to her village and finds her mother ailing and widowed in the meantime. She lives in utter poverty and becomes completely alone. The villagers believe that the crocodile which took her into deep waters married her after she herself turned into a crocodile in the process. After observing her sadness about the change, he taught her the mantra to resume her human form as and when she liked. She would swim to the shore, recite the *mantra* and roam about in places of pilgrimage as a woman and return to the bank to swim into the waters as a crocodile again. This was made possible by another *mantra* recited by the husband crocodile countering the effect of the previous one.Once she visited her village resuming her human form but could not return to the waters as her ailing mother required attention. Unable to bear the separation the creature arrived to take her back. The villagers thrashed the crocodile to death. The villagers had no need to investigate into what really had happened to the lady. They rather called her 'the crocodile lady' and thought of her presence in the village as a boon because that would prevent crocodiles nearby from harming them. The references to ghosts, the mysterious birth of the saint Languli Bābā, The *Mālikā*, an ancient folk epic of prophecies, the benevolent attitude of the villagers towards the old lady construct a complete picture and evokes the Indian ethos. The interaction of the rural people with the white professor Dr. Batstone creates the juxtaposition of two kinds of attitude to life – the emotional and the rational.

Apparently absurd the story is told so lucidly that the readers suspend their disbelief. Manoj Das's style of telling transforms the social realistic events of here and now into something mysterious, remote and layered with multiple meanings. The decade long disappearance of a young woman could be an act of her choice, courage and escape from deprivation and the story cooked by her could be intended to veil the facts. But the veil matters more than the actuality elaborated with fidelity. The appeal of Manoj Das's stories lies in his art of integrating the fictive and the factual.

In *'The Submerged Valley'* there is a character called Abolkarā who is the crazy son of an insane woman. After the death of her mother, he is found wandering on the hills and talking to birds and beasts. The villagers do not mind his abnormal ways and are sympathetic towards him. Construction of a dam begins and the valley containing the village gets submerged. The people are displaced leaving their ancestral land. Five years after the construction the level of the reservoir falls unusually low due to delayed monsoon. At the top of the village there was Shiva temple and the hillock behind it could be seen. The displaced people get the news and rush to the spot by boats under governmental supervision. The former residents witness the sight with excitement and agony and discover to their utter dismay the forgotten young man Abolkarā. They believe that Abolkarā was there on the spot all these years more or less fasting and clinging to the submerged rock all the while. As waters rise all are asked to vacate. But Abolkarā does not listen. The story ends when an engineer (father of the child narrator) rescues him in torrentialrains in a launch. The story not only relates the village with civilizations like Harappa and Babylon but foregrounds the ecology of Indian village that sustains the retarded and the healthy; where the humans are in oneness with the birds and the beasts. The intense bond between land and the people come to surface when the rupture is imminent and the ancient habitat is terminally lost to the natives. Provision of alternativesite and money cannot compensate for the loss. Abolkarā's defiance seems to be a gesture of rebellion that springs from mysterious depths of the unconscious. The narrator says: "In the how lingwind, I heard the cries of the ghost of the drowned village".(76)

A Story entitled *'Farewell to a Ghost'* is a superb piece of writing that transports the reader to another order of reality. The story was included in October 1975 issue of the 'Malahat Review, An International Quarterly of Life and Letters'. The ethereal ambience is built through description of a river-bank, long silences, a phantom castle floating on an unreal sea. The story relates to the process through which stories of past generations are carried forward to the present. At the center of the story is a ghost of a girl. The girl was killed a century ago in a mansion now abandoned but since it is believed that 'ghosts do not grow in age', the boys of the village are fascinated and the boy narrator even falls in love with the ghost. The story unites the whole village who respond to the ghost with sympathy, love, and respect. The girl who was the illegitimate daughter of a Sahib by a tribal woman was kidnapped and brought to the villa by three 'feringhees'. The girl poisoned them with the help of the keeper but the treacherous keeper stabbed her to death and escaped. This backdrop is implicated with white man brown woman relationship in the colonial context and needs further interpretation. When Government decides to demolish the old mansion, the villagers find another place for the ghost through a mendicant. The elderly men looked upon her as one of their unlucky daughters. The story too represents the customs, cultural practices and moral makeup of the villagers.

'The Bridge in the Moonlit Night' is a love story presented through a conversation between two friends who are in their old age. They reminisce of events that had happened sixty years ago. Sudhir confesses that he had torn Meena's letter in response to Ashok's many love letters out of envy

and attachment. Ashok who is older and suffering from amnesia is deeply moved and says that he should have known about her love for him earlier so that he could have been happy for a longer duration. Meena had invited Ashok to meet her near the bridge. But the letter torn into shreds were thrown and blown under the bridge. The old bridge was already demolished by the time Sudhir confessed. What was left with Ashok was only moonlight acting as a bridge between past and present, between unrequited love and death wish. The pathos of the story is heightened through a dream like fusion of mystery and memories.

Not only on subjects of love and reminiscence but while writing on light or humorous themes he never allows the appeal of the stories to diminish. The frailties and frivolities of characters are exposed by an intelligent sequencing of juxtapositions and construction of irony. The satire perceived in his story *'The Mystery of the Missing Cap'* is built around the sudden intervention of a monkey who is half-domesticated, half-wild. The monkey takes away the cap of the Minister kept on a stool by the window making Shri Maharana, the ambitious host thunderstruck. Both the guest and the host in their own peculiar ways try to cover up and conceal the truth of the missing cap. Shri Maharana's fictive 'nobleman'and Babu Virkishore's willingness to be robbed of his clothes as a price for love acquire new meaning at the climactic moment when Jhandoo(the monkey) appears, sits between both and returns the minister his cap.

The plot of *'A Night in the Life of a Mayor'* is based on political context but the total effect of the story leaves the readers awed at the realization of how helpless man could be at the prime moment of glory and power. Maturity comes not by scaling heights in the ladder of power but by encountering crisis. The moment of making existential choice is the moment of a new beginning. The Mayor comes face to face with naked truth at a time when he is literally naked and desperately tries to hide from public gaze. Mayor Divyasimha offends his old Professor Sudarshan Roy when the professor raises the issue of the menace of stray cows in the city speaking at the Corporation meeting. But his pride is shattered by weird chance incidents taking place when he is immersed in celebratory narcissism. The humour and satire embedded in the story cannot be communicated through explanation and one needs to read the story proper to enjoy and understand them. When we listen to the Professor who shouts with deep resentment: "In a city with such a jubilant corporation, a cow would dare to chew up, of all things, psychology, that too in broad daylight and you the mayor laugh and say that it was no tragedy?", (227-228) our attention goes to 'psychology'. 'Psychology' here not only refers to the notebook of Professor's grand daughter chewed up by a cow but becomes a metaphor of the psychology of a corrupt administration.

With each story one discovers something unique that either leads him to profound musing or sheer wonder and amusement at varied situations in which men get stuck. A Story like 'A Letter from the Last Spring' opens up a world of human relationship in which intimacy is formed where language plays no role. The 'delight of an inaudible exchange'between a retired professor and Rina, the little girl, ending with a peculiar reciprocation is charged with a pathos. The forgetting habit of Bhola Granpa in 'Bhola Grandpa and the Tiger 'evokes pure laughter. The reader enjoys the story both despite and for the improbabilities involved. His famous story 'Sharma and the Wonderful Lump' highlights Sharma's physical deformity as instrumental in bringing money and fame in America for which he postpones the surgery there. He is tempted to earn more and complicates his position abroad and ultimately returns to India. His lump disappears as a block of ice by the power of his mother's Guru. The subtle undertones that run throughout the story is intended against mercenaries in business and politics. But all his stories lift the readers beyond their immediate social and political contexts to other mental planes where thoughts and feelings of empathy, creativity, values and spirituality emerge.

Manoj Das says: 'The sudden exposure of our people to the new political dispensation created quite a few minor and major predicaments for many. This has been the premise of *"The Misty Hour", "The Irrational", "The Mystery of the Missing Cap", "The Assault", "The Brothers", "The Old Man and the Camel"* and indirectly of *"The Bull of Babulpur", "Statue-breakers are coming!"* and *"Two Slippers and a Soul"*. I must hasten to say that these situations are by no means the themes of my short stories. They have constituted the context, they have provided me with the elements that form the outer sheath of the stories–like the five elements composing our body –they have provoked me, but the themes, the souls of the stories, I have always felt, have come to me as inspirations from the elusive horizons of life–or rather from the many-tiered and many-splendoured consciousness, both manifest and unmanifest, the source of our life and all life." (Das:xiv)

While reviewing 'The Vengeance and Other Stories' in *'Poetry Time'*, critic A. Russell stated, *"There is little doubt that Manoj Das is a great story teller of the sub-continent and he has too few peers, no matter what yardstick is applied to measure his ability as an artist… he shows how powerfully all artifices of storytelling can be used to write a story in realistic genre without any attempt at being faithful to the photographic details of facts. His world has the fullness of human psyche, with its dreams and fantasies, its awe and wonder, the height of sublimity can be courted by the depth of the fictive. He proves that the reality is richer than what realists conceived it to be".* (Russel:1987)

His autobiographical work *"Chasing the Rainbow in an Indian Village"* containing twenty-eight chapters speaks about a village of Odisha by the sea recounted from his childhood memories. The work is not merely a journey into one's personal memories marked by nostalgia but offers a picture that could evoke in the reader an endearing response to identify with the narrator and feel the spirit of rural India of colonial period. Critic Amiya Dev observes: *"For no matter how sequestered, history catches up with a community with its long hand. Hitler trickles through as 'Hitlord' and rumors spreads his highhanded humiliation of the British. Even 'Japan' is not unheard of and in the midst of the fear that Japanese may land anywhere anytime and claim victory, a British airplane is seen to catch fire and crash-land, quite a lure to the schoolboy Manoj to go and look up. A jeep too is a novel sight."* (Dev:200)

His travelogue *"My Little India"* depicts India through many travel accounts. The "little" in the title metaphorically refers to author's intimacy with his country and not the size. The Odia version is entitled *"Antaranga Bhārata"*. The accounts are written with ease and felicity without eliminating the history and legends of the places. There is an intertextual quality in his travelogues. While talking about the Andamans he speaks about the British policy of lifelong deportation and the Cellular Jail and when the scene changes to *Dandakāranya* he relates the account with memories of 'Aranyakānda' of *Rāmāyana*. Talking about Rajastan he refers to Tod's '*Annals of Antiquities*', Sister Nivedita's '*Studies from an Eastern Home*', Mark Twain's '*More Tramps Abroad*' and E.M. Forster's '*Adrift in India*'. The book is an attempt at showing the cultural diversity and heritage of India ranging from Buddhism to modern times. In a review article of this book Amiya Dev refers to Manoj Das as *"a seeker of diversity of Indian traditions"*. (Dev:203)

P. Raja has fairly said: *"ManoJ Das has been a crusader against the invasion of India's intellectual climate by decadent values. He has not only been a 'social critic of the first order', but also, what is more important, he has stressed the divinity and psychic splendour inherent in man, through his creative writings."* (Raja.1993:4)

Manoj Das had started writing from an early age. "*Samudrara Khyudhā*", his first ever short story written during his adolescence emanates the spark of his creativity and considered a classic in Odia prose. Living as an ashramite of Sri Aurobindo Ashram, Pondicherry since 1963, and working as an English professor at the Sri Aurobindo International Centre of Education, Pondicherry, he has explored life through literature and mysticism.He has received many awards like Odisha Sahitya Academy Award 1965 and 1987, Kendra Sahitya Academy Award, 1972, Saralā Award, 1981, Vishuba Award, 1986, Saraswati Sammān, 2000, Padma Shri, 2001, Atibadi Jagannath Das award, 2007, NTR Literary Award, 2013,Mystic Kalinga Literary Award, 2000. He was conferred the Padma Bhushan award in 2020.The following year (on 27 April 2021) in Puducherry he passed away at the age of 87.

As one of the best storytellers of our times Manoj Das will continue to inspire generations of readers to come. The inimitable Manoj Das will be remembered for telling stories the traditional Indian way.

REFERENCES :

Dev, Amiya. *Indian Literature* : 227, Delhi : Sahitya Akademi, 1998.

Das, Manoj. *The Bridge in the Moonlit Night and Other Stories*, Delhi: NBT, 2015.

Green, Graham. (https://en.wikipedia.org/wiki/Manoj_Das).

Raja, P. *The Hindu* (Online edition). Sunday, March 18, 2001.

Raja, P. Manoj Das: An Introduction. *Many Worlds of Manoj Das.*, Delhi: B. R. Publishing Corporation, 1993.

Rao, Raja. *Kanthapura*, NewDelhi: Orient Paperbacks,1971.

Russel.A.(http://www.worldofmanojdas.in/english_story_writer.php).

Autobiography of Pratibha Ray– "Padmapatrare Jibana"*

Basanta Kumar Panda

"It's my strong belief that in the near future in our sacred motherland many writers will emerge who will author their autobiographies. I have created merely a base for them." (*Ātmacharita* – Fakir Mohan)

At the outset of his autobiography Fakir Mohan had written regarding his expectation of many autobiographers to emerge in Odia Literature in the near future. What he had predicted has come true. Many have proved to be his inheritors in the true sense and have enriched the life-writings produced in Odia. Keeping this in mind if we come across the autobiographies of reputed story writers like Godabarish, Kalindicharan, Gopinath and Surendra Mohanty as successors of Fakir Mohan. After Surendra Mohanty, Pratibha Ray has been able to endear the readers through her autobiography *"Padmapatrare Jibana"*. Author of many novels like *Shilapadma, Jājñaseni, Māhmoha, Ādibhumi,* and *Mahārāni Putra* that offer varied characters against vast canvasses Pratibha has rendered the story of her life which reads almost like a novel. But unlike the novels she has tried to abstain from creating fictive worlds inhabited by characters. She has rather tried to present the real world that she has experienced as a real human being. She has emphasized about the basic purpose of autobiography: *"What one records in her journal, diary and memories are not her own personal possession but are a part and parcel of time and collective life. Many characters and events stay imprisoned in memories and to free them and bring them to limelight is possible through the only medium called autobiography."*

In a truthful and lively manner, she has narrated the story of her life that started in a rural setting under the supervision of her teacher-father. Though the narrative at some points seems too metaphorical and steeped in hyperboles the narrator figures as a round character poised at the center of a non-linear novel who is constantly present immersed in self-reflexivity. The author has adequately and genuinely represented both the positive and negative dimensions of life. In addition to personal facts and experiences she has offered her analyses on major events and prominent personalities of her time and in detail. By this she has transformed the autobiographical work into a social document. One perceives from the book a subtle appeal of a life devoted to literature while going through her world-view, life-style and values. The writer has not only described the ecstasy of success life has bestowed on her but has tried to construct an identity of the self that stays hidden behind tormenting incidents left unsaid. Her work *"Life on a Lotus Leaf"* reflects all the four major qualities of autobiography: 1) Historical chronology 2) social and psychological analysis 3) Ethical angle 4) Aesthetic values. She has made the work significant by liberating the characters and incidents from the confinement of memories and pages of diary. Pratibha's life is not marked by political events and she has not been interested in becoming a social activist. Moreover, she neither does pursue a spirit of scientific enquiry nor does she adhere to any particular method of philosophical inquisition. One doesn't come across grandiose and pompous utterances in her narrative. Despite all these the autobiography has become educative and appealing in depicting the struggle of a village girl who has been able to accept all hostilities and succeed in turning most of them as a test of her strength. This is the most notable feature of *"Padmapatrare Jibana"*.

The first story of Pratibha Ray's autobiography was published in *"Amrutāyana"* under the title *"Amruta Anwesā"* (Search for Nectar). But in the autobiography this section is named *"Alakā Naira Gita"* (Songs of the River Alakā). Pratibha was born as the fourth child to the parents Parashuraam Das and Manorama Devi. Her father Parashuraam Das was a teacher who was working as the headmaster of Balikuda High School situated on the banks of the river Alakā. She was born on January 21,1943 the full moon day of Pausha. Her horoscope says that she has a longevity of 128 years. May the prediction come true. May the author live a long life and enrich our literature through her creativity. From childhood the ideal for Pratibha was her father. In different places of the autobiography, she has said about this. Still, it seems as if she has not been able to speak all about it in a complete manner. Because Parashuram was multi-talented, unique as a human being. Inspired and instructed by the scientist Prana Krushna Parija he had left his lucrative job, attractive salary and high position in Tata Company at Jamshedpur and accepted the responsibility of being the headmaster of the newly established Balikuda High School that was burdened by a plethora of problems. The author describes: "Father was a moralist, a devoted Gandhian. He had lived his life on the basis of some principles and never desisted from them at the cost of his life.

From childhood Pratibha had developed an interest in the rural and natural surrounding and was fond of walking the distance to the primary school regularly past the old banyan tree called 'Budhapira'. Her world-view grew with the devotion and a sense of surrender to the ancestral deity Gopaljiu coupled with trust and faith in ordinary human beings." How simple and dependable was the world of my childhood! But time taught me - how untrustworthy is man."- she says.

In 1956, while she was in Class VII her poem was first published in 'Mina Bazar' entitled "Morning Breaks: Spring Arrives". She has described her feelings of this moment; "The publication of my poem in Mina Bazar and the ample praise I received from my teacher cum father endorsed the idea of the poet present in me. That moment was exhilarating. It was the greatest reward in my life I have received as a creative writer. The first ever feeling of a simple and unassuming self at the instance of being applauded for creativity was far beyond the thrill the plethora of awards I received later. This excitement was incomparable." Later in life she earned reputation and received many awards like *Murtidevi, Jñānapitha* and *Padmashri*. While writing her autobiography the author is reminded of the unique and blissful moment her maiden work had brought her way back during early childhood.

Maybe there was no plan of writing novels but the

passion for reading them might have built up an interest in her to know about the complex structures required in the making of a novel. Again, the words of mother were always in the backdrop as a warning: *"the day our daughter would author voluminous books like my Kanhu uncle and Gopa uncle would be the day she would be known as a poet."* These words must have agitated her like a challenge. Her first novel came entitled *"Adekhā Hāta"* (*Unseen Hand*). This marked her glorious entry into the world of novel. Then followed all reputation, position and expectations.

"In my adolescent heart there were sky high dreams. There was the dream of becoming a writer. In addition, I had the dream of becoming a singer and a dancer. Father was able to compose modern songs of prayer, patriotic songs, set the tune and teach us singing them with the accompaniment of harmonium. "Pratibha was singing in the children's programs as a child artist of All India Radio.

Projecting herself as the daughter of river Alakā the author has devoted more space to the memories of childhood and adolescence in her autobiography. Through powerful expressions in her narrative, she has reconstructed the picturesque landscapes, scenes, individuals, bits and pieces of emotion and agony as a sequence. Her style of narration has been more effective than language in communicating her take on life. The work is full of such instances.

"Probably there are more tears than blood in this body. Not only mine but children tears are more in quantity than blood. Therefore, frail children of village shed rivers of tears at a moment's notice. When one grows the amount of blood increases and tears drop in the body. That is the reason why the grown-ups are stronger than the youngsters and never feel like crying." The author had to take leave from the river Alakā as she had to go to Cuttack – enticed by Mahānadi. She had to take her High School Examination. The journey was in search of a new life, to build a future and fulfill her dreams and ambitions. Father wanted her to pursue medical studies and become a doctor. But the daughter was firm in her mind – her ambition was to become a writer. She was to take admission in Ravenshaw College, Cuttack as a science student. *"Exhibiting a sense of pride in being a Ravenshaw student and hiding the guilt of giving father a fake assurance, I boarded the bus with him."*

The story of Mahānadi began. This forms the second section of the autobiography packed with memories and meditative recollections. The dream destination Cuttack now is the workplace of real life.

The historical city of Cuttack which is a vast chronicle of glories and downfalls changed the course of Pratibha's life. Cuttack plays a significant role in instilling in her knowledge, insight, literary sensibility, social and familial values. It has created for her a reading public and admirers. In the autobiography this middle phase of her life has claimed a considerable space.

A girl from a rural area now stays as a border of World Women's Hostel after joining a science course in Ravenshaw College. She is full of promises and dreams. City life with friends offer new experiences that make her more inspired to write. She gets the opportunity of receiving prize from reputed poets like Kalindi Charan, Kunja Bihari, and Harihar Mahapatra as a result of her participation in Poetry Competition. She becomes a favorite student of the Literature Professor and poet Chintamani Behera. In 1961 her poem was published in "Jhankāra" for the first time. On the other hand, she regrets the fact that she could not learn music in Kalā Bikāsh Kendra as it involved strict regulation and control. Pratibha during this period comes across the personality of the Principal Sadasiba Mishra who was a distinguished economist. She feels inspired by his sense of commitment. Her talent unfolds and gets enriched through her participation in numerous programs of All India Radio. She was appreciated by Kalindi Charan Panigrahi for her role in the radio program "Turyanāda". She was more excited to receive a letter of encouragement and blessings sent by her father who had listened to the same broadcast in his village. She has preserved that letter as the most valued citation of her life.

Father's dream could not be actualized. She turned down the opportunity of medical studies and joined graduation course in Ravenshaw College. She informed her mother: "From childhood my goal has been to be a writer and not a doctor. My father had encouraged me in that direction by citing the example of Kuntala Kumari. But I know that I am not that competent and knowledgeable like Kuntala Kumari to combine the talent of a doctor and a writer. So, I left medical studies. I don't have the courage to meet father. "After the end of B.Sc. Examination, she leaves Ravenshaw College. Later in life she comes back to Ravenshaw and joins as a lecturer in Education. This Ravenshaw College is a repository of myriad dreams. In the mean while she had completed two novels. Her novel *"Duiti Dheu"* (*A Couple of Waves*) came out in 1967 with a cover designed by Shiba Panigrahi.

Her professional career begins as the first ever graduate Headmistress of Balikuda Minor Girls' School. After some days in 1965 she joined a training institute at Satyabhamapur, the birth place of Madhubabu. The institute was being managed by Sumitra Choudhury, daughter-in-law of Maa Rama Devi. There she came across the fiery Gandhian Baidehi Panda. Later she(Panda) appears as the character 'Maithili' in the novel "Uttaramārga"

From Satyabhamapur Pratibha went to Angul Basic Training College to study B.Ed. During those days training colleges were adhering to strict regulation and known as centers of excellence providing proper training to teachers and conducting cultural activities. The foundation of Pratibha's life as a teacher was built there. She exclaims at the mysterious ways life flows swayed away by time: *"Many events take place in the flow of time that are beyond control. That is called destiny. Love, affection, deceit, envy, jealousy, friendship, enmity all seem to be pre-designed as parts of a drama. They look like illusion, lies, like games children play, like roles played by actors on the stage."* She remembers those days and adds: "Had it not been for a teacher who came in my life I would have ended up as a worldly housewife of an orthodox family of Rays. I could never have been a lecturer. Whatever followed as a sequence affecting my passion and profession would not have happened at all. He is none other than Debendra Nath Rout of Berhampur."

After taking the B.Ed. Examination at Angul Training College she returned to village and then arrangements were made for her marriage. The bridegroom was

Engineer Akshaya Chandra Ray of Kaduapada. As she was a poet, she had to write the wedding verses on behalf of the groom's family on request. The wedding took place on July 4, 1963.The marriage involved no dowry. However, after the wedding Pratibha took a few things including a bound picture of Lord Jagannāth she used to worship to her in law's place. At the moment of leaving all resolves dissipated. She burst into tears at the time of parting from her paternal home.

Her professional life had started almost at the same time her marital life begun. First, she worked in residential schools and then taught in different colleges as a lecturer. While performing her duties sincerely she kept her passion for writing burning and struggled to strike a balance between the two. In 1974 her book *"Barsā Basanta Baisākha"* was published. It received huge applause from the readers which inspired her to write more novels. The confluence of education and literature boosted Pratibha's genius in varied directions. She worked as a researcher and earned her doctorate degree from Regional College of Education. While she was working as a Senior Reader she was selected as a member of Orissa Public Service Commission. She retired from Government service working as a member of the Commission.

During the 80's of last century a transition took place in the literary output of Pratibha. A new age dawned on her literary world. After *"Shilāpadma"*, her *"Jājñaseni"* is considered as a significant event not only in Odia Literature but in the whole of Indian Literature. Translated into many Indian languages the book brought unprecedented fame to the author. In 1986 in a bilingual seminar involving Odia and Kannad Nagaraju suggested a Hindi translation of the book which was published by Rajpal and selected for Moortidevi Award by Bhāratiya Jñānapith.

She found herself swaying between the prominence she received from the literary world and the responsibilities of the two sons Anwes and Ayaskant and daughter Adyasha on the family front. The transition that life offers in its cyclic process is often monotonous and at times lively with a fresh newness. The author has included such moments in the story of her life.

After changing her residence from Cuttack to Gajapati Nagar, Bhubaneswar she has authored a number of significant novels and short story collections. This duration is described as *'Mahodadhira Māyā'*, the last section of her autobiography. Works like *"Dehatita"*, *Uttaramārga"*, *"Ādibhumi"*, *"Mahāmoha"*, *"Magnamāti"*, and *"Mahārāni Putra"* are unique creations. Each book stands singularly remarkable for the exceptional merit it embodies. Among these works *"Magnamāti"* claims to be recognized as a classic. Written against the backdrop of the super cyclone of 1999 this novel is a superb testament of undying human relationship. The work is an epic on reality and corporeality exploring the nature of human existence on earth. It can be read as a sequel to earlier works like *"Mātira Manisa"*, *"Hidamāti"*, and *"Māti Matāla"* by other writers. The author has received Saralā and Sahitya Akademi awards for her work *"Ullanghana"*. She has been honored by the Government of India with *Padmashri* award. Her stories, translated into different languages and acclaimed throughout India have earned ample fame for her. From Odia literature she has moved to the pan Indian literary world and has been considered as a major Indian author. Taking all these into account *Bharatiya Jñānapitha* award has been conferred on her. She is the fourth Odia litterateur and the second Odia novelist to have received the Jñānapitha. Viewed from this angle she is an inheritor of Gopinath Mohanty. Not only in terms of awards but considering the bulk of her output she can be called a true a successor of Gopinath. Her popularity among the Odia readers, the greatness assigned to her works by Indian critics and reviewers have installed her as one of the greatest writers of India. The author in her autobiography has briefly mentioned about these as remembrances. In future this book as a primary source will help others to prepare an authentic biography and a chronological framework for her works furthering research and criticism. Utkalmani Gopabandhu has said that human life should be measured in terms of one's contribution and not the duration of time one lives on earth. In the light of his view Pratibha's life and creative contributions will continue to be discussed by generations to come.

Kaviguru Rabindranath wrote in his *"Jibansmruti"*: *"Who paints the picture of life on the canvass of memory one never knows. But whoever he may be, he draws the pictures. In other words, he does not hold his brush to replicate all that has happened. Selectively he chooses what to include and what to abandon. He in consonance with his taste enlarges the petty things as great and reduces the significant ones as trivial. He never hesitates to reverse the sequence of events. He adorns the past events in subsequent slots and later events prior to past. On the whole his work is to paint a picture, not write history."*

Pratibha has painted the pictures of life in *"Padmapatrare Jibana"*. There one may find the chronology of events distorted, some events missing as mind erases many of them in time. But a sense of wholeness depicting the entirety of life emerges from the work. Since she is actively engaged in her creative pursuit this work is but a part and not the whole of her life. Maybe in future she would produce works more wonderful. The readers will definitely wait for that. But let no reader think *"Padmapatrare Jibana"* as another novel by Pratibha. This kind of assumption is not new in Odia literature. Fakir Mohan's "Ātmacharita" was termed as his fifth novel and not autobiography. Such wilful controversies are not desirable. May this autobiography be treated with reader's genuine ardor. May this work be received as an invaluable addition to the gamut of life writing in Odia.

* Translated by **Dr. Chittaranjan Misra.**

Prof. Harekrishna Satapathy : Renowned Sanskrit Scholar and Academic Administrator

Arun Ranjan Mishra

Prof. Harekrishna Satapathy is one of the remarkable educationalists, a prolific writer, an erudite sanskrit scholar and an Academic administrator that Odisha has witnessed. He has a deep love for the Odia community. He could establish himself at the National level in a very short span of time. Right from his birth (5.8.1956) in Kendrapara district he showed the signs of exceptional oratory and intelligence that impressed the elders. His students, and colleagues in Ravenshaw College took instant benefit from his wide range of knowledge in Sanskrit language and other literary fields. Prof. Satpathy started his teaching career in Ravenshaw College and subsequently transferred to other eduational institutions. He has uncommon depth in Classical Sanskrit as well as Modern Indology, the seraphs of wisdom at Puri, the citadel of ancient learning, keenly wanted his valuable service at Sri Jagannāth Sanskrit University where he joined as Reader in Sāhitya on 6.1.1988 and later became the Professor of classical Sanskrit Literature on 23.7.1999. He not only served in Sāhitya Department but also dedicated himself for various causes of the university. Thus he came back to the spiritual jurisdiction of Lord Jagannāth where he had spent his formative period as a sanskrit scholar (in Acharya Class at Sadāshiv Sanskrit College, Puri). Sometimes during 21.3.2000 to 24.10.2000, he took the charge of Vice-Chancellor there besides being the Head of Sāhitya Department and Chairman of the P.G. Council. He organized All India Oriental Conference twice at Puri and then at Tirupati.

Later on, Prof. Satapathy became the Vice-Chancellor of National Sanskrit University, Tirupati for ten years (two terms) from 19.4.2006 to 31.3.2016. This was the golden period of the university since he was successful in drastically enhancing the overtone and undertone of it. The university was accredited with NAAC A++ grade. He tinged the whole campus with various layers of divine beauty. The life of inmates of the campus were smooth and peaceful at low cost through various means. He increased the number of the faculty members and non-teaching staffs by appointment and recruitment. The quality of teaching and research was enhanced and enriched by research publication. By organizing All India Oriental conference, International and National seminars, the university was converted into a national hub of think –tank.

Prof. Satpathy joined as the first Vice-Chacellor of Kalinga Institute of Social sciences (KISS Deemed to be university) for a term of three years w.e.f. 1.9.2017. He engaged himself for the welfare of downtrodden strata of our society.

Prof. Satpathy is a genuine scholar and a sincere social worker. For the intellectual growth of young mass, he is very keen and enthusiastic. He is associated with many councils, academic and executive bodies for the promotion of Sanskrit. His active participation in academic bodies and council for formation of policy for the advanced course is praiseworthy. He being the General Editor of more than one hundred seminal books in Sanskrit are published propagating rich cultural heritage and wisdom of India. Prof. Satpathy has excelled in the field of publication. Almost all these works were undertaken during his tenure at National Sanskrit University, Tirupati. However, he has his own original works in Sanskrit: numerous books on history, grammar for the unity of Indian value and culture. Some of his works are as follows;

1. Āchārya Sankara
2. Dharmapadam (Khanda Kāvyam) in Translation
3. Kabisatakam (Sataka Kābyam)
4. Gangā Jala Dushitam (Khanda Kāvyam)
5. Janani (Sataka Kāvyam)
6. Bhāratayanam (Mahakāvyam)
7. Pātu Nah Saradāmba (Khanda Kāvyam)

In *Acharya Sankara*, Prof Satpathy reminded people of the country about the spritrtual value and the essence of history and cultural tradition. *Dharmapada* symbolizes supreme sacrifice which is central to Indian Culture. Utkalmani Pandit Gopabandhu Das was an icon of sacrifice who wrote "*Dharmapada*". His life is a life of sacrifice for the people of his own country. He left his only son in the death bed and went to flood affected area to serve the distressed people. By translating *Dharmapada* into a Sanskrti *Khanda Kāvya*, Prof Satapathy depicted the vision of Gopabandhu, the ideal of sacrifice in human life for the cause of the motherland.

The *Khanda Kāvya "Gangājala Dushitam"* written by

Prof. Satapathy is to generate a sense of awareness among Indians towards the spiritual and economic value of river Ganga. We should make the water of the Ganges pure and keep her free from pollution.

Prof. Satapahty is out and out a patriot. In his *"Janani Satakam"*, he highlights the glory of the mother and motherland. The new generation under the sway of consumerism and materialistic attitude is forgetting the role of parents of this country who try to sacrifice their own comfort for the sake of their children. But in the long run, the parents are neglected in their old age. Indian cultural value gives emphasis on Pitru ṛna and Mātru ṛna, each man should repay these debts.

In the *Khanda Kāvya Pātu Nah Saradamba*, Prof. Satpathy describes Goddess Saradamba seated in Sringeri Peetha of Ādi Sankarācharya, she is the conglomeneration of *Saraswati. Laxmi* and *Durga* symbolizing the spiritual uplifement of people. Prof. Satapathy spelled out his inner personality with the secrets of *Yoga Sāstram*. His intention of spiritualizing everybody's life is very much evident form the divinely charged verses.

The poetic and patriotic feelings of Prof. Satapathy is reflected and manifested in *"Bhāratayanam"*, the first *mah k vya* of the poet. It depicts the spiritual glory of India. Each Indian should feel proud that he has taken birth on this enlightened land. *Srikhetra*, the adobe of Lord Jagann th, *Dw raka* the seat Lord Krishna, *K shi* the divine seat of Viswanatha and *K nchi*, he seat of Goddess *K m ksi* etc. are the most spiritual places famous on the earth for providing fourfold *mok a*.

Prof. Satapathy who is decorated with highest degrees in Sanskrit and law is also widely honoured with awards, titles and prizes by numerous prestigious institutions. He was the recipient of Odisha Sahitya Akademy Puraskar (1992), Delhi Sanskrit Academy Puraskar (2005) Viswakabi Rabindranath Puraskar (Kolkata) Sri Jayadev Samman (2007), Ramakrishna – Jayadayal – Dalmia – Srivanya Lanka Rana Puraskar (2010). He was conferred with the title *"Brahmarshi"* conferred by the President of India (2011), Sahitya Akademy, Delhi Puraskar for the epic *Bh ratayanam* (2011). Title *"Mah mahop dhyaya"* conferred by Kavimoula- Guru – Kalidas Sanskrit University, Nagpur (2012), Title *"Kavikulaguru – Kalidasa Sadhan Puraskara* conferred by the Government of Maharastra (2013), Certificate of Honour from the President of India (2020) and many other awards.

All these prestigious awards signify the contributions of Professor Satapathy in enriching thoughts and sensibilities. His love and affection for students is unparalleled. He has written around two dozens of books with Odia annotations to Sanskrit originals annexed with indepth study helpful for researchers in Indology. His Odia translation of Sanskrit *"Skanda-Pur a"* received readers approbation. Prof. Sataptathy is a source of inspiration for scholars, researchers and millions of people of Odisha and India.

Subroto Bagchi: One Man, One Mission and a Million Dreams

Disha Bhatt

An Indian entrepreneur, business leader and best-selling author, Mr. Subroto Bagchi is the co-founder of Mindtree and Indian technology MNC who has represented his life in his book *"Go Kiss the World"* has been inspiring the youth. Born on 31st May 1959 in Patnagarh, Odisha, he studied Political Science at Utkal University. The young and courageous Bagchi underwent training with the Parachute Regiment of the Indian Army and successfully completed the 5 mandatory jumps to earn the "Para Wings" in the year 1974. A year later, he was adjudged best NCC Cadet of India at the Republic Day Parade, New Delhi where he was awarded the Prime Minister's Cane Honour.

Subroto Bagchi wears myriads hats, he started his early professional career as a clerk in the Industries Department of the Government of Odisha in 1976 after a year he qualified as a management trainee in DCM in 1977 where he worked for five years. He worked for various computer companies from 1981 to 1999 in various capacities like sales, marketing and operations. He rose to the position of Chief Executive of Wipro's

Global R&D before working for the Chairman of Azim Premji as corporate Vice-President, Mission Quality. Shri Bagchi expanded his horizon by leaving Wipro and joining Lucent Technologies in 1998 and translated his dreams into reality by co-founding Mindtree a year after leaving Lucent.

A prolific writer, which Mr. Bagchi is, has the credit of penning many books: *"High-Performance Entrepreneur"*, *"Go Kiss the World: Life Lessons For The Young Professional"*, *"The Professional"*, *"MBA at 16"*, *"The Captainship: First-gen Entrepreneurs"*, *"The Elephant Catchers"*, *"The Professional Companion"*, *"On Leadership and Innovation"* and *"Sell"*. He created a niche for himself. As time passed by, Mr. Bagchi came into the world of skill development in 2016 and was entrusted with the responsibility of setting up the Odisha Skill Development Authority. Soon, it became his mission to create employable skills for 1.1 million youth mostly school dropouts.In his passionate endeavor of skilling the youth he raised moot questions like why focus on minimum wages and not sustainable wages and reducing gender balance at workforce. A man who truly believed in the real skilling of the youth and not mere skilling just for the sake of it. In a short span of time, Odisha Skill Development Authority grew to be a major hub for skilling, training and development for youth in vocational areas and the like.

Mr. Subroto Bagchi made Odisha as the sandbox for innovation in creating Nano-Unicorn programme. Trained 215 ITI teachers and officials in Singapore and Odisha has been the best performing state at the short-term employment linked skill development programmes like DDU-GKY. In wake of the Covid-19 pandemic, Mr.

Subroto Bagchi was given additional responsibility to be the Government's Spokesperson for the 45 million people in the state of Odisha during the pandemic in addition to his endeavours in the areas of entrepreneurship development, industrial investments in the state, leadership development and innovation.

The mayhem caused by the Covid-19 pandemic is well-known and needs no explanation. The entire world was floating in troubled waters and had disturbed the entire ecosystem with people dying, economic imbalances, people losing their jobs, psycho-social issues, fears, virtual working, social distancing, lockdown and the pressure of balancing work from home. Mr. Bagchi shouldered the responsibility of being the Chief Spokesperson of the Odisha government on Covid-19. He led the IEC team which was responsible for spreading awareness on Coronavirus in Odisha. He became the point person for every development in the fight against this deadly virus in the State. It is under his leadership and guidance that Odisha received the praises of removing the obstacles and blocks early in arresting the measures for the spread of the virus. He was appreciated for the use of thoughtful choice of words, wearing an empathetic approach during the disaster, and eloquent speaking.

In one of his deliberations, Mr. Bagchi underscored the importance of leadership communication during crisis. "Leaders should listen to the voice of the dissent. Most leaders fail to do this in the face of crisis", said Mr. Bagchi. This explains volumes about his critical thinking, unwavering confidence, and unbeatable skills of leading a team. Sharing his experiences, he said that innovation is key during a crisis. Under his initiative Odisha received the credit of giving Gram Panchayat

Sarpanch the power of a collector. This impacted the way in which the migrant workers were handled in Odisha. A man known for his foresight, leadership, communication style and vision received many accolades and appreciation in dealing with the crisis.

In 2021, he and his wife committed US $50 million to help and to set up a philanthropic cancer hospital in association with Sri Shankara Cancer Foundation and Karunashraya respectively.

A man who rose from a very humble background back in time where there was no electricity, primary school nearby and water. His father (a government servant) had a transferable job and as a child Mr. Bagchi had to be home-schooled. He gives the credit of his success to his parents and respects and acknowledges their role in laying the foundation of his life. Sharing some of his life lessons in his blog "you treat small people with more respect than how you treat big people. It is more important to respect your subordinate than your superiors"; "it is important not to measure personal success and sense of well being through material possession"; "it is not about what you create for yourself, it is what you leave behind that defines success". With these magical words, Mr. Subroto Bagchi has been waving his magic wand to inspire minds and to change lives.

A personality worth emulating Mr. Bagchi once defined success as "success to me is about Vision. It is the ability to rise above the immediacy of pain. It is about imagination. It is about sensitivity to small people. It is about building inclusion. It is about connectedness to a larger world existence. It is about personal tenacity. It is about giving back more to life than you take out of it. It is about creating extra-ordinary success with ordinary lives."

Among his many achievements, Mr. Subroto Bagchi has been inducted into the *Order of Engineers* by the University of Florida, and honored for his contribution in management and information technology by the Utkal University with an *Honorary Doctorate in Literature* and by the Veer Surendra Sai University of Technology with an *Honorary Doctorate in Science*. On 4th August 2023, Mr. Bagchi has been appointed by Govt. of Odisha as Chief Advisor to Govt. of Odisha for Institutional Capacity Building across all civil services and training institute of the state. Mr. Subroto Bagchi stands as a role model for the youth of our generation.

Hockey Legend – Dillip Tirkey

Harischandra Sahoo

Dillip Tirkey is a well-known figure in the history of Hockey. He is known as Rahul Dravid of Indian Hockey team. As an internationally acclaimed hockey player, he could set records by participating in 412 games. Dillip was born on 25th November 1977 in Saunamara village of Balisankara block of Sundargarh district, a place of Odisha adjacent to Jharkhand and Chhatisgarh. The inhabitants of this place prefer to speak in Hindi than Odia language. It may be reminded that Dillip belongs to Oram Tribe and is a Christian. His place of birth is in a tribal dominated area full of natural beauties like waterfall, deep and dense forest, full of flora and fauna. The villagers are poor but simple and honest to the pie. Sundargarh district is popularly known as *"Nursery of hockey."* Due to the influence of Britishers, the villagers are inclined to play hockey, the game that has given them identity and self-respect. Hockey is not a mere game for them. They never play hockey for material or financial gain, rather it is more than that. "Michel Kindo" belongs to this area who was the only hockey player and a tribal member in Indian hockey team in the year 1975. Dillip's father, Vincent Tirkey, was an employee of Indian Railways and was the main source of his inspiration. Both of Dillip's brothers Ajit and Anup were playing hockey for the railways. Dillip was inspired from his childhood to play hockey. Sometimes he walked several miles to see the hockey matches. Once he remarked;

"Hockey is in our blood.
We have watched our fathers
and grandfathers play."

It will not be out of place to mention that in Sundargarh district, when a boy is admitted to a school, he must be carrying a hockey stick with him (which is a prerequisite while taking admission into a school). Sometimes the village disputes are settled by hockey matches. After one cultivation is over, the brazen field in that locality is converted to a hockey practising ground for people of nearby villages. This shows the popularity of hockey in Sundargarh district.

The contribution of Sundargarh district for the sports is immense. It has given hockey players moral strength, ability, attitude and desire to win games. The aggressive nature of tribals is one of the factors for playing as well as winning matches. In Dillip's career, he considers Pargot Singh, a frontliner player to be his icon with whom he had a chance to play. Furthermore, Dillip is proud of hockey tradition in Sundargarh.

Dillip's life is full of events. He started his career at Ispat stadium, Rourkela (SAIL Hockey Academy). In the initial stage, he faced disqualification but he was never disappointed. With a challenge he continued to play. His coach is Mr. Ajay Kumar Bansal. Mr. Bansal in the year 1989, joined as a new hockey coach in Bhawani Shankar High School, Sundargah, who happened to be his mentor during the formative year of his career. Bansal speaks high of him. Dillip has played more than 400 matches. He was the captain of Indian team. Since, Dillip was the defence player in hockey matches he was called as the "Wall of the Indian Hockey." He is considered to be the "world's best defender."

Dillip represented 3 Olympic games. In 2003, India won gold medal in Afro-Asian game defeating Pakisthan when Dillip was leading the team as the captain. In 2004, India won Summer Olympic at Atlanta. In 1966 and 2000 (Sydney) Dillip represented India in Olympics. Once upon a time, players like Dhanraj Pillay and Baljit Singh Dhillon were in Indian Hockey Team. Dillip had a chance to play with Lazarus Barla, Birendra Lakra, Amit Rohi Das and Dipsan Tirkey. All are defenders in Indian team. Dillip carried forward the legacy of Indian Hockey Team. In 2002, he captained the team and won silver in Asian games. In the year 2002, he received most prestigious award i.e. Arjuna Award. He is the only tribal to receive such an award. In the year 2004, he received the most prestigious *Padmasri Award*.

In 2006, his biography "*Dillip Tirkey*" written by K. Arumugam has been released. If we analyse his career, we find him to be a striker first, then a mid-fielder and finally he played as a full back. By nature and temperament, he is shy, humble and quiet. He is not extrovert. He speaks less as and when required. He is a man above all controversies. At age of 36 he got married to a girl belonging to his clan. In May 2010, he himself declared his retirement from hockey at Kalinga Stadium, Bhubaneswar. His retirement is definitely a disappointment for the hockey lovers and his fans.

In this connections he says; "*Years from now when I think back on the height of my career, I'll definitely remember this day (02-05-2010). I had to pack my hockey sticks forever, which was never my choice. But I knew, there is a time for everything and a season for every activity."*

But then a new chapter was added after his retirement. From Biju Janata Dal on 22nd march 2012, he became the Member of Parliament (Rajya Sabha) to represent the voice of people of Odisha. In 2018, Hockey World Cup was organised in Kalinga Stadium, Bhubaneswar and it was a grand success. In 2022, Dillip was elected as president of hockey India. Regarding some other assignments, it can be stated that Dillip was the former Chairman of OTDC (Odisha Tourism Development Corporation) and he was former Chairperson of Odisha Hockey Promotion Council. He is the founding President of DTSRD (Dillip Tirkey Sports Research Development Foundation) for the promotion of hockey.

The life of Dillip Tirkey brings important messages to the young players. He advocates that one should know his innate (inborn) talents and potentialities. The second message, he gives is that one has to try hard and struggle hard to achieve success. It goes without saying that the physical fitness is one of the basic prerequisites of a sports man, he adds.

Once upon a time, India was proud of Hockey players like Dhyan Chand. Now DillipTirkey is an embodiment of success. He is really a hero, a living legend for the hockey players of our country.

Sudarsan Pattnaik : Magical hands capturing the beauty of Sands

Kashmira Murmu

Sudarsan Pattnaik, an internationally renowned sand artist, who was born on April 15, 1977 in Marchikote Lane, Puri. Sudarsan, a youngman who was born to a poor family and raised outdoors, was surrounded by nature as a child. He used to create sculptures of Gods and Goddesses while playing in the sands of Puri's Golden Beach. The sculptures' initial forms were immature because he lacked professional assistance. Despite these obstacles, he persisted in his work and gave sand art its current elevated status, which brought him recognition both at home and abroad. He accepted the challenge of popularizing sand art as a professional art form and began exhibiting sand art in various locations throughout India by giving it new content and meaning. In 2014, the Government of India bestowed the prestigious 'Padmashri' award on him.

Sudarsan Pattnaik has the credit of being the pioneer in popularizing Sand Art as a means of expressing one's creativity which one cannot even fathom as it is impossible to protect and preserve such an art and adding to the existing challenges, there are no ways and means to encash this form of art. He has worked to raise awareness and enthusiasm among the general public. In an endeavour to keep this art form alive, Sudarsan has contributed in training the youth in order to keep the legacy alive.This could not have been possible if he wouldn't have been an avid traveller and demonstrated his magic across the country and the world through workshops. He runs a sand art institute in Puri as well.

He used the language of sand art to raise public awareness about issues such as world peace, endangered wildlife species(such as the Olive Ridley turtle), terrorism, HIV/AIDS, international sports, and global warming. His work has been extensively covered by print as well as electronic media, national and international media outlets like the BBC, CNN, ABC, Doordarshan, Discovery, National Geography, Aaj Tak, and NDTV. The state of Odisha and India has earned name and fame because of son of the soil, Padmashri Sudarsan Pattanik.

Sand art is a popular professional art form in many countries around the world. Various international sand art competitions and festivals, such as the World Championship and the US Open, are held on a regular basis. The International Sand Art Committee selects sand artists from around the world to represent their country, just like any other sporting event. Thousands of people gather to witness the mega event as the artists give a live demonstration.

Sudarsan Pattnaik has captured his work in calendars for corporates like NALCO, created sand animations, sand paintings, and sand installations on canvas in addition to sand sculptures. Sand animation is the most popular form of art now and has the power of telling a story to the people. Sudarsan Pattnaik has made the state and the country proud by performing sand animation show at the Opening Ceremony of the Commonwealth Games in New Delhi in 2010. He recently exhibited his Sand art photographs on canvas at the Lalita Kala Academy Gallery in Bhubaneswar, Odisha, and Kolkata.

Sudarsan Pattnaik has bagged several awards at the domestic and international level. He is the first Indian to receive Italian Golden Sand Art award in Italy in 2019. He won People Choice Award at Boston International Sand Art Championship in 2019. He participated in International Sand Art Festival at Sand Museums Japan in 2019. He also conducted a sand art workshop for all school teachers at Behrin was and felicitated by the Ministry of Education Govt. of Behrin in 2018. He participated in Sentosa Sand station in 2017 at Singapore. He won Gold Medal in 10th Moscow Sand Sculpture Championship in 2017. He won People's Choice Gold Medal at Sand Art World Championship in 2016 at Bulgaria. He is a recipient of Gold medal at Moscow Sand Art Championship 2016. He participated in India festival at Seychelles and was honored by the Government of Seychelles in 2015. He won People's Choice Prize in World Cup for sand sculpting at Atlantacity,USA in 2014. He exhibited Sand Sculpture in Cannes Film Festival in France in 2014. He bagged First Prize (gold medal) at 12th International sand art competition 2013 held at Saint-Petersburg. He also participated in World Sand Sculpting Championship in 2013 at Atlanta city, USA. He won the Danish Grand Prize at 2nd Copenhagen International Sand Sculpture Championship in 2013. He won Moscow museum prize at Moscow World sand art championshipin 2013. He also won Public prize at Copenhagen International sand sculpture championship in 2012. He won double gold medal at Solo International sand art contest in Mervala 2012. One was for the people choice and another for the most positive sculpture. He won 1st prize at Copenhagen International sand sculpture championship in 2012. He bagged Gold medal for People's Choice at 3rd Moscow World sand sculpture championship in 2011. He won 3 medals in North American Solo Sand Sculpture Championship in 2010. He won People's Choice Prize at CNE International Sand Sculpture Championship 2010 at Canada. He secured 1st place in People's Choice at 8th International Berlin Sand Sculpture Championship 2010 (Sudarsan Pattnaik won the People's Choice Prize for the fifth time). He won People's choice prize at 2nd Moscow World Sand Sculpture Championship in 2010. He won People's Choice Prize at 2nd USF World Championship in 2009 at Berlin, Germany. He won Korea Sand Sculptor Award 2009 at 4th Haeundae Sand Festival at Busan, South Korea. He also achieved Special Prize at World Sand Sculpture Championship in 2009 by Russian Government.

Sudarsan Pattnaik secured 1st Prize at USF World championship 2008, Berlin, Germany and got the title of World champion. He also achieved People's Choice Prize at 1st International Sand Sculpture Festival in 2008 held at Moscow, Russia. He represented India in Tottori Sand Museum in 2008 at Japan. He won Audience Prize at 1st International sand sculpture festival in 2007 at Ruhr, Germany. He won Public Prize at 5th Berlin International Sand Sculpture/Festival in 2007. He represented India at 1st Istanbul International Sand Sculpture Festival held in 2007 at Turkey. He represented India in 1st International Sand Sculpture Festival in 2007 at Malayasia. He demonstrated sand sculpture at International student's conference in 2007 at Abu Dhabi. He represented India at 34th Sapporosnow sculpture festival in 2007 at Japan. He demonstrated on 15th Asian Games in 2006 at Doha,Qatar. He represented India on tournament of World championship sand sculpture in 2006 at Canada. He won 1st Prize at 3rd Berlin International Sand Sculpture Competition in 2005. He also participated in Houston International Festival-2005 at Houston, Texas. Here created The Taj Mahalin sand. He also participated at Sand Sculpting Australia 2004 at Melbourne.He also participatedat Sand World Festival at Travemunda at Germany in 2003-04. He also won Public Prize at 2ndBerlin Sand Station Competition in 2004. He also participated in Sand Sculpture Demonstrationat Muscat Festival in 2004 at Oman. He secured 4th Prize at China International Sand Sculpture Competition in 2003. He on 3rd Prize at Berlin International Sand Sculpture Championship at Germany in 2003. He got 2nd Prize in International Sand Sculpture Championship at Valadoli,Spain in 2003. He won the 3rd LuilangColour Sand Festival Demonstration prize at China 2003.He bagged the 1st China Ningxia Sand Lake International Sand Sculpture Event in 2002. The eventwas held from 3rd to 10thAugust, 2002. He participated in the Dutch Sand Sculpture Festival 'Thorn 2002-2003' held at Holland in July 2022. He participated in the Sand Sculpture Festival Blankenberge 2002 held at Belgium in June 2002.He won the Champion Medal in "29th International Snow Statue Contest -2002" held at Sapporo, Japan. He participated in Singles International Sand Sculpting Competition held at Scheveningen, Netherlands on 6th May 2001 and 6th May 2002. He secured 3rd Prize in World's Master Sand Sculpture's Championship 2001 on16th July 2001 at Italy. He won International Sand's Sculpture's Festival 2001 Blokhus held atDenmark on 25th June 2001. He participated in SANTOSA SANDSTATION 2001 on 3rd

June "SPLENDOURS OF GOLDEN ASIA" at Singapore. He won International Sand SculpturingFestival 2000 at Glasgow. He won the International Sand Sculpturing Championship 2000 atChina. He won the World Sand Sculpturing Championship at France 2000. He exhibited during the World Cup Cricket' 99 held at Edgbaston, United Kingdom during May-June'99. He exhibited during the World Travel Market held at Earls Court, London in November 1998 with support ofGovt.Of IndiaTouristOffice, London.

Apart from winning awards, SudarsanPattnaik has also initiated special activities for budding artists. He provided training to artists through Open Air Sudarsan Sand Art Institute at Puri beach which he started in 1995 with a view to make the students learn and develop sand art as a professional art form. Students from India and abroad are enrolled for projects, regular and short-term courses. His objective is to create professional artists through regular curriculum in this school of art and culture in a Gurukul concept. He has also published a book regarding sand art.He has conducted training and workshops and demonstrated the art form in different Fair andFestivals in and around the countries to promote and popularize this art. He has created World records on sand sculpture at Puri beach from 2006 to 2016. This was placed in Limca Book of World record. He also portrayed sand animation show at the opening ceremony of CommonWealth Game 2010 at New Delhi. He has been appointed as President of Odisha Lalita Kala Academy by Department of Culture, Government of Odisha. He has been appointed as Brand ambassador for International sand art festival by Odisha tourism from 2011 to 2019. He was appointed as member of National Tourism Advisory committee in 2013-14 by

Tourism Dept., Govt. of India. He was Executive member in EZCC. He participated in WTM and NYT for The Odish Tourism Dept in 2014-15. He created Guinness World Record for building World's tallest sand castle in 2017 at Puri beach.

Sudarsan Pattnaik also bagged "Padmashri" Award in 2014 by the Govt. of India. He was honored with "Honorary Doctorate" in LL.D. by Berhampur University, Odisha in 2012 and ICFAI University, Hyderabad in 2017. He bagged the "Godavari Award" by Kusumagraj Pratisthan at Nasik, Maharastra in 2012. He got "National Tourism award 2005-2006" for most innovative tourism project by Ministry of Tourism, Government of India. He achieved "NATIONAL YOUTH AWARD 2004-2005" organized by Ministry of Youth Affairs and Sports, Government of India at Patna, Bihar. Mr. Pattnaik was felicitated and awarded by the Hon'ble President of India Smt.Pratibha Devi Singh Patil at Puri beach in Odisha. He got Young Indian Leadership Award 2010 by CNNIBN. Limca Book of Records honoured him as "People of the Year 2009"

Sudarsan Pattnaik has bagged "Sarala Award" by the state government in the year 2008. "Limca Book of Record"honored him as India Extraordinary for sand sculpture on the occasion of the celebration of sixtyyears of India's Independence on Sept. 25, 2007, in New York. He received "EXCELLENCY AWARD 2006" held in July 2006 at New Delhi by The Sulabh International and The Society of Sri Lanka Justice of the Peace Human Rights Organization. He got "BHARAT JYOTI AWARD 2001" at Kolkata and "Award of Excellence" by State bank of India BBSR Circle. He created Black Taj Mahal in black sand infront of the white monument at Agra on the occasion of the closing ceremony of the Taj Mahotsav celebrations commemorating 350th year of Taj Mahal organized by Govt. of U.P. to honor the wish of Shahjahan. He demonstrated sand art at India International Trade Fair at Orissa pavilion at New Delhi on 2003-2004 organized by Govt. of Orissa. Further, he participated in different Tourism festivals like Konark Festival, Puri Beach Festival, Goa Food and Cultural Festival, Bhramhaputra Beach Festival, Assam, Travel and Tourism Fair etc.

Sudarsan Pattnaik, an out of the box thinker, a personality worth emulating, has been an example of courage, perseverance, integrity and hard work for millions today. In the present era he is the pioneer of sand art and will be remembered forever as the worthy son of Odisha.

Contributors' Profile

1. Dr. Preetinanda Roy, Assistant Professor of English, Kalinga Institute of social Sciences (Deemed to be University), Bhubaneswar.
2. Prof. Laxmikanta Mishra, Former Professor of History, Ravenshaw University, Cuttack.
3. Dr. Chittaranjan Bhoi, Associate Professor of English Program, KISS (D.U.) Bhubaneswar.
4. Prof. Harekrushna Satapathy, Former Vice-Chancellor National Sanskrit University, Tirupatti and KISS (D.U.) Bhubaneswar.
5. Prof. Bijayananda Singh, Professor, Gopabandhu Research Chair, KISS (D.U.) Bhubaneswar.
6. Prof. Harihar Panda, Former Professor of History, National Defence Academy Pune and member of Indian Council of Historical Research, New Delhi.
7. Dr. Netaji Abhinandan, Associate Professor and Head Dept. of Political Science, Ravenshaw University, Cuttack.
8. Mr. Soumya Ranjan Gahir, Research Scholar, Dept. of Political Science, Ravenshaw University, Cuttack.
9. Prof. Harischandra Sahoo, Professor, Bhima Bhoi Research Chair, KISS (D.U.) Bhubaneswar.
10. Prof. Prafulla Kumar Mohanty, Professor of English and Formerly Principal, Ravenshaw College, Cuttack and Khallikote College, Berhampur.
11. Dr. Hemanta Kumar Parija, Retd. Reader in History, Bhubaneswar.
12. Durga Charan Panda, Acomplished bilingual poet, Sambalpur.

13. Professor Baishnab Charan Samal, Retd. Professor of Odia, Viswa Bharati University, Santiniketan.
14. Mr. Sanatan Mallik, Retd. Special Secretary, Govt. Of Odisha, Bhubaneswar.
15. Dr. Niranjan Mohanty, Former HOD, Dept. of Philosophy, Christ College, Cuttack.
16. Prof Siba Prasad Adhikary, FNASS, Former Vice-Chancellor, F.M. University, Balasore.
17. Prof. Sarat Chandra Panigraphi, Former Professor and Head Dept. of Philosophy, Utkal University, Bhubaneswar.
18. Prof. Ganesh Prasad Das, Former Professor and Head Dept. of Philosophy, Utkal University, Bhubaneswar.
19. Dr. Pabak Kanungo, Former Head Dept. of Political Science, Christ College, Cuttack.
20. Dr. Sunamani Rout, Former Associate Professor of Odia, Sailabala (Auto) College, Cuttack.
21. Dhaneswar Sahoo, Former Reader and Head, Dept. of Philosophy, BJB (Auto) College Bhubaneswar.
22. Dr. Niranjan Barik, Former HOD Political Science, Ravenshaw College, Cuttack.
23. Dr. Rabi N. Patra, Visiting Professor, Council of Analytical Tribal Studies, Koraput (Odisha).
24. Prof. Udaynath Dash, Formerly Professor of Psychology, Utkal University and Delhi University.
25. Dr. Sayantani Behura, Former Asst. Professor of Psychology, Ravenshaw University, Cuttack.
26. Prof. Himansu Sekhar Pattnaik, Former Professor and Head, Dept. of History, Utkal University, Bhubaneswar.

27. Prof. Haris Chandra Panda, Former H.O.D., History, Ravenshaw College, Cuttack.
28. Dr. Kharavella Mohanti, Former H.O.D. of History, S.B. (Auto) College, Cuttack.
29. Dr. Disha Bhatt, Asst. Professor of English, KISS D.U. Bhubaneswar.
30. Dr. Chittaranjan Misra, Former Associate Professor and Head, Dept. of English, BJB (Auto) College, Bhubaneswar.
31. Prof. Basant kumar Panda, Director, Centre of Excellence in Classical Odia Language (Govt. of India), Bhubaneswar.
32. Prof. Arun Ranjan Mishra, Professor of Sanskrit, Viswa Bharati University, Santiniketan.
33. Miss Kashmira Murmu, Asst. Professor of Philosophy, Ravenshaw University, Cuttack.

Abhiram Paramhansa

Swami Prajnanananda

Pranakrushna Parija

Hrudananda Ray

Jitendranath Mohanty

Ganeswar Mishra

Binode Kanungo

Bhikari Bal

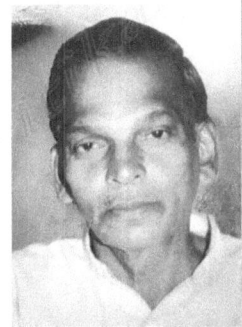
Chittaranjan Das

BLACK EAGLE BOOKS

www.blackeaglebooks.org
info@blackeaglebooks.org

Black Eagle Books, an independent publisher, was founded as a nonprofit organization in April, 2019. It is our mission to connect and engage the Indian diaspora and the world at large with the best of works of world literature published on a collaborative platform, with special emphasis on foregrounding Contemporary Classics and New Writing.

www.ingramcontent.com/pod-product-compliance
Lightning Source LLC
Chambersburg PA
CBHW060547080526
44585CB00013B/477